De

APPLETON SERIES IN SPECIAL METHODS

EDITED BY

PAUL KLAPPER

THE TEACHING OF LATIN

THE TEACHING OF LATIN

BY

MASON DeWITT GRAY

LATE DIRECTOR OF ANCIENT LANGUAGES IN THE
EAST HIGH SCHOOL AND IN THE JUNIOR
HIGH SCHOOLS OF ROCHESTER, NEW YORK

D. APPLETON AND COMPANY
NEW YORK : : : LONDON

PREFACE

The author of this book felt very keenly the need for improvement in teaching methods. He believed that such improvement should be based not merely upon opinion but upon a scientific analysis of the educational possibilities of a given subject, the extent to which such values were actually being realized in the classroom, and the methods which might best be adapted to promoting progress. If this book makes a real contribution to that end, it will fulfil the purpose which he had in mind.

The chapters which follow are the product of twenty years of teaching experience, supplemented by supervision of Latin instruction in senior and junior high schools and by the teacher-training courses which the author gave at various universities. In addition to this, he had the perspective secured by his participation as special investigator in the nation-wide survey of Latin teaching conducted by the American Classical League. This book summarizes the professional experience of a lifetime whose abrupt ending was directly due to the very intensity of interest and self-forgetful devotion which he gave to his chosen work.

For the completion of the bibliography, which my husband left unfinished at his death, I am deeply indebted to Miss Sara Schwendler of East High School, Rochester, New York, and to Professor W. L. Carr of the University of Michigan, who also undertook the final revision of the manuscript.

FRANCES A. GRAY

EDITOR'S INTRODUCTION

Teachers of Latin, as a class, have done more than any other group to lower the prestige of Latin as a school subject. Their severely synthetical and grammatical approach, their lessons unrelated to the language of the pupils, the character of the reading texts, their dogged pursuit of mythological and historic allusions, their attention to language irregularities,—all these teaching practices, rooted deep in narrow humanism, have kept the teaching of Latin on a low plane.

Unsuccessful in maintaining a place for Latin coördinate with that accorded to the sciences or mathematics in modern high-school and college curricula, the teachers of Latin fell back on a second line of defense, its cultural and disciplinary values. But this position also proved untenable. It was not difficult for the opponents to demonstrate that all the cultural stimulation which the average high-school pupil derives from the study of Latin can be obtained by reading, under proper guidance, the translations of a few of the old classics and by well planned lessons in word study—all of which may be introduced with profit into the course of study in English.

The disciplinary line of defense held stubbornly. Does not the study of Latin grammar sharpen judgment and develop conceptualization,—processes that are the very essence of thinking? Language is the external instrument of thinking; what better agent for teaching the logic of language than analysis of Latin text and the search for reasons to justify the use of the case or the mood in question? Statistical studies of students' grades yield data to prove that students who studied Latin show greater proficiency not only in a modern language like French, but also in mathematics, in physics, and in the social sciences. The skills developed in the study of Latin, it was assumed, flowed into a mental reservoir that could be tapped to meet the mental needs of any experience. More recent studies, that employ improved research techniques, refute such smug conceit. They reveal the fact that the languages hold no preeminent place in the mental training afforded by high-school studies; that persons of marked mental power show the greatest gains from any study; that Latin does not maintain its reputed place as a school discipline. True, there was a high correlation between the grades in Latin and those in the other subjects of high-school curricula, but Thorndike explains: "When the good thinkers studied Greek and Latin, these studies seemed to make good thinkers. Now that the good thinkers study physics and trigonometry, these seem to make good thinkers."[1] Our recent researchers say no more and no less for Latin than they do for mathematics or the sciences as school disciplines.

The time seems ripe for an informed scholar to take stock of changing conceptions in educational values and to formulate a progressive program for the teaching of Latin. This book, published posthumously, is the product of ripe scholarship and rich experience of many years as a teacher and supervisor of Latin in the high schools. Dr. Gray's active membership on progressional committees representing

---

[1] E. L. Thorndike, "Mental Discipline in High School Studies," *Journal of Educational Psychology,* Vol. 15 (1924), pp. 1-22 and 83-89.

Broyler, Thorndike and Woodyard, "A Second Study of Mental Discipline in High School Studies," *Journal of Educational Psychology,* Vol. 18 (1927), pp. 377-404.

teachers of Latin, gave him an intimate knowledge of current theories and practices in the teaching of Latin.

Dr. Gray bases his entire pedagogical program on definitely posited aims. The reader is led to formulate for himself the objectives of and the reasonably expected outcomes from the learning of Latin. In well organized and critical analyses, the author then sharpens and refines the reader's conceptions of aims. A solid basis is thus laid for the study of those methods of teaching and that content of instruction which are designed to attain these guiding aims. The discussion is well-balanced and practical and always related to classroom needs because it springs from clearly conceived aims. Strictly speaking, few of the traditional teaching practices are bad; a specific teaching technique, *per se,* is frequently neither good nor bad; it is effective if it achieves its purpose. Our quarrel with the highly formalized and humanistic teaching of Latin is less with the methods than with the aims.

The Teaching of Latin gives expression to deep-seated convictions, but it does not ride a hobby. While Dr. Gray courageously recommends a specific teaching practice and condemns another, he is neither propagandist nor prosecutor. His discussions of these questions are always complete, always fair, and never contentious. His decisions are reached with due regard to the findings of recent inquiries and to generally accepted psychological theories. The prospective teacher of Latin and the novice will find guidance that is definite, practical, and in harmony with the best thought of the day. To the experienced teacher, Dr. Gray brings a systematic and integrated summary of the findings of professional committees working under the auspices of a society of scholars and a clear discussion of objectives and teaching procedures in terms of which one may evaluate his own classroom practice. The supervisor and the teacher of high-school methodology will find most of their problems critically and constructively treated. The appendices contain helpfully arranged teaching and testing material and a classified bibliography.

PAUL KLAPPER

CONTENTS

CONTENTS

THE TEACHING OF LATIN

THE TEACHING OF LATIN

CHAPTER I

THE STATUS OF LATIN IN SECONDARY SCHOOLS

During the many centuries through which Latin has occupied a position of major importance in education, its function in society has undergone several radical transformations, each reflecting the spirit of the particular period. Still another transformation appears to be in process at the present time. In this brief preliminary survey we shall give consideration only to the period beginning in 1894 with the publication of the report of the Committee of Ten on Secondary School Studies.[1]

Report of the Committee of Ten. The report of the Committee of Ten was the accepted basis for the content of the curriculum in Latin in secondary schools from its publication in 1894 until the publication of the report of the Classical Investigation [2] in 1924. The report of the Committee of Ten crystallized the prevailing practice regarding the content of the course which had gradually developed in this country and gave it an authoritative stamp. The traditional standard course in secondary-school Latin, consisting of four books of Cæsar, six orations of

---

[1] "Report of the Committee of Ten on Secondary School Studies," National Education Association publication (American Book Co., 1894), pp. 60-75. A general committee of ten was appointed by the N. E. A. with nine subcommittees on various studies, each consisting of ten members. The Committee of Ten may thus refer to the general committee or to any one of the subcommittees. In this discussion it naturally refers to the subcommittee of ten on Latin.

[2] *The Classical Investigation* (Part I): *General Report.* (Princeton University Press, 1924.)

1

Cicero, and six books of Vergil, derives from this report; for the suggestions regarding the possible substitution of Nepos or Viri Romæ for parts of Cæsar proved ineffective. Furthermore, this committee seemed to recognize only the "preparatory" function of secondary Latin, and the justification offered for the study of Latin in secondary schools rested chiefly, if not wholly, upon the theory of "postponed returns." The committee's "preparatory" conception of secondary Latin is frankly stated on page 65 of the report: "The teacher of elementary [secondary] Latin need not concern himself too much with the remoter ends of the study [that is, with its educational objectives]. To him, the question should be: What knowledge is of prime importance as the foundation for subsequent work [in Latin]?"

Latin word-order method. This report is noteworthy in that it set up authoritatively for the first time the reading and understanding of Latin in the Latin order as the proper goal of Latin instruction. This goal and what may be called the Latin word-order method of teaching has received the endorsement of all subsequent reports. Teachers of Latin have been officially committed to that method since 1894. It is, therefore, somewhat surprising to find opponents of the *General Report of the Classical Investigation* (1924) criticizing it because of its revolutionary proposals in respect to the method of attacking the Latin sentence, when in this, at least, it is thoroughly orthodox.[3]

Other recommendations regarding methods. This report also anticipated largely the recommendations of the report of the Classical Investigation with respect to the methods to be employed in the mastery of the elements, and the function of these elements as simply means to an end, namely, the understanding of the thought of the Latin

---

[3] The passages in the earlier report bearing on the method of attacking the Latin sentences are quoted in the *General Report* of the Classical Investigation, pp. 288-290 (*see* footnote on page 1).

sentence. The point of view held by the Committee of Ten is clearly indicated in the following quotations from their report:

> Special vocabularies attached to separate exercises or selections should in no case be committed to memory before the study of such *pensa*, but should be used for reference first, and memorized last of all; that is, words should be studied in a sentence before they are studied in isolation.[4]
>
> For the student who is preparing for college it [syntax] is merely an indispensable means to an end, namely, the power to read. . . . No question upon construction should be put except as a means of guiding the class to an understanding of the meaning of the Latin; and consequently, every question of this type should precede the translation.[5]
>
> Particularly should dependence not be made wholly or even chiefly on the repetition of tabulated forms. . . . The mastery of inflection, so that the number, case, person, mood, tense, etc., can be *instantly recognized*. . . .[6]

Some reasons for failure of these ·recommendations. These recommendations regarding method in the teaching of vocabulary, syntax, and inflection, although pedagogically sound, failed of acceptance. The excessive amount of reading from classical authors required in the standard course placed a premium upon covering ground rapidly, rather than upon the use of sound methods. The same cause encouraged the artificial vertical division of the work by which the elements of grammar were "covered" during the first year, and the reading of continuous Latin begun in the second year. The recommendations as to method in the report of the Classical Investigation are in harmony with those of the Committee of Ten, but a determined effort was made to remove the causes which made them ineffective in the earlier report.

---

[4] "Report of the Committee of Ten on Secondary School Studies" (American Book Co., 1894), p. 69.

[5] *Ibid.*, pp. 69, 71-72.   [6] *Ibid.*, pp. 65, 68.

Report of the Committee of Twelve. The report of
the Committee of Twelve of the American Philological
Association,[7] published in 1899, was a reactionary document of remarkable character. This committee professed to
discover a demand for more extensive reading of the classical authors than had been provided by even the excessive
amounts recommended by the Committee of Ten, and it
therefore set up four to five books of Cæsar, six to nine
orations of Cicero, six to nine books of Vergil's Æneid, and
1,000 lines of Ovid as the desirable standard. Naturally this
report had little effect upon an already overloaded curriculum. The committee did not feel constrained to formulate
any justification whatever for the study of Latin, and appears to have been inspired by the feeling of elation and
overconfidence resulting from the marked increase in the
number of pupils studying Latin in high schools during the
years just preceding the preparation of the report. The
committee's concern seems to have been what these pupils
could do for Latin, not what Latin could do for the pupils.
There was, apparently, no interest in method, although the
recommendation regarding the Latin word-order method,
proposed by the Committee of Ten, who were otherwise
ignored, was repeated.

Report of the Commission of Fifteen. The report of
the Commission of Fifteen of the American Philological
Association and the College Entrance Examination Board,[8]

---

[7] "Report of the Committee of Twelve on College Entrance Requirements," National Education Association, July, 1899, pp. 50-77.

The report of the committee on courses in Latin and Greek, contained in the general report, is entitled "Report of the Committee
of Twelve of the American Philological Association on Courses in
Latin and Greek for Secondary Schools" (*see Transactions and Proceedings of the A. P. A.*, Vol. 30, 1899, pp. 78-122. Also published
separately under the same title by Ginn & Co.).

[8] "Report of the Commission (of fifteen) on College Entrance Requirements in Latin"; A. P. A. and C. E. E. B., 1909 (*see Transactions and Proceedings of the A. P. A.*, Vol. 41, 1910, pp. 135-140).

published in 1909, is an important document, since its definition of requirements for Latin remained the official basis for college entrance examinations until 1929. This report is noteworthy for its attempt to encourage more varied reading in secondary schools. The effect, however, was negligible because of its rigid adherence to the traditional kind and amount of reading. The influences which fostered the continuance of the traditional standard course are analyzed in the report of the Classical Investigation, pages 119-123. The report of 1909 also recommended strongly the use of the Latin word-order method and its description of the desirable procedure [9] is to be found in the announcements of the College Entrance Examination Board and in the catalogues of most colleges. Even in this report there is no recognition of the fact that secondary Latin has any other service to perform than to prepare the pupil for college Latin, and there is no attempt to set up or evaluate educational objectives.

Report of the Committee on Classical Languages of the National Education Association. The first document in which any consideration is given to the attainment of the educational values of Latin is the "Report of the Committee on Classical Languages of the Commission of the National Education Association on the Reorganization of Secondary Education." [10] This report marks the first step in the gradual emergence of the idea of specific educational objectives which has been increasingly dominant in subsequent documents. The vigorous arraignment of some of

---

Identical with present requirements of C. E. E. B. (*see* "Tenth Annual Report of the Secretary of the C. E. E. B.," 1910, pp. 4-7, *also* "Document 101 of the C. E. E. B.," August 1, 1921).

[9] *The Classical Investigation* (Part I): *General Report* (Princeton University Press, 1924), p. 291.

[10] Preliminary report, United States Bureau of Education Bulletin No. 41, 1913, pp. 32-40. Final report completed 1921, but not yet published.

the evils of the traditional course contained in the preliminary report, published in 1913, gave promise of a final report of great significance. It is much to be regretted that the final report, completed in 1921, has never been published. It should be published even yet as a document of importance for an understanding of the development of those conceptions which are dominant in the report of the Classical Investigation. A quotation from this final report will indicate that it was the first report to recognize the proper dynamic function of the potential values of Latin. "The aims and values of a given study must be considered with care before the organization and the methods of that study can be discussed intelligently." Axiomatic as this statement now seems, it struck an entirely unprecedented note in the official pronouncements in regard to the secondary course in Latin.

Denial of automatic transfer. The report also explicitly recognized that the potential values of Latin are not realized automatically:

> The Committee further holds that in proportion as such potential values are consciously the aim of the work in Latin and are consciously developed, in like proportion conditions are favorable to their realization as actual results of the work in Latin.[11]

The main significance attaching to the report lies in its relegation of the "preparatory" function of Latin to the background, and its insistence that Latin should be so taught in secondary schools as to be worth while, whether it is continued in college or not. Neither the term "preparatory" nor "college preparatory" nor even "college" occurs in the report.

Evils of congestion. The report recognized that congestion was the most serious evil of the traditional course, but

---

[11] A. J. Inglis, *Principles of Secondary Education* (Houghton Mifflin Co., 1918), p. 462.

its recommendations to remedy the evil were entirely inadequate. The traditional amount was impliedly recognized as representing the proper standard.

Report of the Classical Investigation. The committee charged with the preparation of the report of the Classical Investigation,[12] published in 1924, employed two important innovations in its procedure.

Tests and experiments. In the first place, the committee sought to secure factual data as a basis for its final recommendations, and through tests and experiments endeavored to find out the extent to which both the immediate objectives of Latin and its ultimate educational values were being attained under existing conditions. The results proved highly significant.

Opinions of teachers. In the second place, it sought to secure the detailed recommendations of a large number of successful and experienced teachers of secondary Latin throughout the country as to the proper function of Latin in secondary schools, its valid objectives, and the content and method appropriate to those objectives. For the first time the actual teachers of the subject were given a comprehensive opportunity to contribute the results of their experience to the formation of the Latin curriculum. This also proved an immensely valuable procedure.

Favorable reception of the report. There have been few educational reports in recent years which have met with so favorable a reception from the teachers of that subject, and so prompt an acceptance of its chief recommendations, as have been accorded this report. The reason for this favorable attitude lies apparently in the fact that, although based mainly on comprehensive data secured through experimentation and testing over a wide area, its recommen-

---

[12] *The Classical Investigation* (Part I): *General Report* (Princeton University Press, 1924). For additional references see the bibliography.

dations at the same time gave expression to the clearly defined views of the great majority of Latin teachers, who had reached the same conclusions independently as a result of their own experience and reflection. In fact, the most striking feature of the report is the remarkable agreement disclosed between the conclusions drawn from the experimental data and the judgments of experienced Latin teachers whose views were obtained in sufficient numbers to impart an impressive significance to the consensus of opinion disclosed. The report simply gave moral support to an already insistent desire on the part of the great body of teachers of Latin to do the very things recommended by it. Thus the report, especially the chapters dealing with objectives, content, and method, rapidly assumed the place of a teachers' manual.

Benefits of a coöperative investigation. Another factor which contributed to the favorable reception accorded the report was the fact that literally thousands of teachers actively participated in one or more of the many projects undertaken during the investigation. One inevitable defect of a purely "round-table" report is that its production has an educative effect only on the members of the committee itself and, hence, upon the publication of such a report, few teachers other than the members of the committee are really in a position to digest and apply it. The report of the Classical Investigation represented a huge coöperative enterprise to which thousands of teachers of Latin had contributed, and it is, therefore, safe to say that even before the report was issued the investigation had already influenced the teaching of Latin in a great many schools.

Chief findings. The chief findings of the report of the Classical Investigation may be summarized as follows:

1. Latin is taught in secondary schools primarily for ends to be achieved during the secondary period.

a. Of every 100 pupils beginning the study of Latin in high school, fewer than five will study it for four years in high school and continue it in college.[13] Most of these five study Latin for not more than one year in college. A computation based upon the number of pupils taking Latin for one, two, three, four, and five, or six years discloses that approximately 50 hours are spent in secondary schools in "preparation" for each hour's work in college. It is obvious that in the legitimate original sense of preparing pupils to continue Latin in college, the preparatory function of Latin has all but disappeared. Yet the control until recently exercised by the single college hour over the fifty secondary hours is one of the amazing phenomena of our educational history. The situation has long existed. Hecker[14] said in 1909: "I should like to inquire by what divine right colleges are allowed to dictate studies in secondary schools, seeing that a very small per cent of high-school students ever go to college."

b. Latin is a one-year course for 31 pupils out of every 100 beginning the study of Latin, a two-year course for 38, a three-year course for 17, a four-year course for 9, and a five- or six-year course for 4. It follows that 95 out of the 100 must secure their returns from the study of Latin during the secondary period, if at all. In fact, more than two-thirds must secure them during the first or second year.

2. The chief evil in the traditional standard course is the congestion resulting from the attempt to cover all the so-called elementary work in grammar and vocabulary during the first year, and from the requirement of excessive amounts of reading in the later years. As a result, there is neither mastery of Latin itself nor a satisfactory realization of the educational values of Latin. Furthermore, the pressure to "cover ground" has fostered the use of undesirable methods.

a. This is abundantly demonstrated with respect to Latin itself by the tables on pages 92, 137-138, and 142 of the report of the Classical Investigation.

b. The unsatisfactory results in the attainment of the ultimate educational objectives are discussed in Chapter III of the report in connection with the particular objectives. See the summary on page 90 of the report. All of Section 3 of Chapter IV of the report (pages 90-123) should also be read in this connection.

---

[13] *Ibid.*, p. 31.

[14] E. A. Hecker, *The Teaching of Latin* (Schoenhof, 1909), p. 50.

3. The report concludes, as did its immediate predecessor, that automatic transfer cannot be counted on to any considerable extent, and that, consequently, the educational values of Latin should be consciously aimed at through the appropriate organization of content and method. For a further discussion of this topic see Chapter III of the Report (pp. 55-62).

4. The facts disclosed in paragraph 2 above indicate that the traditional course does not provide a proper basis for the mastery of Latin even from the strictly "preparatory" point of view. The traditional course not only does not create favorable conditions for such mastery but it in effect prohibits it.

> It should be particularly borne in mind that there never has been any issue between teachers of college and secondary Latin over the desirability of high standards, or, indeed, over the necessity of higher standards. The issue has been over the insistence by colleges of the right to prescribe the means by which the desired standards should be attained. Secondary teachers are naturally in a far better position to determine that point. In fact, it might with reason be maintained that secondary teachers are in a better position to suggest what should be included in the fifth year of Latin than the college teacher is to prescribe how that year shall be prepared for in the first, second, third, and fourth years of Latin.

New requirements of the College Entrance Examination Board. "The New Requirements in Latin" [15] adopted by the College Entrance Examination Board in April 1926, to go into effect in June 1929, were based upon the report of a special committee appointed to study the recommendations of the report of the Classical Investigation. This special committee gave its unanimous approval to those recommendations of the Classical Report which aimed to relieve the present congestion of the secondary course in Latin, placed the emphasis upon quality rather than upon quantity by abolishing requirements as to *amount*, and encouraged a wider choice of reading material from classical authors by limiting the prescriptions as to *kind*

---

[15] College Entrance Examination Board, Document No. 120, December 1, 1926, p. 30.

to one semester for each of the last three years. This significant action now makes possible the gradual development of a national policy for the teaching of Latin in the secondary school from the point of view of the secondary pupil. The future of Latin in the secondary schools now rests in the hands of the secondary teachers of Latin.

CHAPTER II

THE PLACE AND PURPOSE OF LATIN

The justification of the study of Latin on the part of so large a proportion of the boys and girls in secondary schools has been the subject of debate, often acrimonious, for many decades. Despite the attacks upon Latin, belief in its efficacy as an instrument of education has persisted since the middle ages. This long continued popular insistence upon Latin as an almost indispensable element in a sound education is a fact the significance of which cannot be eliminated by superficial references to "tradition." Where the popular will has manifested itself so consistently in its estimate of educational values, it may be assumed that there exist at least potential justifications for it, even though the motives may be operating more or less unconsciously.

The cumulative values of Latin. The justification of Latin in the secondary curriculum must ultimately rest upon an accurate appraisal of the extent to which its potential values, as analyzed, for example, in the report of the Classical Investigation, are actually realized. The strength of Latin lies in its many-sided and cumulative aspects. Critics of Latin in failing to recognize these aspects have been grossly and at times deliberately unfair in their judgment. It is absurd to assert that the improvement in English expression secured through Latin could be more economically attained by devoting all the time now devoted to Latin directly to English. This proposal assumes that all the time spent upon Latin is properly chargeable to this

12

one objective alone. Yet this type of argument is frequently applied not only to the value of Latin for English, but to its historical-cultural and to its disciplinary values.

Improvement of the mother-tongue as an instrument of thinking. Yet among the potential values of Latin, each and all of which must be fairly considered in any final appraisement, one seems to provide for a most vital need through an agency for which there is no adequate substitute. The potential capacity of Latin to develop the habit of exact thinking, through the improvement of the mother-tongue as an instrument in thinking, is of such unique significance that it deserves first consideration in the justification of the presence of Latin in the secondary curriculum. The unconscious recognition of this immensely significant function may have been one of the controlling factors in the long continued popularity of Latin. In attaching this importance to the value of Latin in facilitating exact thinking, especially through insistent practice in adequate translation, the author finds himself in complete agreement with the assertion of Inglis that "the language studies of the secondary school should find their fundamental values and primary aims in the development of the ability to employ language as an instrument of thinking."[1]

It should be noted that the power implied in the definition of this value is of much deeper significance than simply "training in the vernacular," which Bennett[2] set down as the first and most important reason for studying Latin, and one outweighing all others combined. The value now being discussed includes that which Bennett so convincingly set forth, but it considerably transcends that value.

---

[1] A. J. Inglis, *Principles of Secondary Education* (Houghton Mifflin Co., 1918), pp. 433-434.

[2] Bennett and Bristol, *Teaching of Latin and Greek* (Longmans, Green & Co., 1899), p. 11.

Purposes of the study of the mother-tongue. Inglis[3] points out that the study of the vernacular has two main purposes: (1) to develop the mother-tongue as the most potent of all instruments for facilitating and conditioning the individual's thinking; and (2) to develop it as a medium of communication. However, "teaching pupils to express themselves in speech and writing is psychologically dependent upon, and pedagogically subordinate to, the process of making language an effective instrument for the individual's own intellectual enterprises."[4] The present author believes that upon the transcending importance of this fundamental ability, and upon the unique capacity of the study of Latin to contribute to that end, rests the chief, if not the supreme, justification for the study of Latin in secondary schools.

Recognition of these functions in the report. This conception of the function of language is embodied in the following paragraph taken from the report of the Classical Investigation, about which many of the specific values of Latin, instrumental, cultural, and disciplinary, might have been made to center.

Since language is an instrument not only for the expression of thought, but also for thinking itself, improved efficiency in the use of the mother-tongue for these two interdependent functions is of unquestionable value to every pupil. Because of the synthetic character of the Latin language as contrasted with English and modern foreign languages, and because of the relatively remote aspect of the ideas expressed in the material read in Latin when compared with those involved in the everyday activities with which English is commonly associated, we believe that the process of translating Latin into adequate English provides a peculiarly valuable instrument for developing the power of thinking and of expressing thought "by increasing the extent of vocabulary, by rendering vocabulary more precise and accurate as an intellectual instrument, and by aiding the development of

---

[3] Inglis, *op. cit.*, p. 427-428.   [4] *Ibid.*, p. 428.

the habit of interrelating words so as to facilitate consecutive thinking and consecutive discourse." [5]

Broad significance of this objective. The careful study of this paragraph from the report is recommended. It appears in the discussion of the objective: *Increased ability to speak and write correct and effective English through training in adequate translation;* but it will at once be recognized as of deeper and broader significance than the specific objective under which it occurs. With this paragraph and its implications the author is in complete accord, except that he would not limit the potential contributions of Latin in this field to the process of translating, although this activity undoubtedly provides the most important source of growth.

How we think. It is to Dewey [6] that we are indebted for the illuminating analysis of the relation of language to thought embodied in Inglis's discussion and in the paragraph quoted above from the report. Dewey's analysis is of the utmost significance to all teachers of language, whether foreign or vernacular, for it has profoundly modified our conception of the function of language by demonstrating that, important as language is as a medium of communication, it is enormously more important as an indispensable instrument for thinking itself. "Thinking is impossible without language." It will be worth while for us to examine Dewey's analysis of the relation of language to thought in more detail.

Dewey's conception of the function of language rests upon two main theses, (1) the relation of words to meanings, and (2) the relation of words to the organization of meanings.

---

[5] *The Classical Investigation* (Part I): *General Report* (Princeton University Press, 1924), p. 45.

[6] John Dewey, *How We Think* (D. C. Heath & Co., 1910), Ch. xiii.

Language is the vehicle for conveying thoughts to one another.

1. *Meanings.* Thought deals not with bare things, but with their *meanings*, their suggestions; and *meanings* in order to be apprehended, preserved, and reapplied, must be embodied in signs, which for all but a slight proportion of meanings take the form of *words*. "Learning in the proper sense, is not learning things, but the *meanings* of things, and this process involves the use of signs, or language in the generic sense. . . . A word is an instrument for thinking about the meaning which it expresses." [7] These three functions of words (apprehension, preservation, and reapplication of meanings) are fully described by Dewey.

a. In discussing apprehension of meanings, Dewey says:

Everyone has experienced how learning an appropriate name for what was dim and vague cleared up and crystallized the whole matter. Some meaning seems almost within reach, but is elusive; it refuses to condense into definite form; the attaching of a word somehow (just how, it is almost impossible to say) puts limits around the meaning, draws it out from the void, makes it stand out as an entity on its own account. . . . The delight that children take in demanding and learning the names of everything about them indicates that *meanings* are becoming concrete individuals to them, so that their commerce with things is passing from the physical to the intellectual plane. It is hardly surprising that savages attach a magic efficacy to words. To name anything is to give it a title; to dignify and honor it by raising it from a mere physical occurrence to a *meaning* that is distinct and permanent. To know the names of people and things and to be able to manipulate these names is, in savage lore, to be in possession of their dignity and worth, to master them.[8]

Inglis's treatment of this point is also illuminating.

The appropriate naming of anything is closely related to the identification of that thing—so closely that there is a necessary parallelism between the development of vocabulary and the development of clearly defined percepts, concepts, feelings of meanings, and the like. The development of individual meanings cannot

[7] *Ibid.*, pp. 176, 178.   [8] *Ibid.*, pp. 173-174.

proceed very far without the development of the corresponding vocabulary.[9]

b. Dewey thus describes the function of words in preserving meanings:

A meaning fixed by a linguistic sign is *conserved for future use.* Even if the thing is not there to represent the meaning, the word may be produced so as to evoke the meaning. *Since intellectual life depends on possession of a store of meanings, the importance of language as a tool of preserving meanings cannot be overstated.*[10]

c. The third function of words, reapplication of meanings, is thus described by Dewey:

When a meaning is detached and fixed by a sign, it is possible to use that meaning in a new context and situation. This transfer and reapplication is the key to all judgment and inference. It would little profit a man to recognize that a given particular cloud was the premonitor of a given particular rainstorm if his recognition ended there, for he would then have to learn over and over again, since the next cloud and the next rainstorm are different events. No *cumulative* growth of intelligence would occur. . . . To be able to use the past to judge and infer the new and unknown implies, that, although the past *thing* has gone, its *meaning* abides in such a way as to be applicable in determining the character of the new. Speech forms our great carriers: the easy-running vehicles by which *meanings* are transported from experiences that no longer concern us to those that are as yet dark and dubious.[11]

Dewey summarizes these three functions of words in relation to meanings as follows:

Combining these various functions in a mixture of metaphors, we may say that a linguistic sign is a fence, a label, and a vehicle —all in one.[12]

---

[9] Inglis, *op. cit.,* p. 426.
[10] Dewey, *op. cit.,* p. 174.
[11] *Ibid.,* pp. 174-175.
[12] *Ibid.,* p. 173.

It is clear from these quotations that the crucial element in the learning of a language is appreciation of *meaning*. Teachers can at once apply this criterion and test the extent to which their teaching of Latin makes genuine appreciation of meaning, whether of Latin as Latin, or of the English translation, the *sine qua non*. One practical result of the application of this criterion is the demand that continuous Latin reading material be made the basis of the work of the first year. Detached Latin sentences are commonly the very embodiment of meaninglessness.

2. *Organization of meanings.* But important as words are in relation to specific meanings, they are still more important in enabling us to make logical connections. To quote Dewey again:

The chief intellectual classifications that constitute the working capital of thought have been built up for us by our mother-tongue.[13]

and again:

[Linguistic] signs not only mark off specific or individual *meanings*, but they are also instruments of *grouping meanings;* they also form *sentences* in which meanings are organized in relation to one another. When we say "That book is a dictionary," or "That blur of light in the heavens is Halley's comet," we express a logical connection—an act of classifying and defining which goes beyond the physical thing into the logical region of species, genera, things, and attributes. Propositions, sentences, bear the same relation to judgments that distinct words bear to meanings or conceptions; and just as words imply a sentence, so a sentence implies a larger whole of consecutive discourse into which it fits.[14]

Inglis's summary is instructive:

Language is an instrument even more important for the individual's thinking than for the expression of his thought, or for his understanding of the thoughts of others expressed through

---

[13] *Ibid.*, p. 175.   [14] *Ibid.*

language. The point cannot be too strongly enforced that language is an instrument on which must depend the individual's actual thinking to a very considerable extent. . . . Failure to recognize properly [this value] . . . constitutes one of the most serious defects in the teaching of the mother-tongue in the secondary school.[15]

The problem of the school in relation to language. As the practical outcome of his analysis of the function of language, Dewey [16] defines the problem of the school with reference to language as: "to direct the pupils' oral and written speech, used primarily for practical and social ends, so that gradually it shall become a conscious tool of conveying knowledge and assisting thought." It is the process of making the mother-tongue "a conscious tool of conveying knowledge and assisting thought" to which the activities of the Latin classroom are potentially able to make so significant a contribution as, in the opinion of Inglis,[17] to justify its presence in the curriculum.

Main function of the study of foreign languages. Inglis [18] analyzes with great acuteness the inevitable limitations of the mother-tongue as an instrument for developing language-thought relations. His discussion deserves careful study by all teachers of languages, whether foreign or vernacular. He concludes that "the most general and fundamental values of the study of foreign languages in the American secondary school are found in connection with language-thought relation, and serve to aid the study of English at the points where the limitations of the latter are greatest."[19] In analyzing the relative potential values of the various foreign languages studied in high school in developing the mother-tongue as an instrument of thinking, he assigns the first place to Latin.[19]

---

[15] Inglis, *op. cit.*, pp. 427-428.
[16] Dewey, *op. cit.*, p. 179.
[17] Inglis, *op. cit.*, pp. 434, 474.
[18] *Ibid.*, pp. 434-438.
[19] *Ibid.*, pp. 471-474.

Improvement of vernacular for thinking purposes distinguished from "transfer value." Before undertaking the task of analyzing the learning processes through which the proper study of Latin may contribute to the development of the ability to think through improved efficiency of the mother-tongue as an instrument of thinking, it will be pertinent to call attention to the difference between this potential value of Latin and the so-called "transfer values," which will be discussed in a later chapter. Improved efficiency in the use of the mother-tongue does not necessarily involve the transfer of elements from one language to another or the transfer of mental functions. Yet the development of this improved efficiency in the use of the mother-tongue through its use "as a conscious tool for assisting thought" should tend to create conditions favorable for such transfer. For in proportion as a pupil improves in his ability really to appreciate meanings and to make terms for these meanings more precise, in that proportion is he more likely to recognize common elements in his experiences, because of his more exact understanding of the one element common to these experiences, namely, his mother-tongue. It is, for example, reasonable to suppose that, if a pupil has shown by his translation of a Latin sentence that he has fully appreciated and adequately expressed the meaning of certain Latin words, he will more readily grasp the force of those Latin words when he meets them in English derivatives. Or, if a pupil has shown by his rendering of a paragraph of Cicero that he has fully appreciated and adequately expressed the meaning, his recognition of analogous elements in other social or political situations will be facilitated.

Value of Latin for improving the mother-tongue as an instrument of thinking. We are now prepared to examine the potential values of Latin in developing the mother-tongue as an instrument of thinking in the specific ways in which Dewey has indicated that the improvement of language improves thinking; namely, in the development of a capital stock of words (apprehension and preservation of meanings); in the development of increasing precision and accuracy in the use of words as related to thought; and in the development of habits of interrelating those words so as to facilitate consecutive thinking and consecutive discourse. Inglis's treatment of the potential contribution of Latin to the development of these three elements of thinking is so comprehensive and illuminating as to deserve quotation practically in full.

1. *Enlargement of vocabulary*. With respect to the enlargement of vocabulary, Inglis puts the main emphasis upon the practice of translation, although he recognizes also the contribution made by the systematic study of English words derived from Latin.

a. Attention has been called previously to the fact that there is a constant tendency for the individual to accumulate verbal symbols, particularly abstract and general words, and words representing qualities and relationships, without clear consciousness of their meanings. In the development of our use of language there comes a time when the ability to understand words heard or seen (especially in a context) far outstrips our ability to use those words to assist thought or to express thought, and only partially to grasp the thought expressed by those words when heard or seen in any new context. In the study of a foreign language, especially in the process of translation, consciousness of the meaning of the word of the mother-tongue is a necessity before the thought can be interpreted, though exception to this statement must be made in cases where the term to be translated has a single equivalent in the mother-tongue. That conscious attention to the meaning of terms which may be minimized in the use of the mother-tongue when its use becomes more or less mechanical is highly fostered in the study of a foreign tongue, particularly in the process of translation. This arises from two facts: first, that in a large proportion of cases terms of the foreign language have not exact equivalents in the mother-tongue; second, that the context does not give meaning to the specific term in the same ready way in which the context of the mother-tongue has rendered aid to its interpretations.

b. The amount of aid afforded to the enlargement of vocabulary by a knowledge of words in a foreign tongue from which words in the mother-tongue have been derived or to which they are etymologically related is doubtless at times much exaggerated. This should, however, not blind us to the undoubted fact that such etymological values exist and ought not be minimized. The number of words in the English language derived directly or indirectly from the Latin has been estimated as high as 50 or 60 per cent of our total vocabulary. It should be noted also that words of the English language derived from Greek, Latin, and French sources are those most closely related to precise and accurate meanings (many were introduced for that very purpose), while our Anglo-Saxon words are the more common terms for "ordinary affairs and conveniences." [20]

2. *Rendering vocabulary more precise.* It is clear that the process described above of enlarging vocabulary through practice in translation is at the same time a process of rendering vocabulary more precise and accurate. The particular value of practice in translating a foreign language for rendering vocabulary more precise is thus described by Inglis:

Importance may be attached to the study of a foreign language because of the practice which it affords in relating words to the thought. Terms in any one language seldom have exact equivalents in any other language. Hence the interpretation of one language in terms of another necessarily involves a constant comparison and weighing of terms more or less similar, a selection and choice of the correct words to express the thought, and a judgment of the thought to be conveyed by the word or words employed. Thus, consider the amount of comparison, discrimination, and choice involved in the translation of the Latin word *res* under varying conditions—thing, object, event, circumstance, occurrence, matter, condition, situation, act, property, factor, fact, reality, effect, substance, possession, benefit, profit, advantage, interest, weal, cause, reason, ground, account, business, case, suit,

---

[20] *Ibid.*, pp. 463-465.

etc., etc. Now, increased precision and accuracy in the use of language and thought must result almost exclusively from practice in comparing, discriminating, and selecting the appropriate word for the desired thought element, and conditions favorable for such comparison, discrimination, and selections for the better relationing of words and thought are those which *do not merely permit, but actually demand,* the operation of those processes. Those conditions may be amply provided in the study of a foreign language.[21]

However, the procedure of requiring pupils to memorize single English equivalents of Latin words to be used in translating is fatal to the attainment of the desired end, as Inglis clearly shows:

It is to be noted in this connection that, wherever single exact equivalents are associated in the foreign and the mother-tongues, no such comparison, discrimination, selection, and relationing can result, the mere substitution of symbols results, and hence increased precision and accuracy is impossible.[22]

On the other hand, Inglis points out that languages differ radically in the extent to which they invite the use of single exact equivalents in translation, and estimates the relative educational value of language in the reverse order of their susceptibility to such treatment.

Since the proportion of exact equivalents differs in the various foreign languages, this factor permits some measure of the relative values of the study of foreign languages with reference to those now under consideration.[23]

Inglis repeatedly indicates the conclusion that the ancient languages are superior to modern foreign languages from this point of view.

One measure, therefore, of the relative values of the study of foreign languages is to be found in the differences in their vocabu-

---

[21] *Ibid.*, pp. 465-466.   [23] *Ibid.*, p. 466.
[22] *Ibid.*, p. 466.

laries demanding careful comparison, discrimination, and selection of terms in the mother-tongue as expressing the intended thought. Now in this respect there is a great difference between the modern languages and the ancient languages. The modern languages all express modern thought in the modern way. Both the thought and the manner of expressing the thought are much closer in the case of modern languages than in the case of an ancient language and a modern language. At first thought this might appear to offer an advantage in favor of the study of a modern language. The opposite is, however, the case where not content but practice in comparison, discrimination, and selection are the important elements involved. . . . The more different the vocabularies and the manner of expressing thought, the greater is the opportunity and necessity for careful comparison, discrimination, and selection without which the interpretation into the mother-tongue is of little value other than for content. If this be true, we cannot do otherwise than assign superiority to the study of Latin and Greek as far as these linguistic values alone are concerned.[24]

3. *Development of habits of interrelating words to facilitate consecutive thinking and discourse.* It is in this connection that Inglis concludes that the study of foreign languages is indispensable in view of the inevitable and inherent limitations of the study of the mother-tongue.

The English language, with its unusually large vocabulary of words borrowed from almost every possible source, with its abundance of approximate synonyms well adapted to express numerous shades of meaning, and to permit extensive discrimination in thinking and expression, is well adapted to its needs as an instrument of expression, and for intellectual enterprises. To these ends also it is well adapted by reason of the relative flexibility which permits its easy manipulation. However, acquired in the early stages for purposes of social intercourse, and employed commonly for purposes of everyday use in circumstances which do not emphasize its use as a precise and accurate instrument of thinking or expression, its use does not enforce such conscious relationing of words and expressions as is involved in the use of a more syn-

---

[24] *Ibid.*, p. 473.

thetic language. Without a certain amount of such conscious relationing, conditions are not favorable for the transformation of the use of language for the ordinary affairs of everyday life into its use as an intellectual instrument.

It is just here that the study of a foreign language, especially a language which is more synthetic, may be made of service for the accomplishment of such a transformation. In the study of a foreign language, that conscious relationing of terms and phrases not only may but must take place, and wherever translation is involved it must take place in the mother-tongue as well as in the foreign language. Such a process becomes necessary as a result of vocabulary differences previously emphasized, and as a result of differences in word order and differences in inflectional usages in the mother-tongue and in the foreign language.[25]

Again Inglis concludes that Latin provides a better medium for the development of the desired processes than do modern foreign languages:

Here the factors involved in evaluating foreign languages as assisting this process are (a) differences in word order, and (b) differences in inflectional and syntactical usages. The greater these differences, the greater the necessity imposed on the pupil of consciously attending to the interrelating of terms employed for the expression of thought. In point of the amount of difference in word order, there can be no hesitation in classifying the Romance languages, French and Spanish, in a class closely similar to English, classifying Latin and Greek as far removed from English, and German as occupying a position between the other two classes, nearer the first than the second. Such values as arise here affect the languages in ascending order: French and Spanish, German, Greek, Latin.[26]

---

[25] *Ibid.*, pp. 466-467.   [26] *Ibid.*, p. 474.

CHAPTER III

THE OBJECTIVES OF LATIN

It has been asserted in the preceding chapter that the ultimate justification of Latin as an instrument of secondary education must depend upon the successful attainment of its potential educational values. It follows that, if these educational values are to be realized, teachers of Latin should have as definite a conception of these values, and of the relation of the daily tasks to them, as they have of the traditional elements of Latin which constitute its indispensable immediate objectives.

Values not realized automatically. First of all, the teacher must realize fully that for the great majority of pupils studying Latin, the attainment of its educational values to a degree sufficient to justify its study requires that these values become objectives consciously aimed at through the use of appropriate content and method.

The elaborate defenses of the "values" of Latin published during the decades preceding the report of the Classical Investigation commonly assumed without the support of any objective evidence whatever that these values were the normal products of the study of Latin and that they were being realized automatically; that is, if pupils studied and learned Latin, the potential values of Latin accrued without any definite efforts on the part of the teacher to secure those values beyond, perhaps, calling the attention of the pupils to their existence.

However, few teachers of long experience in instructing pupils in Latin in secondary schools labor under any such delusion. They have been too constantly confronted with the difficulties of securing, even within the limits of Latin itself, an accurate application of principles learned, to be able to cherish the comforting belief that pupils whose powers seem so limited in the comparatively easy problem can or do, on their own initiative, perform the much more difficult task of generalizing and applying outside the Latin class what is being learned in it. This opinion, generally held by thoughtful teachers, has been confirmed by the practically unanimous verdict of psychologists, and by the overwhelming evidence of data derived from tests and experiments.

Introspection suggested. Were any doubt still remaining as to the extent to which the average pupil realizes automatically the "transfer values" of Latin, it might be removed by a frank introspection on the part of Latin teachers of their own personal experience. It may be assumed, since the opponents of Latin assert it, that teachers of Latin are as a group superior to other teachers in their native mental endowment. As language students they presumably possess superior linguistic ability and a high degree of that ability to generalize upon which automatic transfer depends. If the claims of the "automatic" school are correct, teachers of Latin who have studied Latin for six or eight years, and have taught it in addition, should be conspicuous for their mastery by automatic transfer over all the fields of knowledge to which Latin is intimately related. They should be past masters of derivation without ever having studied it; thoroughly familiar with the relations of Latin to the Romance languages, because they automatically note those relations. They should possess a wide historical background and a keen appreciation of the influence of Roman civilization upon our own, since these products are implicit in the Latin texts read. They should be especially strong in their understanding of general language relationships, because the languages they studied are potentially able to develop these conceptions. Yet few teachers of Latin will claim to be in possession of these related fields of knowledge, unless they have made them a special object of study. Tests given to groups of teachers of Latin show conspicuous lacks, unless they have supplemented through definite study what knowledge they secured merely as students of Latin.

No criticism of Latin teachers is implied in these statements. They are made simply to show that automatic transfer cannot be relied upon to any considerable extent even in the case of a highly selected group.

General principles of "transfer." For these reasons, it may be asserted that the conclusions regarding transfer set forth in the report of the Classical Investigation [1] are abundantly justified. The main paragraphs are:

1. Automatic transfer is a function of the intelligence of the pupil, and comparatively few young pupils possess capacity for independent generalization in a sufficient degree to justify the adoption of methods of teaching Latin which assume the occurrence of automatic transfer to any large extent.[2]

In other words, pupils having very high intelligence quotients may possess the ability independently to see relations and make applications of Latin outside the classroom on their own initiative. Doubtless many personal testimonials to the value of Latin have been not only sincere but justified because their authors brought to the study of Latin the requisite generalizing ability. For other pupils automatic transfer can be counted on only in situations where the application is so nearly identical with the original material that recognition is a matter of course.

[1] *The Classical Investigation* (Part I): *General Report* (Princeton University Press, 1924), pp. 55-62, 183-188.
[2] *Ibid.*, p. 184.

2. For the great majority of pupils studying Latin, the development of the habit of generalization and consequent transfer calls for <u>continued practice</u> in it by teacher and pupil.[3]

In other words, for most pupils "the transfer of training has become a problem of training for transfer."

3. When a particular habit, trait, or aim has been generalized and has been repeatedly applied to other fields, it may be expected to become automatic.[4]

In other words, it is not expected that the total value of Latin in assisting pupils to learn French will be limited to the applications to which attention is specifically called. If the mental barrier has been broken down and the <u>habit</u> formed of associating the facts of Latin with French through a limited amount of systematic application of Latin to French, it may be expected that most pupils will continue the process independently.

Contemporaneous realization of values. A second fundamental element in the situation is the necessary abandonment, in view of the facts, of the theory that pupils will reap the returns of their efforts in later courses. The theory of "postponed returns" was the dominating note in the report of the Committee of Ten, in 1894. Even at that period it is an open question whether a sufficiently large number of those who began the study of Latin in high school continued it in college to justify the claim that very many reaped the postponed returns for which their four years of Latin was held to be the necessary preparation. Even for those who studied Latin for four years the term "college preparatory" became less and less legitimately applicable to the course as a preparation for continuing Latin in college. Latin came to be recognized as a "selective agent," and four years of Latin as a certificate of intellectual ability.

---

[3] *Ibid.*, p. 185.   [4] *Ibid.*, p. 187.

As to the situation at present the facts are clear. They are summarized in Chapter I, and abundantly justify the conclusion reached that "the work of each year, therefore, beginning with the first, should be so organized as to be worth while in itself, whether or not the pupil is to go further in the study of Latin."[5] It might be affirmed that the course should be so organized that a week or a month or a term or four years would yield results commensurate with the time spent.

In view of the facts, there can be little ground for refusing to admit that Latin is studied in high school primarily for purposes to be realized during the secondary period. It has ceased to be merely a college-preparatory subject.

Ultimate and immediate objectives. A thorough understanding of the objectives of Latin, both of those pertaining to Latin itself and of those involving educational values, is for the reasons discussed above an indispensable part of the equipment of all teachers who accept the present situation as their working basis.

In discussing the objectives of the study of Latin, it is necessary at the outset to emphasize the important distinction between immediate and ultimate objectives. By ultimate objectives are meant those which involve educational values upon which the justification of Latin as an instrument in secondary education depends; namely, those abilities, knowledges, attitudes, and habits which continue to function after the school study of Latin has ceased; for example, the ability to determine the meaning of an unfamiliar word derived from Latin, the habit of sustained attention, or an appreciation of the influence of Roman civilization on the course of western civilization. By immediate objectives are meant those indispensable aims in which progressive achievement is necessary to insure the attainment of the ultimate objectives, but which may cease to function after the school study of Latin has ceased; for example, the ability to conjugate a Latin verb or to translate a passage from Cæsar.[6]

---

[5] *Ibid.*, p. 31.   [6] *Ibid.*, p. 32.

The intimate interrelation of these two sets of aims is repeatedly and vigorously insisted upon in the report of the Classical Investigation.

These two fundamental aims, namely, attainment of the immediate and ultimate objectives, should be concurrent and mutually supporting throughout the course from the very beginning of Latin all the way to the end.[7]

The continual interdependence of these two aims should be explicitly recognized in the content of the course and in the methods of instruction employed. For example, the reading material selected should be of such a character as to provide the best basis for developing progressive power to read and understand Latin, and at the same time to make the largest possible contribution to attainment of those objectives which depend primarily on the thought-content, such as development of a general historical background.[8]

The development of these immediate and ultimate objectives should be continuous, concurrent, and interdependent.[9]

The argument has been advanced in opposition to the doctrine outlined above, that pupils cannot apply what they do not know, and that they should first learn their Latin and later learn to apply it. It is difficult to understand what is meant in such arguments by "learning Latin." At what point in the course may it be assumed that pupils have learned Latin? The fact is that they will not know all the Latin there is at the end of a postgraduate course and a lifetime of study. On the other hand, pupils know or should know *some* Latin at the end of the first day. From that point progressive mastery continues. Waiting until pupils have "learned their Latin" is simply the discredited theory of "postponed returns" in a slightly disguised form. Furthermore, there is conclusive evidence to show that pupils "learn their Latin" more rapidly and more thoroughly as a result of the mental processes involved in applying it as they learn.

---

[7] *Ibid.*, p. 83.   [8] *Ibid.*, p. 84.   [9] *Ibid.*, p. 182.

Primary immediate objective. The Classical Investigation defines the primary objective of Latin as "the progressive development of ability to read and understand Latin." [10] Translation into English is regarded either as one of the means of testing a pupil's understanding of Latin, or as an exercise in English expression.

The elements of Latin not ends in themselves. The classical report properly emphasizes the fact that the study of vocabulary, syntax, and inflections is secondary and only a means to the primary end of developing power to read Latin. It particularly deprecates the teaching of forms and syntax in a way which seems to make them ends in themselves. What is here meant by teaching forms and syntax as if they were ends in themselves will be made clear in the later chapters on those topics. Translating English into Latin is also regarded as an important instrument for teaching forms and syntax, that is, as a means to a means, as a *method* and not an objective.

Primary and secondary immediate objectives. The author would, therefore, classify the immediate objectives in the study of Latin as follows:

Primary: Progressive development of power to read and comprehend Latin   *Ch. V* -
Secondary: Progressive mastery of vocabulary   *ch VI.*
   Progressive mastery of inflections (*forms*)   *ch VII*
   Progressive mastery of syntax (*rules*)   *ch VIII*

The distinction between the primary and secondary immediate objectives is a vital one. Much of the congestion in the work of the first year could have been eliminated long ago if the elements to be mastered, especially syntax and inflections, had been rigorously limited to those which really function as means by which reading power is secured. There is no point at which the dynamic function of objec-

---

[10] *Ibid.*, p. 32.

tives in determining relative emphasis is more decisive than
here.

The ultimate objectives of Latin.   The ultimate objectives approved by the Classical Investigation are in general
accepted as the basis for the present discussion. They are
as follows: [11]

1. Increased understanding of those elements in English which
   are related to Latin.
2. Increased ability to read, speak, and write English, and
   increased efficiency in the use of the mother-tongue as an
   instrument of thinking itself.
3. Increased ability to learn other foreign languages.
4. Development of correct mental habits.
5. Development of an historical and cultural background.
6. Development of right attitudes toward social situations.
7. Development of literary appreciation (last two years).
8. Elementary knowledge of the simpler general principles of
   language structure.
9. Improvement of the literary quality of the pupil's written
   English (last year).

The more specific objectives which are comprised in certain of these general objectives will be discussed in Chapters
IX-XI.

**Relation of the ultimate objectives of Latin to general
objectives of secondary education.**   What is the relation
of the objectives just defined to the general objectives of
secondary education? In 1918, the Commission of the
National Education Association on the Reorganization of
Secondary Education published a bulletin that should be
familiar to all Latin teachers, entitled "Cardinal Principles of Secondary Education." [12] It set up seven main
objectives of secondary education, as follows:

1. Health
2. Command of fundamental processes

---

[11] *Ibid.*, pp. 78-79.
[12] United States Bureau of Education, Bulletin No. 35, 1918, pp. 10-11.

3. Worthy home membership
4. Vocation
5. Citizenship
6. Worthy use of leisure
7. Ethical character

It may be said that the objectives listed in "Cardinal Principles" have received wide acceptance in theory, but that only gradually are they modifying practice in the schools.

Perhaps the most completely worked out set of objectives for the secondary schools is that published in 1927 by the North Central Association of Colleges and Secondary Schools.[13] This report sets up four main ultimate objectives. As will be seen, these represent the seven objectives of the "Cardinal Principles" in condensed form:

1. To maintain health and physical fitness
2. To use leisure time in right ways
3. To sustain successfully certain definite social relationships, such as civic, domestic, community, and the like
4. To engage in exploratory-vocational and vocational activities

This report also sets up four immediate objectives "which serve directly as guides in the selection of subject matter and in determining emphasis and neglect in teaching."[14] These are:

A. Acquiring fruitful knowledge
    1. Preparatory to acquiring other knowledge
    2. Knowledge which functions directly in developing dispositions and in discovering and developing abilities
    3. Knowledge which is useful in the control of situations of everyday life
B. Development of attitudes, interests, motives, ideals, and appreciations

---

[13] *North Central Association Quarterly*, Vol. 1, No. 4 (March, 1927), pp. 1-16.
[14] C. O. Davis, *Our Evolving High School Curriculum* (World Book Co., 1927), pp. 96-101.

    C. Development of definite mental techniques in memory, imagination, judgment, and reasoning
    D. Acquiring right habits and useful skills

More recently, a committee of the National Education Association on the Objectives of Secondary Education has defined the four main objectives of secondary education as follows: [15]

    1. To promote the development of an understanding and an adequate evaluation of the self
    2. To promote the development of an understanding and an appreciation of the world of nature
    3. To promote the development of an understanding and an appreciation of organized society
    4. To promote the development of an appreciation of the force of law and of love that is operating universally

Identification of particular with general objectives. In organizing the curriculum of a particular subject in the secondary school, there are evidently two methods of approaching the problem of identifying its objectives with the general objectives of secondary education.

Analysis from the point of view of general objectives. We may accept these general objectives as the explicit bases from which to work, and analyze the potential capacities of the particular subject to contribute directly or indirectly to the general objective. An illustration of this method will be found in the report of the Latin subcommittee contained in the report of the North Central Association referred to above.[16] This is one of the best syllabi that has been produced in Latin since the publication of

---

[15] National Education Association, *Sixth Yearbook,* Department of Superintendence, 1928, pp. 51-56.
[16] "Report of the Committee on Standards for Use in the Reorganization of Secondary School Curricula: Latin Committee Report," in *North Central Association Quarterly,* Vol. 1, No. 4 (March, 1927), pp. 55-76.

the classical report, but in the judgment of the present writer the attempt to bring each of the potential educational objectives of Latin under one of the general categories seems unnatural and forced. It does not appear that we are ready for that step yet. We have not been thinking long enough in terms of general objectives to be able to make a convincing appraisal of the specific activities of a subject in terms of its potential contributions to the general objectives. The potential educational values of Latin are clear, definite, and undeniable, yet they cut through the general categories at a different angle. It would be difficult to say, for example, to which of the seven (or four) general objectives a knowledge of English derivatives primarily contributes. Before this type of procedure can be expected to be fruitful, the general objectives of education must be analyzed in much greater detail. Such an analysis has been attempted, but it is significant that only so long as committees confine themselves to general objectives is there any widespread agreement.

Analysis from the point of view of the particular subject. The alternative procedure available to the teacher of a school subject who fully recognizes his obligation to make the study of his particular subject contribute to the larger objectives of education is to analyze its potential capacities independently and *from within the subject* with the general objectives of education sympathetically in mind, and with an earnest scrutiny of the possibilities of the subject from that point of view. This was the procedure adopted in preparing the report of the Classical Investigation. If teachers of Latin and of other subjects conscientiously and uncompromisingly analyze the genuine educational values of their subjects, and if, in the meantime, the general educational objectives are resolved into particulars that command general acceptance, a gradual rapproachement may be anticipated. For the present, and probably for some time to come, the most promising avenue of approach is from within the subject to the general educational objectives, and not from the general educational objectives to the subject.

CHAPTER IV

Interest

Justification vs. **motivation.** The recognition in recent years that the study of Latin, especially in the first year, has values for English as its main justification is reflected in the tendency, manifested in a number of recently published elementary Latin books, to explain to pupils in the introductory lessons the reasons why they are studying Latin, and to analyze the values which they will derive from it. The typical book of fifteen years ago contained little indication to the pupils either through content or method of any sound reasons for studying Latin. The natural reaction has led to the practice of listing the values of Latin as furnishing the motives for its study. From the point of view of intellectual honesty this practice is altogether healthy, but the motives which actuate immature pupils, and the valid reasons why they should study Latin, rest upon entirely different bases. Motives, to be genuine and powerful, must spring from the emotions and not from intelligence. An intellectual understanding of the educational values of Latin cannot be expected to inspire the pupil with a keen desire either to undertake the study of Latin or to persist in his efforts to overcome its difficulties. Pupils will not normally undertake or pursue a subject with zest merely because it is good for them, even though the fact be demonstrated to their complete satisfaction. Still less are such analyses of values early in the course likely to influence the pupil, especially when the returns promised the pupil are chiefly indirect. Even direct vocational appeal has very slight effect upon pupils of secondary-school age, as has been conclusively shown by the experience of teachers of commercial subjects.

Desire to learn Latin the chief motivation. The only sound, permanently active motivation for the study of any language must, in the nature of things, spring from the desire to learn the language, and from a consciousness of steady progress in the mastery of it.

Lack of motivation in the traditional course. It was one of the most serious defects of the traditional course that it afforded little or no opportunity for the development or operation of that motive. Pupils normally entered upon the study of Latin with zest and with the healthy interest and curiosity which provides the basis for any real learning. Except in the case of specially endowed pupils, that interest and zest soon faded away, for it was quickly discovered that progress *in the language* was not the objective to which the pupils' efforts were being directed, but progress *in learning forms and syntax.* Language had been associated in the minds of these pupils with the expression or comprehension of thought, and it was with this point of view that they began the study of Latin. When this object was lost ·sight of, through the inevitable pressure of excessive requirements in grammar, with it disappeared the interest of the average pupil. The emphasis in the report of the Classical Investigation upon the reading of Latin, and especially the recommendations that continuous Latin be introduced at the beginning as the basis of the course, is an explicit recognition of the necessity of capitalizing, rather than diametrically opposing, the natural interests and capacities of adolescent boys and girls.

Progress in the language the chief satisfaction. Progressive development of the ability to read and understand Latin, then, provides the strongest direct appeal to the natural language interest of the pupil, and the most power-

ful incentive to vigorous application. The ultimate success
of the pupil depends in the main upon the extent to which
this motive is preserved unimpaired.

Motivation of the study of the elements. If learning to
read and understand Latin becomes the main motivation
in the pupil's mind for the study of Latin as a whole, this
reading and understanding of Latin in turn furnishes the
most effective motivation for the mastery of vocabulary,
syntax, and inflections. If interest in the material being
read and satisfaction at the sense of progress exist, the
necessity of understanding a new fact in order to understand the story results in a more vigorous attack upon the
unknown fact than a formal presentation could be expected to excite. And it is precisely the attitude with which
a new fact is attacked that is most decisive with reference
to retention and later recall. Many experiences with new
facts will normally be necessary before mastery is attained,
but if the initial presentation arouses the pupil to the fullest
exercise of his interest and powers, the number of repetitions required will be appreciably diminished.

Differences between the elements in their appeal. The
amount of motivation needed for attacking new problems
of vocabulary, syntax, and inflection differs markedly.
Pupils are already word-conscious when they undertake
the study of Latin. Many of them have played at making
up languages, and this play consists of substituting new
words for old. They, therefore, have little difficulty in
recognizing a new word as new and as requiring explanation. The case is quite different with new problems of forms
or syntax. English-speaking pupils are not only *not* form-
conscious, but their previous preoccupation with words as
all-sufficient for the understanding of language creates a
serious obstacle to developing sensitiveness to forms either
new or old. Accordingly, the learning and instinctive recognition of forms and their functions requires a powerful and

conscious motivation. Suggestions regarding this problem will be found in chapters on Inflection (Chapter VII) and Syntax (Chapter VIII).

The values of Latin explicitly embodied in the course. At the same time, the course should provide copious illustrations of the educational values of Latin which pupils may at any given stage be expected to appreciate for themselves. It is far more convincing for pupils actually to encounter derivatives whose meaning is obviously made clearer by a knowledge of their Latin origin, than to be told in the introduction to the book that "Latin is valuable for English." To let the content of the course and the tasks assigned regularly illustrate the potential values of Latin is much more effective than to preach about its values. Instead of telling the pupil that the study of Latin will provide him with a valuable historical background, let the content of the Latin read and the teacher's treatment of the content consistently exemplify that potential value from the beginning. Instead of pointing out that Latin will assist him to write grammatically correct English, let him discover that fact through solving tangible and appropriate problems in which errors are commonly made. Instead of telling him that Latin has great training value, let the mental processes employed in his study of Latin be such as to build up desirable mental habits. In short, let the teacher's practice do his preaching for him.

Consciousness of values of Latin from experience. Consciousness of the values of Latin should, therefore, develop from continuous experience of their realization. And consciousness of the values of Latin, if developed through experience, has an important bearing upon motivation by supplying a rational justification for an initial spontaneous language interest. Every normal boy or girl will sooner or later, either of his own accord or through some external stimulus, ask himself and his teacher, "What's the use of

Latin?" Explicit consciousness of values provides the answer to this question, but if the answer is to be sincere and not simply material for an argument, it must have arisen from the consciousness that those values are actually being realized. Consciousness of values being realized provides for the pupil the intellectual motivation for the study of Latin, as a natural interest in a new language provides the emotional motivation.

1. must see it as a language.
2. are word conscious but not form conscious.

CHAPTER V

THE IMMEDIATE OBJECTIVES: COMPREHENSION AND TRANSLATION

CONTENT

Reason for uniformity of content. The uniform content of the secondary curriculum in Latin in this country has been the result of the uniformity of requirements for college entrance examination, especially as to *amount*. These requirements have exercised not only a direct control over schools which emphasized this preparatory function, but also a potent indirect influence in maintaining the traditional course even in sections of the country professedly not affected by them. Freedom in the choice of *kind*, introduced in 1910, has been so restricted by inflexibility as to amount, that it has been largely illusory. The situation is fully discussed in the report of the Classical Investigation, pages 115-123.

Elimination of prescriptions as to amount. The elimination of prescriptions as to amount in the new requirements announced by the College Entrance Examination Board [1] in 1926, has now brought flexibility and variety in the selection of reading material within the realm of the practical. The question, "What Latin should be read in secondary schools?" becomes for the first time more than an academic question. It cannot be expected that any

---

[1] College Entrance Examination Board, Document No. 120, December, 1926, pp. 30-32.

authoritative answer to that question will be reached except through an extended period of experimentation.

Continuous Latin from the beginning. The report of the Classical Investigation urges strongly that "the reading of continuous Latin should begin at the earliest possible moment" in the first semester, and that "for at least the first three semesters a large amount of simple well graded easy Latin should be included in the course, and that the first classical authors should not be introduced, at least in unmodified form, before the beginning of the fourth semester." [2] These recommendations are in harmony with the judgment of the large majority of teachers of Latin. They had been, in fact, anticipated in many places throughout the country and, notably, in the unpublished report of the Committee on Classical Languages of the National Education Association.

Criteria for selection of reading content. The chief criteria set up in the report of the Classical Investigation for the selection of the reading for the first three semesters are as follows:

1. *Capacity for developing the power to read Latin.*

This reading material should be abundant, repetitious, simple and varied in form, attractive in its content, and carefully adapted to the capacity of young boys and girls. . . . It should, from the beginning, conform to the genius of the Latin language, should illustrate the synthetical character of Latin, and should embody the essential problems of Latin word order and suspense of thought. . . . The first brief sentences should advance not merely in length, but in complexity, slowly approaching the structure of the developed periodic sentence.[3]

2. *Capacity of subject matter to provide for the attainment of the historical-cultural values of Latin.* The

---

[2] *The Classical Investigation* (Part I): *General Report* (Princeton University Press, 1924), pp. 124-125.

[3] *Ibid.,* p. 127.

following list of important topics which should be represented in the reading material of the first three semesters
is taken from page 128 of the classical report:

Classical mythology
Roman traditions and dramatic events in Roman history
Biographical sketches
Home life of the Romans
Ideas of the Romans about their environment
Examples of Roman wit and wisdom
Anecdotes and fables illustrative of Roman life and thought,
particularly those which have a moral and embody the charac-
teristic virtues of the Romans
Legends and stories heroic in character, such as were used by
the Romans themselves to inculcate true standards of conduct,
which because of their heroic quality appeal to the imagination
of youth
Stories on ancient themes which have a human appeal analogous
to that found in stories used in teaching modern foreign languages

It is not intended to suggest that any one topic be long
continued. Rather there should be an interweaving of topics
and returns to earlier topics to provide variety. The writer
believes that the dominating topic during the first semester
should be the life of the Romans, including their home life
and their other normal activities; that during the second
semester especial attention should be given to Roman traditions and dramatic events in Roman history, especially
those that are inspiring and "heroic in character, such as
were used by the Romans themselves to inculcate true
standards of conduct and because of their heroic quality
appeal to the imagination of youth"; [4] and that Greek
mythology, although represented in the earlier semesters,
should be given more consideration in the third semester.

Emphasis upon the Roman element in the content.   The
reason for the emphasis upon the Roman element during

[4] *Ibid.*, p. 128.

the first year seems obvious. It is the language of the Romans that is being studied, and it is to a knowledge of the Roman background that the reading material of the first year should mainly contribute. Fortunately, there is an abundance of material of this sort to be derived from Livy and other Latin authors.

Objections to "Fabulæ Faciles." The writer is inclined for several reasons to doubt the advisability of giving to Ritchie's *Fabulæ Faciles* as much time as is frequently given to them during the first three semesters. In the first place, the reading of all the *Fabulæ* including the Argonauts focuses a disproportionate amount of time, especially in the case of two-thirds of the pupils who study Latin for two years or less, upon a few Greek stories at the sacrifice of the Roman element, which constitutes the main ingredient in claims for the historical-cultural values of Latin. In the second place, it would be an astonishing arraignment, if justified, of the poverty of Latin literature, if with all its resources it cannot furnish interesting and valuable material, especially for the work of the third semester. Livy and other authors are abundantly able to furnish genuinely Roman material. Why, then, devote so large a proportion of the time to made Latin based on Greek ideas? In the third place, the *Fabulæ Faciles*, while built around interesting stories as a nucleus, were prepared chiefly to illustrate grammatical principles systematically, and not to provide stories inherently interesting. The Perseus story is sufficiently short so that interest does not pall; but the long-drawn-out story of Hercules becomes intolerably monotonous to many pupils. It is frequently asserted that the Argonauts is of great interest to pupils. On the basis of the author's own experience and that of many others, he is inclined to believe that most pupils find it dull. It is told with too great detail to hold the interest. As stated above, the *Fabulæ* are altogether too long to warrant the devotion of so much time to so few stories. Greek mythology should be included, but the striking features of a dozen myths with all their atmosphere can be presented in much less space.

Complete reappraisement of Latin literature necessary. The need that is increasingly felt as one attempts to select and adapt reading material for the first three semesters, and which becomes imperative with the fourth semester is a complete reappraisement of Latin literature on the basis of its relative potential values for use in secondary education. The same criteria are recommended in the classical report for selecting material from classical authors, as were employed in selecting material for the first three semesters: (a) "suitability of the Latin as a medium for the progressive development of power to read and understand Latin," [5] and (b) suitability of the thought content "for the development of the historical-cultural objectives." [6] With reference to the first criterion, the factors which the author considers especially important are:

In observation look for these

a. The extent to which the material is adapted in difficulty to the ability of the pupil.
b. The suitability of the thought content to the maturity of the pupil.
c. The suitability of the material for creating in the pupil a sense of progress in the mastery of the language.
d. The attractiveness of the material to the pupil.[7]

Certain negative considerations. In the application of these criteria certain negative considerations are pertinent:

a. Pupils are not interested in authors as such. This interest is appropriate to maturity, but there has always been a tendency

[5] *Ibid.*, p. 129.
[6] *Ibid.*, p. 130.
[7] J. Allison Stevenson, "Pre-Cæsar Reading in Latin: Contents of the Ideal Second Year Book," New York Board of Education, *Bulletin of High Points*, Vol. IX, No. 5 (May, 1927), pp. 32-33.

in any attempt to broaden the course to have certain authors represented because of their importance in Roman literature. Thus the new college entrance requirements suggest that Phaedrus, Aulus Gellius, Eutropius, Rufus, Valerius Maximus, and Nepos be introduced. The recommendations of the report of the classical investigation (pages 149-151) read apart from the preliminary discussion (pages 129-132) might be interpreted in the same way. But the intent there is something quite different. Pupils cannot be expected to feel or acquire any natural interest in these authors as such. All of them and, in fact, the entire range of Latin literature, should be open to examination for material conforming to the criteria recommended. Availability of material, from whatever sources, to exemplify the aims set up, is the primary object of the search, not an acquaintance with a given author for its own sake.

b. Another point of view appropriate to maturity but highly inappropriate to immature secondary pupils is the traditional conception that particular works of authors should be read completely through, or, at any rate, should constitute an entire year's work. This supposed satisfaction in *completing* a work is an unjustified imposition of the adult mind upon the adolescent. It is the sense of progressive mastery of a subject which makes the strongest appeal, and the inherent interest of the material read, whether a long or a short selection, is the main desideratum. If considerable material from one author is read, a topical arrangement appears to be better adapted to stimulating and maintaining interest in the content than long unbroken selections.[3]

c. The pupils were not made for Latin; on the contrary, Latin should be selected and adapted for the pupils. No original text should be considered sacred at any stage of the secondary course

---

[3] "Our text must be arranged so that it can be assigned topically, going far in the matter of simplification, if necessary, to connect it with the type of reading that has been the custom of the preceding term. It should, at the outset, be simple and amply repetitious, progressing gradually in difficulty. . . . Then we can take up topics, such as 'The Helvetians Cross the Rhone.' This would, of course, be simplified and rewritten to bring out one or two constructions. Objection may be made that we are not reading Cæsar's Latin; to which I should reply that Cæsar did not write his commentaries with a view to having our boys read them. If we sincerely desire to have our pupils get the benefit of his works, we should be willing to present them in the form in which their worth may be most readily assimilated." J. Allison Stevenson, *loc. cit.*, p. 33.

if its modification will make it a better medium for developing a sense of progress. Textbook writers and teachers are frequently obsessed with an attitude toward an original Latin text which makes of it something sacred and inviolable, forgetting that the needs of pupils should be the chief consideration.

d. The range of Latin literature open for appraisement should not be restricted by the reservation of particular authors for use in college. Livy, for example, probably contains more material available for secondary use than any other author. His histories are commonly read in college and have for that reason been avoided in high school. But it is unjustifiable to deprive ninety-five pupils of material because five may read it in college, and there is no real duplication even in the case of the five. Stories from Livy to be read in the secondary school must necessarily be adapted to an early stage of progress.

Place of Cæsar. It is difficult to prophesy what Latin authors will ultimately prove to be most suitable for the needs of the secondary school. It is open to question, for example, whether, in view of the wide range of interests of Roman literature, and of the genius of our own civilization, we are justified in this country in devoting even a half year to the military campaigns of one Roman general. In certain European countries the emphasis upon Cæsar is probably justified by the fact that his commentaries furnish the introduction to the history of these countries.

A growing number of schools throughout the country not infrequently postpone the reading of a classical author until the fifth semester, on the ground that the decisive consideration which determines the time at which the first Latin author should be taken up by any given class is not any arbitrary number of semesters but the attainment by the pupils of actual power to read the easier Latin with some degree of facility. This practice affords an opportunity to experiment throughout the two years with reading material selected as to content solely on the basis of its suitability for interpreting to young pupils the most significant and appropriate phases of Roman life and thought.

In any case, the reading material during the first two years should introduce pupils to those phases of Roman life which offer the most helpful and inspiring lessons to the youth of to-day. Particularly should emphasis be placed upon the three great loyalties of the Romans; loyalty to the family, devotion to country, and fulfillment of obligations to the gods.

Place of Cicero. Again, the orations of Cicero require, for any real comprehension, a degree of maturity not possessed by the majority of pupils at so early a stage in their Latin course. In no other country are the orations of Cicero read with so limited an amount of previous experience.

Vergil satisfactory. Vergil is the only author whose works appear to be properly placed pedagogically in the traditional secondary course. The greater liking which pupils evince for Vergil as compared with Cæsar and Cicero [9] is not to be accounted for by the greater command of Latin possessed in the fourth year. The relative appeal of these authors varies too much to be thus explained. Vergil is a story, the thought content of which is suited to the level of ability reached. Neither of these conditions is supplied by Cæsar's *Commentaries* or those works of Cicero commonly read. The new requirement of the College Entrance Examination Board, prescribing one semester each of Cæsar, Cicero, and Vergil, should encourage authors and publishers to attempt seriously "to select from Latin literature as a whole the material they believe will make the greatest direct contribution to the attainment of the historical-cultural objectives." [10]

The following list of the topics of major interest which should be represented in the material read is taken from page 131 of the report of the Classical Investigation:

[9] *The Classical Investigation* (Part I): *General Report* (Princeton University Press, 1924), pp. 73-74.

[10] *Ibid.*, p. 131.

The attainments of the Romans in government, politics, law, commerce, economics, literature and art.

Religious ideas and practical philosophy of the Romans.

Characteristic Roman virtues.

Private and public life of the Romans.

History and traditions of the Romans, including selections from narrative, oratorical, poetic and biographical literature.

The continuity of Græco-Roman civilization and its influence upon western civilization.

Significance of Rome as a whole, especially as a governing state and a consequent stimulus to the imagination of mankind.

Background sources for the teacher. Whatever Latin material may be selected for any given stage of the course, it is vital that the teacher should not only be thoroughly familiar with the Latin itself, but should have a comprehensive grasp of its setting, background, and historical significance. This can be secured only by study for that purpose.

For the general course of Roman history two books may be mentioned as particularly valuable for teachers, *A History of Rome* (Macmillan Co., 1921) by Boak, a rather dry account but one which gives an exceptionally clear and lucid view of the successive epochs, and *A History of Rome* (Henry Holt & Co., 1923) by Tenney Frank, an excellent corrective of the first-mentioned book, emphasizing the larger aspects of Roman history and giving due consideration to economic problems. For more detailed accounts of particular periods or episodes, *A History of Rome* (Longmans, Green & Co., 1896) by How and Leigh is recommended. Two source books for Roman history in translation are *A Source Book of Roman History* (D. C. Heath & Co., 1904) by Munro, and *A Source Book of Ancient History* (Macmillan Co., 1912) by Botsford.

For the period of the revolution with which the authors commonly read in high school are concerned, teachers will profit from reading *Seven Roman Statesmen of the Late*

Republic (Edward Arnold, London, 1923) by Oman, *The Gracchi, Marius and Sulla* (Scribner's, 1896) by Beesley, and the first volume of Ferrero's *The Greatness and Decline of Rome* (G. P. Putnam's Sons, 1909).

Other books dealing with particular contents will be found in bibliography given in the Appendix.

For the private life of the Romans, the best books for teachers are *The Private Life of the Romans* (Scott, Foresman & Co., 1905) by Johnston, and *A Day in Old Rome* (Allyn & Bacon, 1925) by Davis. For the larger social aspects of Roman life, *Social Life at Rome* (Macmillan Co., 1909) by Fowler is the standard reference.

For Roman political institutions, the best books are *Roman Political Institutions* (Ginn and Co., 1911) by Abbott, and *Roman Constitutional History* (Allyn & Bacon, 1902) by Granrud. A more detailed account, especially valuable for the period of the revolution, is *A Constitutional and Political History of Rome* (Methuen & Co., London, 1899) by Taylor. For the fundamental theories of the Roman State, *Roman Public Life* (Macmillan Co., 1901) by Greenidge is recommended.

For the religious life of the Romans, the volume announced in *Our Debt to Greece and Rome* series,[11] entitled *Roman Religion* by Laing should meet a serious need. Teachers are referred to the chapter on Roman religion in any good general history. The *Life of Rome* (Oxford University Press, 1927) by Rogers and Harley contain translations of passages from Latin authors bearing on the religious ideas of the Romans.

Teachers should be well acquainted with books on ancient mythology through such works as Gayley's *Classic Myths* (Ginn & Co., 1911).

The military side of Roman life is less significant for

---

[11] Longmans, Green & Co.

modern times than most other aspects. The traditional high-school course gave it undue importance. The best book on the subject is *Warfare by Land and Sea* (Longmans, Green & Co., 1923) by McCartney.

The best book dealing with the indebtedness of modern civilization to Greece and Rome is *The Legacy of Rome* (Oxford University Press, 1923) by Cyril Bailey. A number of volumes in the *Our Debt to Greece and Rome* series [12] will also be found valuable.

Selected translations from classical authors are of particular value in giving teachers a rapid view of available material. *The Life of Rome* (Oxford University Press, 1927) by Rogers and Hartley, and *Roman Literature in Translation* (Harper & Brothers, 1924) by Howe and Harper are especially recommended.

Emphasis upon understanding the content. In harmony with the emphasis upon the selection of a reading content intrinsically valuable, the report of the Classical Investigation [13] places great emphasis upon the importance of insisting that pupils understand fully the thought of what is read.

We recommend that much more attention be given to a full understanding of the thought content of the reading. We make this recommendation both because of the belief that pupils should be taught to regard language primarily as a means of conveying thought and because of the clues which a clear understanding of the story up to a given point will give for the comprehension of the thought of the passage which follows.

The failure of pupils to understand the thought even of passages translated with apparent accuracy has been, under the traditional course, a widely prevalent evil. There frequently seems to be no expectation on the part of a pupil

[12] Longmans, Green & Co.
[13] *The Classical Investigation* (Part I): *General Report* (Princeton University Press, 1924), p. 199.

that a given passage should have a sensible meaning.
From this disregard of the thought content arises the per-
nicious tendency merely to string words together without
any semblance of rational meaning. Insistence that pupils
understand fully the thought of everything read is the *sine
qua non* for the justification of the study of Latin.

Preliminary study of background of Latin material.
Unless the material read is complete in itself and fully intelligible without any further knowledge of the background,
this background should be provided through preliminary
collateral reading in English and sufficiently intensive work
upon it to make the content of the Latin wholly intelligible.

The dominating motive in the mind of a pupil as he attacks
an advance lesson should be a desire to follow the progress of the
story. If this purpose is to be attained, he must, in the first place,
understand something of the setting of the story. A reading of
Cæsar or Cicero, for example, if not preceded by a careful study
of the historical background, is almost certain to fail of this purpose. It seems quite impossible for the pupil to acquire this necessary background contemporaneously with his reading of the Latin
text. We, therefore, recommend that some prescribed reading in
English should precede the detailed study of Latin selections
dealing with particular events or periods, in order to give the
pupil an intelligent understanding of the background, and to enable him to fit what he reads in Latin into its place in the general
scheme.

Equipped with a preliminary knowledge of the setting of the
story secured from reading in English and from classroom discussions, pupils should then be expected to understand the thought
content of what is being read in Latin from day to day, and to
understand its bearing upon the larger whole of which it forms a
part.[14]

The following devices for emphasizing the thought content of material read as a whole are taken from the report
of the Classical Investigation.[15]

---

[14] *Ibid.*, pp. 204-205.   [15] *Ibid.*, p. 205.

An occasional review of the story from the beginning to the point reached by the class

Frequent summaries of chapters in which important events are rounded out (for example, the mutiny in Cæsar's army during his campaign against Ariovistus)

Maps, plans or outlines upon the board which are modified as the reading proceeds

The use of such devices as the following for vivifying the story:

   a. Class discussions

   b. Debates

   c. Dramatization

   d. Pictures and slides

   e. Reading such books as Whitehead's *The Standard Bearer,* Holmes's *Cæsar's Conquest of Gaul.*

METHOD

Latin word-order method. Probably no section of the report of the Classical Investigation has provoked as much discussion, favorable and otherwise, as its vigorous recommendations that pupils be trained to take in the thought of a Latin sentence in the Latin order. This method will be designated in this discussion as the Latin word-order method.

As was pointed out in Chapter I, there is nothing new in this method. It has been consistently recommended in all national reports since 1894. It has long been an integral part of the requirements in Latin of the College Entrance Examination Board. The report of the Classical Investigation, however, devotes an unusual amount of space to an analysis of the reasons for the general failure to adopt the method and to a fresh presentation of the arguments for it. This discussion has focused the attention of teachers upon the problem.

Definition of method. A good deal of the current debate on this problem has arisen from a failure to define terms. The power to read and understand Latin is defined in the classical report as "the ability to get the thought in the

Latin order and directly from the Latin itself instead of backwards and indirectly through translation." [16] It is more fully defined by the following paragraph quoted from the announcement of the College Entrance Examination Board:

From the outset particular attention should be given to developing the ability to take in the meaning of each word,—and so, gradually, of the whole sentence,—just as it stands; the sentence should be read and understood in the order of the original, with full appreciation of the force of each word as it comes, so far as this can be known or inferred from that which has preceded and from the form and the position of the word itself." [17]

It is obvious that the essential element in the power desired is the ability to take in the thought of a Latin sentence in the Latin order. This process is not, as is sometimes assumed, both by proponents and opponents of the method, equivalent to "thinking in Latin," although it doubtless provides a favorable condition for it.

Arguments for this method. The desirability of training pupils to take in the thought of a Latin sentence in the Latin order rests upon several grounds. In the first place, it would seem indisputable that pupils may most reasonably be expected to develop power over the Latin language in so far as, in their attempt to understand the thought of a Latin sentence, they employ methods which most closely approximate the way in which the Romans themselves took in the thought of Latin sentences. That in doing this they will make *conscious* use of tools used *unconsciously* by the Romans does not affect the argument. The analytical method of attack by which pupils are trained to look first for the subject, then the verb, then the object, and then to fit in the rest of the sentence also depends upon the *conscious* use of specific procedures.

In the second place, the Latin word-order method brings

---

[16] *Ibid.,* p. 93. [17] *Ibid.,* p. 94.

the pupil into immediate contact with the genius of the Latin language, the most important element in which is the suspense made possible by the synthetical character of the language. That not all Latin sentences involve suspense, as the letters of Cicero testify, will readily be granted. Probably most of the conversational Latin involved little suspense; but it may be asserted with confidence that suspense is the characteristic element of all of the classical Latin ordinarily read in school and college. It is unfortunate that in discussions of this type, teachers of Latin should sometimes display the very linguistic provincialism which it is maintained the study of Latin will correct. The assertion that a given procedure is the "natural" course to follow in the study of a foreign language because it happens to be a characteristic of the English language is a serious indictment of the capacity of Latin to develop general-language concepts. Linguistic phenomena in English which are in harmony with the genius of the foreign language studied should certainly be used as a legitimate apperceptive basis, but the linguistic phenomena in English inconsistent with the genius of the new language should not only *not* be used as apperceptive material, but should be eliminated from consciousness so far as this is possible, in as much as they create a constant barrier to any genuine appreciation of the genius of the new language. Allowing or encouraging the pupil to attempt to reconstruct Latin on a basis foreign to its nature is what has given rise to the idea that a Latin sentence is a puzzle to be pieced together, instead of a thought to be understood.

In the third place, it is assumed by those who believe in developing the ability to take in the thought of a Latin sentence in the Latin order, that language is primarily a vehicle for the expression and comprehension of thought; that the method employed in teaching Latin should be such as to keep that primary fact paramount; and that any method which obscures it or relegates it to the background constitutes linguistic stultification. That the analytical or translation method does represent an activity readily separable from, and, therefore, unfavorable to, concentration upon the thought, is one of the most familiar demonstrations of the classroom. Translations are frequently given, and all too commonly accepted, *in lieu of* an understanding of the thought.

In the fourth place, the mental processes involved in taking in the thought of a Latin sentence in the Latin order possess very significant potential values for mental training. If the process is analyzed, it will be found to be almost identical with the process of reflective thinking, as described by Dewey in *How We Think*. The essential attitude of a pupil studying a Latin sentence is suspended judgment, which Dewey denotes as the most important factor in reflective thinking.[18]

Reflective thinking, in short, means judgment suspended during further inquiry; the most important factor in the training of good mental habits consists in acquiring the attitude of suspended conclusion, and in mastering the various methods of searching for new materials to corroborate or to refute the first suggestions that occur.

Dangers of the Latin word-order method. As suggested above in connection with the first argument for the Latin word-order method, advocates of the method will need to be on their guard against the fallacy which has been a very potent factor in the general failure of the direct method of teaching Latin. Attempts to use the direct method to develop the power to understand Latin of any serious grade of difficulty on a purely habitual or *unconscious basis* have been disappointing because users of the method have failed to recognize the fact that Roman children, before they

---

[18] John Dewey, *How We Think* (D. C. Heath & Co., 1910), p. 13.

came to read Latin of comparable difficulty, or even to read any Latin at all, had already heard and come to understand without conscious effort a vastly greater amount of Latin than modern pupils will have heard by the time they attack their first classical author. The ratio of 1,000 to 1 probably does not exaggerate the difference. There is no conceivable possibility of furnishing our pupils with a total number of unconscious experiences with spoken Latin remotely approximating that of the Roman boy. Since the essence of the direct method is *unconsciousness*, its failure as a basis for developing the ability to read Cæsar within the preparatory period allowed is inevitable.

An analogous situation holds with reference to the reading method. It cannot be expected that pupils will develop *unconsciously* the ability to read Latin unless they have had a wide reading experience at each successive level of difficulty, involving an amount of material and a period of time comparable to that which a Roman boy had before he was expected to comprehend *unconsciously* Latin comparable to that of the Manilian Law. Such a provision in the pupil's school program is obviously impossible.

A substitute for unconscious acceptance of thought necessary. It is clear that some elements must be introduced into the learning process which will enormously reduce the number of experiences necessary for the thought of a Latin sentence to be comprehended in the Latin order. *Consciousness* of the process supplies the answer. In fact, it is difficult to believe in the soundness of any theory which would deny to conscious intelligence its proper rôle in the educative process. The power of conscious generalization, that is, the learning and application of principles, provides the indispensable short-cut. Yet the theory is often advanced, not only in connection with the learning of languages, but in other phases of education, that consciousness of the process should be eliminated. This appears to the present writer a wholly untenable assertion. Why should man in his own education deprive himself of the use of his most distinctive faculty? That consciousness may become inhibitory rather than contributory to the formation of a habit no one will deny. We shall all agree that unconsciousness is the goal, but conscious repetition of a habit, it may be confidently asserted, will continue to be the basis for the formation of most unconscious habits, both in the practical affairs of life and in intellectual pursuits.

Technique of Latin word-order method. As applied to the taking in of the thought of a Latin sentence, consciousness means that the pupil, for example, is consciously aware of the uses of the accusative case. That is, he has the ability, *if required*, to state all possible [19] uses in terms of thought relations. The pupil has developed that ability through numerous *conscious* applications until finally he is able to select the pertinent possibility *without conscious debate*. It should be noted that it is not the giving of all possible uses which, on this basis, is the crucial element, but the *ability to do so*. The moment a pupil actually has the ability to call explicitly into consciousness all the ideas potentially expressed by a given form, at that moment it becomes not only unnecessary but undesirable to have him do so.

Absolute consistency not possible. A teacher may be an enthusiastic advocate of the Latin word-order method and yet not commit himself to uncompromising consistency in the use of the method. A pupil will sometimes encounter a Latin passage which is obviously too difficult to be comprehended in the Latin order at his stage of progress. Teachers must remember that the material from classical authors commonly read in high school was not written for

---

[19] The emphasis on *possible* ideas should be noted. An accusative like *puerōs* obviously cannot express time how long, extent of space, or degree.

pedagogical purposes and, therefore, does not constitute an ideal medium for the uncompromising development of *any* method. No one is troubled by a similar lack of consistency in the reading of English. Every one has probably been forced, at times, to analyze difficult sentences of English prose or poetry before he has fully understood the thought, but no one has ever set this experience up as evidence that our normal procedure in taking in the thought of an English sentence is unsound, and still less has anyone advocated that, because of such experiences, pupils should be taught to analyze *all* sentences as a basis for getting the thought. The adoption of the Latin word-order method does not, therefore, commit teachers to an undeviating use of it under all conditions, under pain of exposing themselves to the charge of inconsistency. We are not advocating the use of a method for the sake of the method, but as a tool for penetrating the thought of a Latin sentence. Those who believe in making the Latin word-order method the controlling factor in the methods of teaching Latin, need not be disturbed when they are sometimes faced with the necessity either of modifying the text to fit the degree of attainment reached at any given stage, or of modifying the method to be used in connection with such material.

It may be said that not even the best of Latin scholars will ever get beyond the point of having sometimes to analyze Latin sentences in order to arrive at the thought. The occurrence of such passages has always been the ultimate argument of those who have opposed the Latin word-order method, but it may be asserted that at no stage from the beginning of the study of Latin to the end of a professional career as a teacher of college Latin, does the inevitable occurrence of such occasional problems legitimately affect our choice of a normal method. There can be no such thing as absolute consistency of method in the teaching of Latin or any other subject. Adaptation of method to the immediate situation is one of the most constant demands made upon all teachers.[20]

Place of translation in the Latin word-order method. It is sometimes assumed by opponents and proponents alike, that reading Latin by the Latin word-order method involves doing away with translation. It is difficult to see, if the pupil has actually taken in the thought of the Latin sentence in the Latin order, how the presence or absence of a subsequent activity can have any essential bearing on the problem. The idea that the Latin word-order method must, of necessity, dispense with translation seems an entirely gratuitous assumption. It may fairly be argued that the use of questions and answers in Latin, instead of translation, as a means of testing comprehension, tends to create a favorable condition for the acceptance of the thought of the sentence in Latin, but this is a question of method and depends largely upon the personality of the teacher. The use of translation as the *sole* means of testing comprehension is justly criticized in the report, and the recommendation is strongly made that the amount of the text to be translated be materially reduced in order to make possible the attainment of a higher standard of English; but it is assumed that translation following comprehension will always be a very important activity of the classroom.

"Thinking in Latin." Opponents of the Latin word-order method are also prone to assume that the Latin

---

[20] This point is fully recognized in the report of the Classical Investigation, page 197: "While recommending that a reading method following the Latin word order be regularly employed by the pupil in his attack upon a Latin sentence, we recognize the fact that in the interpretation of difficult passages it will at times be necessary to resort to a detailed analysis. We urge, however, that in all such cases the pupil should be made clearly to understand the difference between this process and the reading method to be regularly employed."

word-order method involves the assumption that pupils
must from the beginning think in Latin. While this is
doubtless a legitimate ultimate goal, the experience of
modern-language teachers forces us to conclude that for
a long time it must be expected that the pupil will do his
thinking in English. Teachers of French, for example, are
fairly well agreed that when the teacher holds up a pencil
and says "un crayon" the pupil does not immediately
associate "un crayon" with the object. What goes on in
the mind of the majority of the pupils is probably "Oh, yes,
crayon means *pencil.*" The argument in favor of such an
activity must rest, then, not on the fact that it immediately involves thinking in French, but that the objective
character of the experience reduces the number of times
that *crayon* must be met before it does convey its idea
directly without the interposition of the English "pencil." [21]
If pupils do actually begin to think in Latin as they begin
to read Latin, so much the better, but the argument for the
Latin word-order method must, in view of the common experience, rest upon other assumptions than that it produces
immediate thinking in Latin.

The test of "reading" ability. It is sometimes assumed
that the real test of whether a pupil or even a teacher is
reading Latin is found in the verbal images that arise during the process, and it is assumed that if any English words
arise the person is not reading Latin. The blotting out of
English words is a desirable goal; absolute thinking in
Latin unquestionably requires it, but we are at present
discussing simply the desirability of training pupils to take

---

[21] It should be noted that reading French, whether or not it is supported by oral work, does not have a purpose analogous to that
which must be regarded as the chief purpose of reading Latin,
namely, the direct insight into the genius of Latin; for no such
contrast in the genius of languages is presented by English and
French as is presented by Latin and English.

in the thought of a Latin sentence in the Latin order as the primary objective, with thinking in Latin as a highly desirable, but secondary aim. In that case, the real test which a pupil or teacher may apply, if he desires to find out whether he is reading Latin, is found not in some difficult and usually inconclusive introspective activity, but in the answer to the simple question, "What do I do when I have read a sentence and find that I do not fully understand the thought? Do I instinctively begin to analyze the sentence and tear it apart, or do I find myself instinctively reading the sentence over again in Latin?" [22] If the latter process has become the natural one, then the reader is taking in the thought of the sentence on the basis of the genius of Latin and is reading Latin, even though English near-equivalents pop into his head from time to time. The obtrusion of English near-equivalents should recur with decreasing frequency, but their occasional presence is not a disproof of one's ability to read Latin as Latin and in the Latin order.

Suggested procedures. The main practical problem confronting the Latin teacher who is convinced of the desirability of training pupils to take in the thought of a Latin sentence in the Latin order is how to conduct that training. It has seemed worth while first, however, to strip the desired aim of certain unessential accretions, and to bring the goal within the limits of practicality. It is precisely these unessential accretions which create in the minds of many teachers the idea that the goal is unattainable. What the present writer is interested in from the practical point of view is not what can be accomplished by teachers

---

[22] The test suggested above is almost identical with that employed by Judd and Buswell in their well-known experiments to determine the eye movements used by pupils in reading languages. Judd and Buswell, *Silent Reading* (University of Chicago Press, 1926), Supplementary Educational Monograph No. 23.

who possess unusual linguistic endowments and temperament exceptionally adapted to the development of the ability to think in Latin, but what Latin teachers reasonably well endowed and reasonably well equipped may accomplish in developing the power of pupils to take in the thought of a Latin sentence in the Latin order.

It will be agreed that the aim of any particular procedure is to secure ultimately the *unconscious* acceptance of the thought of a Latin sentence in the Latin order, but it has been pointed out above that the conditions under which Latin is taught as a school subject preclude the possibility of giving pupils an amount of oral and printed Latin at each successive level necessary to attain, through exclusively unconscious assimilation, the ability to read a classical text. The process must be assisted in connection with each new form and each new word by a conscious understanding on the part of the pupil of what he is seeking ultimately to do unconsciously. The chief desideratum in the conscious procedure adopted is that it be persisted in.

Transverbalization or metaphrasing is sometimes advocated as the proper basis of procedure. In following this procedure, the pupils turns each Latin word or phrase into English in the order in which it occurs in the Latin sentence. While this familiarizes the pupil with the order in which thought is presented in Latin, it does not insure the actual comprehension of the relations of words as transverbalized. The perception of relations, the crucial element, frequently comes about only through a rearrangement of the transverbalized elements into the usual English order so as to make sense. Thus, the chief problem, a direct understanding of Latin forms and their functions, has been evaded.

A more common procedure is to give the pupil constant practice in naming in grammatical terms the function of words or word groups as they appear. The difficulty with this procedure is that it assumes that the application of the correct technical term to the function of a group guarantees that the function of the group has been really comprehended. But it may be affirmed that the correct designation of a word or word group as *means* or *agent*, or even as *subject* or *object*, does not necessarily mean that the function of the word or word group has been appreciated in terms of thought relations. What seems to be required as a preparation for the unconscious acceptance of thought, is training in the conscious acceptance of *the actual thoughts* expressed by the successive words or groups. Pupils need to be trained to feel the contribution made to an understanding of the thought of a sentence which results from the recognition of a word as a probable object; they need to feel that a prepositional-phrase expressing agent informs them that the subject has something done to it by the person mentioned in the phrase. The danger in any word-by-word or group-by-group method that does not explicate the contribution made by each group to the thought of the sentence is that it degenerates into a process of classifying and labelling without genuine appreciation of meaning. The writer, therefore, recommends that the conscious training in taking in the thought of a sentence should repeatedly involve the actual construction by the pupil, as he goes along, of complete sentences, often skeletonized to be sure, into which each group fits. This simply means bringing to consciousness just what was really conveyed unconsciously to the Roman by the form of a word, a contribution not limited to the content of the group, but forming a part of a developing, connected, and frequently completely anticipated sentence thought. For the sentence, not the word or phrase, is the real thought unit.

Details of procedure. There is fairly uniform agreement among all the advocates of the Latin word-order method upon the importance of the following factors:

1. *Insistence upon oral reading* as the first step in the attack upon new Latin, whether in sight work in class or in work assigned for home study. But pupils need to be constantly reminded that the object of such reading is to get the thought; that, in such reading, their energies should be concentrated upon the effort to follow the story. Otherwise, reading the Latin becomes a formal drill in pronunciation. The class work especially should emphasize comprehension as the object. Teachers should rigorously restrain their insatiable desire to correct mispronunications until the main object, comprehension, has been secured. Inopportune correction of pronunciation inhibits comprehension of the thought, and leads pupils to believe that, after all, the object of reading is merely correct pronunciation. The data published in the report of the Classical Investigation [23] indicate clearly that the relation of the oral reading of Latin to the understanding of the thought needs to be made much clearer to pupils. For the majority, the exercise is largely perfunctory and unaccompanied by any intelligent effort to understand the thought of what is read. Such oral reading is a waste of time.

2. *Insistence upon careful grouping or phrasing* in such oral reading in class and in preparation at home. This constitutes the only basis for the hope that pupils will comprehend any but the simplest type of sentence. Sentences which can be comprehended "at a gulp" are few. If we can secure an increasing ability to comprehend group-by-group, we shall have attained the utmost that is practicable for most pupils. The exaggeration of pauses between groups will help in developing the idea. Exercises in translation by ear also afford the teacher an opportunity to illustrate what is desired and to demonstrate the aid which grouping gives to comprehension.

3. *Daily work at sight including*

> *a.* A certain amount of conscious work in following through a sentence group-by-group, by one of the methods suggested above.
>
> *b.* A larger amount of rapid work in which an opportunity is given for an unconscious operation of the processes developed in the slower attack. If all work is done consciously, the result will be simply increasing ability to do it consciously. If

---

[23] *The Classical Investigation* (Part I): *General Report* (Princeton University Press, 1924), pp. 173-174, 190.

unconscious acceptance of the thought is the aim, opportunity for practice in this procedure must be constantly furnished.

4. *Questions in advance on form and syntax* to clear up any difficulties anticipated by the teacher in the more rapid comprehension. Questions on syntax are as important by the Latin word-order method as by any other method, but they should be used to assist the pupil in comprehending the thought, not to give him practice in classifying thoughts already comprehended.

5. *Testing comprehension* either by

   a. translation into standard English
   b. questions in English on the content [24]
   c. questions in Latin to be answered in Latin [25]
   d. other devices such as functional questions on syntax

6. *Literal translation or metaphrasing*, whenever necessary to clear up any question as to just how the thought is expressed from the Roman point of view.

7. *Training in comprehension by ear*, and in direct expression of simple ideas in Latin. "Oral use of easy Latin in brief phrases or sentences, especially in the form of questions and answers between teacher and pupil or between pupil and pupil, will help to give quicker facility in the reading and understanding of Latin." [26]

8. *Home assignments* in which reiterated emphasis and continuous encouragement is given to the use in the independent study of new Latin of the methods developed in the work at sight in the classroom. Classroom methods that do not affect habits of independent study have failed of their main purpose.

It should be fully understood by teachers that the use of the Latin word-order method requires a slower development than the analytical or subject-verb-object method.

---

[24] For illustration see *The Classical Investigation*, p. 200. *See also* the Ullman-Kirby Latin Comprehension test, published by the Extension Division of the University of Iowa.

[25] For a series of type questions requiring the use of various principles of syntax as the answer, see the Appendix (p. 190).

[26] *The Classical Investigation* (Part I): *General Report* (Princeton University Press, 1924), p. 192.

Pupils in the initial stages can cover ground more rapidly by recasting the Latin sentence to conform in word-order to the genius of English. Covering ground must be subordinated to the development of power to read Latin, if the latter is accepted as the actual goal. This fact needs to be faced squarely, since the habit of sacrificing everything to the one object of covering ground has been so deeply implanted in secondary schools by the traditional course that its inhibitive effects are likely to be felt for a long time to come.[27]

Translation. The use of translation as one of the means of testing comprehension has been discussed above. Its use as a training in English expression will be discussed in Chapter IX. The substitution of other methods of testing comprehension is repeatedly emphasized throughout the report.[28] It is urged further that "only so much of the reading assignment at any stage in the course be set for translation into English as the pupil can reasonably be expected to turn into English which will accurately interpret the thought of the Latin, will be grammatically correct, and in the case of the more advanced pupils will approach in style and in beauty the original from which it is translated."[29] Only with such a standard can translation fulfill its primary function of developing the "power of thinking and of expressing thought through the process of putting into adequate English a thought already comprehended in Latin."[30]

It is particularly to be desired that the injunction "translate" shall from the beginning of the work mean to the pupils "translate in good English." When literal translation is desired it should be indicated by a difference in phraseology. The discussion in the report [31] on the confusion

[27] *Ibid.*, p. 126.
[28] *Ibid.*, pp. 126-127, 194-196, 201-204.
[29] *Ibid.*, pp. 202-203.
[30] *Ibid.*, p. 201.
[31] *Ibid.*, pp. 195-196.

of ideals resulting from an indiscriminate use of terms should be read thoughtfully by every Latin teacher.

Review translation. The character of all translation whether of advance or review passages will be discussed in Chapter IX in its bearing upon fundamental educational values. The writer, however, believes that the degree of fluency required and attained in review translations has an important bearing upon progress in Latin itself. By a fluent translation is meant one not necessarily rapid, but free from stumbling, hesitations, repetitions, and interruptions of the thought. If from the very beginning of the work in Latin a definite standard of fluency in the translation of review passages is rigorously insisted upon, it will contribute materially to the mastery of Latin.

In the first place, since there are no new elements in the review passages, there is nothing for which pupils may not be reasonably held responsible to a much higher degree than in advance work. It becomes simply a question of the willingness of the pupil to apply himself to the attainment of that which is wholly within his powers. To secure that willingness the teacher should address himself.

In the second place, a fluent translation of the review saves a great deal of valuable class time, which may more profitably be spent on teaching and learning than upon reciting. It is, of course, purely a relative matter. The standard set by the teacher and illustrated by him from time to time will not always be attained by the pupils called upon, but uncompromising reiteration of the standard, commendation of pupil translations that attain the standard, indication of the unsatisfactory character of review translations that fall below the standard, suggestions as to the number of times pupils should go over the passages set for translations, if persisted in, will establish clearly in the minds of pupils what is expected, and the results will be markedly better than without such emphasis.

In the third place, a fluent reading is highly conducive to the desirable habit of focusing the attention on the thought content of the passage. In a slow, stumbling, disjointed translation, the continuity of thought of a paragraph is often obscured by the mere length of the pauses between sentences or smaller thought units, when the closer juxtaposition of these units would have clarified the thought. Experienced teachers are aware that the meaning of a paragraph which had previously been haltingly translated and obviously not fully understood by a pupil, often dawns upon him as he retranslates it, with no added element except closer juxtaposition of the thought units. Inconsistencies which may have been present in a halting translation tend to disappear when fluency is secured. In other words, fluency makes an actual contribution to the understanding of a narrative or argument as a whole. The story gets an adequate chance to help in the understanding of the story.

A definite standard of fluency that will guide pupils in their preparation is desirable. This will vary with different authors. From five to ten lines a minute represents an attainable degree of fluency with authors commonly read in high school.

Teachers often unconsciously encourage the tendency toward halting and disjointed translations by continuously and unnecessarily interrupting pupils when they are translating. A pupil called upon to translate a paragraph should be permitted to go through with it without interruption. He will thus be relieved of the inhibiting expectations of interruptions, his energies will be concentrated on his problem, and the results will be better with less expenditure of time. Corrections of errors and suggestions for improvement should be religiously postponed until the pupil has finished. This practice, if established as the normal procedure, will also discourage pupils from taking advantage of the inter-

rupting habit by inviting it at critical points, and will pro-
mote their acceptance of full responsibility. The practice is
also recommended of asking all members of the class to be
ready to offer suggestions for corrections of errors and for
other improvements, after the pupil translating has finished
his passage.

CHAPTER VI

THE IMMEDIATE OBJECTIVES: VOCABULARY

CONTENT

The traditional emphasis upon preparation for Cæsar which formerly dictated the vocabulary of the first year of Latin has now happily been abandoned. The healthy trend of the past ten years is given definite expression in the report of the Classical Investigation, as follows:

The vocabulary to be thoroughly mastered during each year of the course should be selected for the purpose of providing the conditions most favorable both for the progressive development of power to read and understand Latin, and for the attainment of the ultimate objectives which teachers consider valid for their pupils, and which dev ~d for their attainment upon vocabulary content.[1]

Words valuable for English. Since teachers commonly agree that the most important educational objective dependent upon the content of vocabulary is "increased ability to understand the exact meaning of English words derived directly or indirectly from Latin, and increased accuracy in their use," [2] emphasis upon this value in selecting the words to be included in first-year texts, and to be mastered, is now general. If attention is given to introducing and emphasizing words important for English through the first two years, during which teachers commonly regard

---

[1] *The Classical Investigation* (Part I): *General Report* (Princeton University Press, 1924), p. 133.

[2] *Ibid.,* pp. 42, 134.

this objective as of special importance,[3] the vocabulary stream may be considered sufficiently broadened out to make unnecessary, thereafter, the use of any criterion other than value for Latin in selecting the words to be mastered. Teachers are thus provided with a valuable basis for judging the extent to which textbooks for the first and second year of Latin meet educational demands.

Types of words to be set for mastery. There appear to be, in general, four types of words that should be represented among those set for mastery during the first two years:

1. *Words important for Latin* (applicable to all four years). For authoritative lists of such words, see *A Latin Word List* [4] of the College Entrance Examination Board (in which the words for the first two years are not separated into years), and the word lists of the 1928 Regents' Syllabus of New York State [5] (given for the first two years by semesters and for the last two by years). In the list of the College Entrance Examination Board, about 900 words are given for the first two years and the same number for the last two years. If 2,000 words are regarded as the normal maximum for the four years, a leeway of about 200 for words important for English only is provided. The New York lists comprise about 2,000 words, but do not include those especially important for English only, and do not make a point of assigning to the first year words which are important for English as well as for Latin. The New York lists are thus open to criticism on the ground that they do not consider the needs of the 30 per cent of pupils who will study Latin for but one year. The lists of the New York Regents for the first two years contain about 175 words not contained in the College Entrance Examination Board

---

[3] *Ibid.*, p. 42.
[4] College Entrance Examination Board, 1927.
[5] New York State Department of Education, 1928.

list for the first two years, while the latter contains about 90 words not contained in the former.

2. *Words important for English* (applicable mainly to the first two years). No authoritative lists of Latin words important for English have been issued. The list prepared by Lindsay [6] is rendered theoretically faulty by the failure in his weighting scheme to take into consideration any other criterion than frequency of occurrence of the derivatives in reading. For example, high rank is given to *longus* as a result of the frequent occurrence of English *long,* although the latter is so familiar a word that *longus* cannot possibly be regarded as throwing light upon its meaning. The distinction between familiar and unfamiliar derivatives, while subjective, must be taken into account in determining the relative potential capacity of Latin words to interpret English derivatives. Nevertheless, Lindsay's list has great practical value and should be in the possession of every teacher. The defect criticized, as it affects the value of individual words, is readily recognized and corrected, and when eliminated leaves a list very similar in content to other lists prepared solely on the basis of subjective opinion. An authoritative list, in which the element of presumptive unfamiliarity of English derivatives is taken into account, is in process of preparation by Dr. Wren J. Grinstead. When completed, it will be published as "Part IV" of the report of the Classical Investigation.

3. *Words important for continuous narrative* (first year). The two lists given in paragraph (1) above do not, in the writer's opinion, accept fully the implications involved in the emphasis given now to continuous narrative in the first year. Included among the words to be mastered during the

---

[6] E. Y. Lindsay, "An Etymological Study of the Ten Thousand Words in Thorndike's Teacher's Word Book," *Indiana University Studies,* University Book Store, Bloomington, Ind., 1918.

first year should be the important connectives showing the relation in thought between successive sentences, a vital element in directing the attention of pupils to consecutive thought. This type is represented by such words as *itaque, igitur, tamen, tandem, nam, enim, interea.*

4. *Words important for oral Latin* (first year). This type will be regarded as especially important by teachers who are stressing oral Latin as a basis for encouraging direct comprehension. Lists will be found in books emphasizing the oral method.

METHOD

In discussing method, a distinction must be made between the procedure followed in getting an understanding of the meaning of any new word, and that followed in acquiring the mastery of those words set for mastery.

Independent solving of new words. Most first-year texts published since the appearance of the report of the Classical Investigation have accepted its recommendations regarding the desirability of training pupils to work out the meaning of many new words by observing their English and Latin relatives, and especially by using the context intelligently. There is still some debate on the desirability of this procedure, and it may be well to summarize the arguments.

"Sensible guessing." It is held by some that the habit of "sensible guessing," as this procedure has been described, is harmful to the pupil in that it substitutes inexactness for the exactness produced by preliminary learning of words through special vocabularies. But no genuine meaning attaches to a word except in context. It may be said that not only does the habit of learning a so-called English equivalent as the first step in learning a new word of a foreign language fail to give the meaning of the word, but it often effectually prevents the pupil from ever getting the

meaning. As will be seen later, one of the most conspicuous defects in pupil translations as disclosed in Miss Woodring's examination of the standard of English used by pupils taking the examination of the College Entrance Examination Board in fourth-year Latin,[7] was the persistent, unreflective use of these so-called equivalents, without regard to the actual *meaning* as indicated by the context in which they were used. This idea of the *meaning* of a word, rather than of some arbitrary equivalent, should have been present in the first contact with the word, and the necessary condition for this is a printed or oral *context*.

Use of general vocabulary. If the habit of learning English meanings of words through special vocabularies before the words are met in context is sound in principle, why should it not be continued throughout the course? No book with which the writer is familiar has ever attempted to carry out the principle beyond the first year. But the regular absence of such special-lesson vocabularies from second-year texts, when combined with the lack of any specific training in how to derive the meaning independently, inevitably develops in the pupil the habit of consulting the vocabulary immediately on the occurrence [8] of a new word, and very frequently on its repeated occurrences, with no serious effort either to see for himself the necessary meaning of the word or to master the word permanently.[9] No one has ever defended the repeated consultation of a vocubulary as a habit favorable either for developing intellectual strength or for developing power over Latin.

---

[7] "The Quality of English in Latin Translations" (Bureau of Publications, Columbia University, 1925), pp. 53-60.

[8] "In their effort to solve the meaning of a new Latin word, the method most commonly reported by pupils is to 'look it up at once in the vocabulary.'" *The Classical Investigation* (Part I): *General Report* (Princeton University Press, 1924), p. 172.

[9] *Ibid.*, p. 172.

Retention of new words. In the discussions of the
recommendations of the classical report bearing on this
topic, there is sometimes obvious on the part of college
men a complete misunderstanding of the actual problems
of teaching secondary Latin. There is an apparent assumption that pupils actually *learn* a word by memorizing its
equivalent as a preliminary step to meeting it in reading.
Teachers of secondary Latin are perfectly aware that the
first attempt to master a word, by whatever method, is
merely the first step, and that only by systematic repetition
is the word finally *learned*. The question of how the word
shall first be met and grappled with is simply a question
of what situation is most favorable for the ultimate mastery of the word with the fewest recurrences. The reflective
process involved in working out the meaning of a word in
context involves a mental activity and a concentration
upon how the word is actually used that probably reduces
considerably the number of times a word must be met before it is *learned*.

Summary of arguments. The arguments in favor of giving pupils systematic training in working out independently
the meanings of new words in context may be summarized
as follows:

1. In this way only may the *meaning* of the word be genuinely
appreciated.

2. By fostering a vigorous mental effort it reduces the number
of recurrences necessary for mastery.

3. The process is identical with that which pupils have been
unconsciously following in the acquisition of the greater part of
their English vocabulary. Comparatively few English words in the
possession of pupils have been acquired by consulting the dictionary. The great majority of words have been acquired through
oral or printed contexts. Pupils are, therefore, not learning some
new procedure but are merely learning to do consciously what
they have been continuously doing unconsciously.

4. From the foregoing statement, it is obvious that the training

recommended has a sound apperceptive basis. To introduce the practice of memorizing the equivalents of words as a first step in acquiring a reading vocabulary is in conflict with all of the previous experiences of the pupil, a situation which will appeal to those only who are desirous of making everything about Latin as foreign to the previous experience of the pupils as possible.

5. The intelligent use of context in deciding upon an appropriate meaning for a word involves just that concentration upon the *content* of the material being read that is most favorable to the development of the highly desirable attitude that the material deals with thoughts and not simply with words. Training the pupil to interpret the new word so that it is consistent with a context will do much to eliminate one of the most serious evils associated with the study of Latin.

6. Since the *meaning* of a word, as worked out by the pupil, will normally be defined by the English word most appropriate to the particular context in which it is met, the training of pupils in giving *good* English translations must inevitably be facilitated.

7. In so far as English derivatives and related Latin words are employed in solving the meaning of a new word, there is produced a further development in the pupils' ability to associate Latin with English and Latin with Latin on the basis of etymological relationship. This procedure will also facilitate the complementary habit of employing known Latin words in interpreting unfamiliar English derivatives. It may reasonably be claimed that favorable conditions are also created thereby for developing the general habit of seeing relations and of recognizing similar elements in different experiences, which may be regarded as one of the valuable "disciplinary" objectives of Latin.[10]

8. Dewey, in his discussion of the relation of language to thought, indicates that context is one of the main contributing agencies to the enlargement of vocabulary, and a necessary condition to the development of the mother-tongue as an instrument of thinking.

Enlargement of vocabulary takes place, of course, by wider intelligent contact with things and persons, and also, vicariously, by gathering the meanings from the context in which they are heard or

---

[10] *See* Ch. X, pp. 152-154.

read. To grasp by either method a word in its meaning is to exercise intelligence, to perform an act of intelligent selection or analysis.[11]

9. Problems of this type arouse much keener interest in the pupils than problems of a purely formal type.[12]

10. The actual training involved in such selection and analysis is certainly of higher intellectual value than any that may be involved in the memoriter method. For a further treatment of this potential outcome see Chapter X.

These various points of view are recapitulated in the following paragraph from the classical report: [13]

The methods to be employed in the teaching of Latin vocabulary should be designed to develop correct habits of independent study, to contribute both to the mastery of Latin vocabulary and to the attainment of the ultimate objectives which teachers consider valid for their pupils, and which depend for their attainment upon a knowledge of Latin words, to involve the use of association and apperception, to enlist the interest of the pupil, and to encourage application of facts and processes acquired in Latin to the activities of life outside the Latin class.

Position of lesson vocabularies. The occurrence of each new word "in an enlightening context, oral, written, or printed" [14] in which the central meaning of the word is faithfully represented would constitute the ideal situation. It follows that the practice of printing lesson vocabularies *before* the reading lessons should be abandoned, since this absolves the pupil from making any effort whatever, even that of memorization.[15]

---

[11] John Dewey, *How We Think* (D. C. Heath & Co., 1910), p. 180.

[12] *The Classical Investigation* (Part I): *General Report* (Princeton University Press, 1924), pp. 174, 183, 209.

[13] *Ibid.*, p. 206.   [14] *Ibid.*

[15] "The textbook which confronts the pupil when he is preparing his lessons should be so constructed as to give the utmost help possible for the use of these methods. Particularly is this true during the first year's study of Latin when permanent habits of study are being formed." *Ibid.*, p. 208.

Absolute consistency impossible. It should be recognized that not all new words can in practice be solved independently. Such an ideal would require a context adapted to the stage of mastery of each pupil, and presenting only as many unknown quantities as that pupil can reasonably be expected to solve. There will be a certain proportion of new words whose meanings will have to be given by the teacher or sought in the vocabulary. The aim, however, should be uncompromisingly set up and continuously illustrated by the solution of new words in sight work, which from this point of view also is strategically the most important part of the class period.[16] Teachers who have not previously given pupils an opportunity to use their minds in solving problems of this type will be gratified at the interest shown and at the increasingly satisfactory results. "We are continually underrating," says Morrison, "the ability of children and overestimating their experience." [17]

Drill necessary for permanent mastery. The ideal method to secure permanent retention of the words set for mastery would be to have the word recur in the reading at intervals just great enough to insure recall. First-year books are coming more and more to provide the repetitious type of reading essential for this purpose, but obviously, the extent to which repetition can be deliberately provided in the text decreases as pupils begin to read selections from classical authors in which no consideration is given to the pedagogical needs of pupils. Even here, repetition can be secured by the use of detached oral or printed sentences for review. The sentences to be translated into Latin may

---

[16] "If pupils are actually to develop a strong habit of attacking new words in this way in the independent preparation of their lessons, it is clear that a more persistent effort must be made to give the necessary guidance through daily practice in comprehension or translation at sight." *Ibid.*, p. 207.

[17] Morrison, *The Practice of Teaching in the Secondary School* (University of Chicago Press, 1926), p. 170.

also assume some of this task. But there probably does not exist any text so perfectly fitted to the varying needs of individual pupils as to eliminate the necessity for some formal drill on Latin words and their meanings. In such drills lies a grave danger of substituting an emphasis upon arbitrary English "equivalents," and thereby nullifying the emphasis previously given to the *meanings* of words, with their English renderings determined by the context. Yet, if pupils are continuously warned that the English "equivalent" called for in formal drills and reviews is intended to aid in the retention of the central idea of a word, and is frequently *not* the word to be employed in translating it, and if this principle is insisted upon in the actual work of the classroom, the dangers of impoverishing the pupil's vocabulary may be avoided. Repeated suggestions to the pupil such as the following are recommended:

There is a certain danger in learning by heart particular English equivalents of Latin words, and you will always need to be on your guard against it when you are translating Latin sentences. There is scarcely any Latin word for which there is one English equivalent that covers exactly the same ground as the Latin word and is always to be used in translating it. Words get their meanings largely from the context in which they are used, that is, from the general meaning of the sentence, and thus have many shades of meaning, which should be brought out by using different English words in translating the same Latin word.

The English equivalent which you learn will assist you in remembering the *central idea* of the word, but it will frequently, and in some cases usually, *not* be the best translation of the Latin word when met in a Latin sentence. This is a very important idea for you to grasp. For if you should go through your Latin course always translating the words given in these lists by the same English equivalents, you would impoverish your English vocabulary instead of enriching it. For example, there are probably ten different English words which you should use in translating *magnus* in different contexts; the equivalent, *great*, commonly given to show the key idea of the word, should rarely be used. Practice in translating Latin will be a valuable means of enlarging your English vocabulary if you constantly seek for *just the right word*.[18]

"Intrinsic" and "extrinsic" meanings. The distinction between the central or *literal* meaning of the word and its varying contextual shades of meaning is not only of practical importance for drill as compared with translation, but is justified by certain more fundamental considerations. It is analogous to the distinction between the *intrinsic* and *extrinsic* meanings of English words analyzed by Inglis.[19]

Aside from what we may call the *intrinsic* meaning of a word—the relatively constant element of the fundamental root idea (that which makes it possible for us to recognize a term in different contexts)—there is always in actual use what we may call an *extrinsic* meaning—the varying element attached to the common element or root idea as a modification of it when used contextually in relation to others terms (that which makes it possible to use the same word with somewhat different shades of meaning determined by its surroundings). As a matter of fact, seldom, if ever, does the same term (auditory, visual, motor, or other image) carry the same meaning in any two different contexts, and therefore the readiness with which varying meanings may be attached to the same term is the real desideratum both for thinking and for the expression of thought. The development of a rather extensive vocabulary in which the *intrinsic* meanings of terms are fairly adequate is a relatively simple task and one which may possibly be accomplished through elementary education. The development of an extensive vocabulary in which the *extrinsic* meanings of terms are adequately mastered is an extremely difficult task of great importance in secondary education. This can be accomplished only by constant practice in the organization of consecutive thinking and consecutive discourse.

Although Inglis is here speaking of English words and of the varying contextual shades attached to them, the

---

[18] Gray and Jenkins, *Latin for Today,* First Year Course (Ginn & Co., 1927), Appendix, p. 4.

[19] A. J. Inglis, *Principles of Secondary Education* (Houghton Mifflin Co., 1918), p. 433.

analogous problem in connection with Latin words is obvious. The central or *literal* meaning of a Latin word is that word which best represents its intrinsic meaning, but it is the varying appropriate translations of the extrinsic meaning of the Latin words in which lies the main educational value of the practice of translating.

Importance of mastering vocabulary. The importance of a thorough mastery of vocabulary by whatever method cannot be overestimated. In the study of the correlation between the scores made by pupils who took the Latin tests of the Classical Investigation,[20] made in order to determine what knowledge appeared to have the closest connection with an ability to comprehend and translate Latin, the highest positive correlation was found between a knowledge of vocabulary and a comprehension of Latin. While this may be due in part to the emphasis commonly placed by teachers upon the formal, rather than the functional, aspects of inflections and syntax, it nevertheless indicates the importance of a thorough mastery of vocabulary.

Words to be mastered vs. other words. It is important that the list of words to be absolutely mastered, be definitely drawn up by the teacher for each semester of the course in the order in which they first occur; and that pupils be systematically made aware of their importance as they occur. The larger reading experience now generally accepted as desirable during the first year involves the introduction of a wider vocabulary than has been commonly included in first-year texts, "unless the reading content is to be . . . so restricted in range as to be neither attractive nor instructive."[21] It is correspondingly more important that teachers and pupils should make a clear distinction between words to be mastered and those not

---

[20] *The Classical Investigation* (Part I): *General Report* (Princeton University Press, 1924), p. 92.

[21] *Ibid.*, p. 135.

to be mastered. Many first-year texts make provision for this. The principle applies, however, just as fully to the work of the later years, although it is commonly ignored in the working apparatus provided by most books for the second, third, and fourth years.

CHAPTER VII

THE IMMEDIATE OBJECTIVES: INFLECTIONS

CONTENT

The general recommendations of the classical report regarding inflections are "a reduction in the number of forms to be included in the work of the first two semesters, a more gradual introduction of these forms than is the common practice at present, provision for a repeated reading experienced with the forms to be learned, and in general emphasis upon functional rather than formal knowledge both in the learning of these forms and in subsequent drill upon them. We wish to emphasize our belief that those forms which are set for learning should be so thoroughly mastered that a recognition of a given inflectual ending and of the grammatical ideas possible for that ending will become practically automatic."[1]

Definition of aim. It will clarify the discussion of inflections if we define more specifically the actual ability aimed at through the study of forms. If this ability is accepted as the actual objective, it will provide the solution of many problems of content and method. We shall define this objective as:

The development of progressive ability to recognize accurately and promptly *when reading Latin* the forms of inflected words as they are met, and to apprehend all possible functions of any given form.

---

[1] *The Classical Investigation* (Part I): *General Report* (Princeton University Press, 1924), p. 141.

Danger of overemphasis on paradigms. Thorndike and other psychologists have criticized the uneconomical practice, prevalent in all subjects in which techniques must be developed, of devoting unjustifiable attention to skills that actually interfere with the development of the ability desired, and which have to be unlearned before this ability is secured. Our traditional emphasis upon the learning of paradigms, as the first and frequently the sole technique employed in the mastery of forms, has tended to give pupils just the limited ability appropriate to that technique, namely, the ability to give paradigms. The result is that the pupil, instead of being able to recognize a given form directly, identifies it consciously or unconsciously by its position in a paradigm. Before the individual forms of a paradigm can be recognized directly, this association deliberately created must be broken down. Pupils may, of themselves, ultimately break up these artificial bonds and learn to recognize forms directly, but the whole procedure has been wasteful.

Identification of individual forms. If identification and recognition of individual forms as they are met in reading is admittedly the end desired, this element should be present from the beginning as the determining factor in the learning of forms. This involves the introduction of the forms of the cases at first very slowly in order that there may be abundant opportunity for practice in the recognition of each new form as an individual form with its own inherent *meaning*, and in order that the point of view may be thoroughly established that, even when paradigms are learned, they are learned solely for the purpose of assisting pupils to recognize individual forms as met in reading.

Paradigms not the test of knowledge of forms. It is probably true that not only has much of the formal drill on paradigms been an uneconomical means of developing the ability to recognize individual forms, but the ability to give paradigms has in too many cases become the real objective. This conclusion is borne out by an analysis of a large number of school examination questions given throughout the country. Questions on inflection, almost without exception, merely require the pupil to give paradigms. Rarely does a question appear reflecting the actual problems arising in reading, and requiring the pupil, for example, to locate a series of individual forms which the teacher knows from experience are likely to be confused when met in reading. The practice criticized illustrates what is meant by the statement that the learning of forms frequently becomes an end in itself, instead of being considered strictly as a means of assisting pupils to get the thought of a Latin sentence.

Wide distribution of forms recommended. No part of the report of the Classical Investigation has met with more immediate acceptance than the recommendation [2] that the inflections traditionally ascribed to the first year should be distributed over two years or more, and that the least important be omitted entirely. The fundamental justification for this wider distribution lies in the fact that, even if the paradigms could all be mastered during the first year, recognition of individual forms, the basic element in reading Latin, cannot be secured in that interval. At no point has the lack of opportunity for functional emphasis, produced by the congestion of the traditional course, been more fatal to the attainment of the end really desired.

Summary of findings on learning of forms. The opinions of teachers are abundantly justified by the data derived from tests.[3] The attempt to include the subjunctive mood in the first year has been an ignominious failure, as it was predestined to be. Thus in the Tyler-Pressey Test, *laudares,* apparently the most familiar subjunctive form in

---

[2] *Ibid.,* pp. 140-143, 160-162.   [3] *Ibid.,* p. 142.

that test, was located correctly by 47 per cent of the pupils at the end of the first year; *auditus esset* by 44 per cent; *posset* by 30 per•cent; and the effect of the attempt to learn the forms of the subjunctive before those of the indicative have been mastered is indicated in the correct location of *capientur* by only 16 per cent. When it is realized that even these percentages include an unearned 25 per cent, due to the fact that the test was of the multiple-choice type with a guessing chance of 25 per cent, raising accordingly the actual zero to 25 per cent, it will readily be seen that a little learning is demonstrably a dangerous thing. Since no definite provision was made in the traditional course for attacking such topics at later stages of the course—for the inflections had all been "covered" the first year—this state of ignorance tended to persist throughout the course. The percentage of achievement on the Tyler-Pressey Test as a whole, which was 51 per cent at the end of the second semester, was only 59 per cent at the end of the fourth semester. Not until the sixth semester of the course was an average of 75 per cent obtained on verb forms supposed to have been learned the first year, and this percentage cannot be interpreted as indicating real mastery, especially in view of the multiple-choice character of the test.

Impossible requirements of traditional course.   There is no depreciation or disparagement of the ability of pupils or of the skill of teachers in these facts. In allowing so short a period for the mastery of the elements, we have been attempting in this country to do what teachers in no other country have ever attempted. In the Realgymnasium of Germany, where pupils begin the study of Latin at about the age of 13, pupils will have spent as much time on the mastery of the elements and simple reading before taking up an author like Cæsar, as our pupils will have spent on Latin by the middle of their fourth year. It might be pertinent to ask those who were responsible for the traditional course on what grounds they credited American children with such phenomenal linguistic ability.

One of the unfortunate outcomes of a course, the mastery of which was impossible, has been to blunt our appreciation of what mastery really is. The argument has been seriously advanced by those opposed to the relief of the congestion, that it would be of no avail to make the redistributions proposed since pupils would not master the reduced amount any more thoroughly than they had mastered the traditional amount. This is assuredly a counsel of despair.

Systematic presentation of forms throughout the course. There is, therefore, no "weakening" of the course involved in the recommendations for a drastic redistribution of inflections throughout the course. The corollary of such a redistribution should be accepted. As definite provisions should be made in the textbooks of the second year for the teaching of the specific inflections assigned to the second year, as is ordinarily now made in the first year. It will not suffice to reduce the number of inflections assigned to the first year and throw the pupil wholly on his own responsibility for those assigned to the second year. The situation points to the same solution as do other factors, the organization of the first two years as a unit.

Forms and syntax inseparable. It will be observed that the definition given above of the objective involved in the learning of inflections includes "the apprehension of all possible functions of any given form." In other words, it is impossible, on any sound psychological basis, to separate inflections from syntax. Any knowledge of forms not intimately associated with the syntactical *ideas* which they may express is not only useless lumber, but is bound to foster the conception that Latin is a purely formal study. This indispensable association of forms with their syntactical implications, again conditions the rapidity with which forms can properly be introduced in the early stages of the study, and mastered. Thus, not only is the attempt to learn forms in mass early in the course certain to fail from the point of view of the forms themselves, but it is sure to preclude any real understanding of the *functions* of forms. For it is precisely in the realm of syntax that the difficulties of real comprehension are greatest. The persistent failure to associate function with form remains throughout the course the chief stumbling block, and any artificial separation of forms from syntax inevitably aggravates the difficulty.

Learning of English case-"equivalents" unsound. Any attempt to short-cut the slow processes of attaining a genuine understanding of the ideas expressed by case forms, by requiring the pupil to learn an English *equivalent* for each form cannot be too strongly condemned. This practice is now happily generally discredited. To set before the pupil *silvae; to a forest,* illustrates a mechanistic conception of language which not only does not put the emphasis upon genuine appreciation of meaning, but sets up word substitution as the aim. The phrase *to a forest* is meaningless except in context. The practice here condemned is an implicit admission that the hope of securing understanding of the ideas expressed by the dative case is abandoned at the outset. It affords the enemies of Latin just ground for charging Latin with pure formalism. Formalism cannot provide a short cut to comprehension; it provides simply a basis for the continuance of formalism.

Order of inflections. The crucial element in the recommendations of the classical report [4] regarding inflections is the necessity of wide distribution and abundant functional exercise. The particular details of the distribution are relatively unimportant. Yet there are certain considerations which suggest the advisability of the order recom-

---

[4] *Ibid.,* pp. 160-162.

mended. The best distribution would appear to be decided by the degree of previous familiarity of the pupils with the ideas expressed, by the inherent logicality of groups of forms, and the extent to which a need for a knowledge of the new forms may be created.

Paradigms of nouns and verbs compared. It should be noted that the declensions and the conjugations present somewhat different problems with respect to the danger of formalism. A paradigm of the six Latin cases has no inherent logic. There is no antecedent reason for expecting these particular six case forms. This is sufficiently evident from the fact that the ideas expressed by the six Latin cases are expressed by four in German and Greek, by eight in Sanskrit, and by three in English. The Latin ablative is the repository of two cases besides the original ablative of the parent tongue, and forms of the locative as a separate case still survive to perplex pupils. Unless, therefore, the function of each case is thoroughly understood for itself, the premature learning of the paradigms of the declensions will inevitably be purely mechanical and formal. The situation is different with verbs. The three persons form a necessary and inherently logical scheme readily anticipated because already thoroughly familiar. The two numbers are equally familiar and ·certain to be anticipated, although they are logical only as far as they go. But the theoretical possibility of finding in a new language special number forms for two persons while an actuality in Greek, Sanskrit, and in the parent tongue does not trouble the pupil.

Thus the six *ideas* expressed by the six verb forms of the Latin present tense are already familiar to pupils, and the paradigm of the individual Latin tense has, from the pupil's point of view, an inherent logic already evident to them through the corresponding English paradigm. Because of the fact that a similar paradigm has been built up in English from individual forms, the learning of the Latin verb paradigm is not open to the objection raised in the case of noun forms; for it is inevitably accompanied by a dissociative process through identification of each Latin form with the idea expressed by the familiar English form corresponding to it.

On these bases we will discuss the appropriate distribution of certain important groups of inflections.

First Semester

Observing

1. The ~~nominative,~~ accusative, and genitive of the first declension (or of the first and second declensions) and of pronouns.

These cases express the case ideas most familiar to the pupil. Furthermore, although the English declension comprising the nominative, possessive, and objective cases has no inherent logic,[5] it is already fairly familiar to pupils and sufficiently identical in scope to provide a basis for introducing pupils to declension in Latin.

2. The paradigm of the present indicative of the first and second conjugations and of *sum*.[6]

3. Remaining cases of the first and second declensions and of pronouns. These cases express ideas usually entirely unfamiliar to

---

[5] It is impossible for the writer to understand the argument sometimes advanced that the full declension of nouns should be presented at once on the ground that it is the "logical" thing to do.

[6] It is desirable to include at once illustrations of both the first and second conjugations in order that the necessity of distinguishing between and building up the forms of different conjugations, the central problem of the Latin verb, may be present from the beginning as an indispensable element of the training. If forms of only the first conjugation are present, the very presence of a logical and universal element in the verb paradigms creates the impression that the formation is also uniform and makes a later discrimination more difficult. The type verb of the first conjugation tends to become the model, not only for the ideas, but for the forms as well. [The danger does not exist to the same extent in the declensions because of the absence of any common logical element.] It furthermore permits directing the attention of pupils at once to the stem as the most important of the three basic elements in the organization of the Latin verb (stem, tense sign, personal endings) which produce uniformity amid diversity.

pupils, and the mastery of their functions requires a slow development.

4. Remaining tenses (except future perfect) of the indicative of the first and second conjugations and of *sum*.

It was shown above that the six forms of the individual tenses in Latin embody a logical scheme which makes the apprehension of each of the six forms, in distinction from the others, the easiest problem in the learning of inflections. It is because of this fact that, given the first form of a new tense, pupils are often able to construct the other forms for themselves and give their meanings. This condition does not exist with reference to the functions of the several tenses *in relation to each other,* and it therefore follows that each tense should be presented separately with corresponding emphasis upon its distinctive function. The majority of the ideas expressed by the six Latin tenses are, to be sure, familiar through experience with the verb in English, but the order of the tenses in formal synopses is different, the names of the tenses are different; one Latin tense expresses ideas expressed by two tenses in the English conjugation, and the expression of the progressive idea, not familiar to pupils as part of the conjugation in English, is a normal function of certain Latin tenses. It follows, therefore, that each Latin tense should be presented separately, with emphasis and practice upon its distinctive function or functions.

Second Semester

1. The third, fourth, and fifth declensions.
2. The third and fourth conjugations in the indicative (except the future perfect tense).

It is a commonplace that the greater difficulty of Latin as compared with French is due to its synthetical character as contrasted with the analytical character of English and French. This means that pupils have great difficulty in establishing the habit of associating function with form. To develop the habit of associating function with form is the major problem in teaching Latin, and this problem is prescribed by the genius of the language. The restriction of the work on declensions during the first semester to the first two declensions and to the pronouns is desirable for three reasons:

1. The number of forms attempted is sufficiently limited to permit uncompromising insistence upon direct association of function with form, and at the same time permit a thorough mastery of the individual forms.

2. The number of forms attempted is sufficiently varied to establish the notion that the same function may be expressed by different forms, and precludes the notion that a given idea is always expressed by the same form.

3. The third declension is notoriously the most difficult, and requires more drill for mastery than do the first two. Its premature introduction fosters undue attention to forms, as such, at the expense of a thorough mastery of the form-function habit.

Third Semester

The entire postponement of the forms and uses of the subjunctive mood to the third semester, as recommended by the classical report, is imperative. A serious congestion in the work of the first year has long been recognized, but the remedies that had previously been proposed were so inadequate that they had no appreciable effect upon the situation. What has been needed is the removal to the second year of a topic large enough to provide genuine relief. This is found in the subjunctive mood, the forms of which, if separated from their functions, are not especially difficult, but the ideas of which make heavier demands upon the analytical powers of the pupils than does any other topic of similar scope. It has already been pointed out that we have, in any case, been only pretending to teach the subjunctive mood in the first year. Its mastery at that time by normal classes, under normal conditions, has been demonstrated by experience to be impossible, and its postponement to the second year in the recommendations of the classical report marks the first official recognition of the kind of remedy demanded by the situation.

METHOD

In discussing method, one must make the same distinction between the problems of initial understanding and permanent mastery of forms as was made in the treatment of vocabulary.

Forms to be met in context. The ideal procedure set up in the report of the Classical Investigation [7] involves a first experience with typical forms in the context of continuous narrative, in which the necessity of comprehending the

---

[7] *The Classical Investigation* (Part I): *General Report* (Princeton University Press, 1924), p. 171.

thought supplies the motive for the study of the new form. The precise method employed in securing a recognition of the new form, and an understanding of its function, will doubtless vary greatly with circumstances. "Adaptation to the immediate problem" furnishes the clue. Sometimes the pupil may easily infer the character of a new form from the context or from similarity to familiar forms, either in Latin or English; sometimes he may be led to identify it by skillful questions; probably in most cases the form will need to be explained. It should be noted that the recommendation that new forms be presented in context does not imply an inductive treatment, as some critics of the classical report have assumed. The purpose of so introducing new forms and syntax is to provide a feeling of need for the new knowledge, and thus supply a genuine motive for mastering the new fact.

Indispensable function of paradigms. The learning of paradigms, and oral and written practice in inflecting words on the basis of the models, is an indispensable means of mastering inflections. The total number of forms is too great to be retained without some organizing agency. It may be prophesied that, if teachers should attempt to require of their pupils the retention of all the individual forms without the organizing assistance of the paradigms, pupils would begin to demand some way of systematizing the forms learned. The main point is that the initial learning of the first paradigms should follow, not precede experience with the individual forms, and should serve a real need by assisting pupils to organize the knowledge gained.[8]

---

[8] "A premature memorization of paradigms sets up habits and associations entirely inconsistent with the process which consists of taking in the thought of a Latin sentence as it develops. If, however, pupils first acquire through repeated experience the habit of associating the appropriate grammatical idea with each of the case forms as they are met, the learning of paradigms should then be

Later, when the habit of associating function with form has been established, entire paradigms of new words may be safely learned provided no new functions are immediately involved. Yet all such learning of new inflections should be preceded by informal experiences with illustrations of the new inflection, to be identified as new forms by the pupil or explained by the teacher.

Similarity of forms in different declensions should permit the informal introduction in the reading material of forms of declensions not yet studied. It will not be necessary, for example, to postpone the use of the accusative singular of fourth and fifth declension nouns until all the other forms of those declensions have been mastered.

Comparison and contrast in learning forms. In the learning of any new forms the utmost stress should be placed upon comparison with forms previously learned, and upon explicit recognition of similarities and differences. This requires giving particular attention to the general inflectional systems underlying them. "This is recommended not only because of the assistance which such a systematic organization will afford in combining and retaining a knowledge of the forms, but also because of its value in giving pupils a conception of the genius of the Romans for order and system as embodied in their language." [9]

Use of Appendix. The grammatical appendix of the textbook used provides the best basis for visualizing the common elements in different inflections, and the systematic study of the appendix should be an integral part of the work.

Organization of the verb. The importance to be attached to a thorough knowledge of the organization of the

---

regarded as a convenient and most valuable method of consolidating and organizing the knowledge gained." *Ibid.,* p. 230.
[9] *Ibid.,* pp. 230-231.

verb (stems, tense signs, and personal endings) can scarcely be exaggerated. If this knowledge is secured in the study of the first two conjugations, the learning of the third and fourth conjugations is greatly simplified; and the learning of the subjunctive forms in the third semester becomes a comparatively easy task.

Apperception. Important also in the initial learning of forms and in later drill on them is the assistance furnished by borrowed, cognate, and derived forms in English.

Borrowed forms of particular pedagogical value are those of the first and second declensions, as, *alumna, alumnæ; alumnus, alumni; memorandum, memoranda.*[10]

Cognate forms of sufficient obviousness to be helpful are few in number but should be stressed particularly, as they present tangible evidence of the common origin of English and Latin in the parent Aryan speech. The most important are:

-m in hi*m* and terra*m*
-m in a*m* and su*m*
's (where the apostrophe represents an original vowel) in boy*'s* and reg*is*
-es in fox*es* and reg*es*
-th in ha*th* and habe*t*

Inflectional elements preserved in English words derived from Latin are of great practical assistance. Of these there are several types:

1. English words showing the stem or base of Latin nouns of the third declension; as, *reg*al, *duc*al, *noct*urnal, *luc*id, *milit*ary, *corpor*al, *tempor*al, *custod*y, *nomin*ate, *gent*ile, *mor*al, *mort*al, *or*al, *oss*ify, *part*ial, *salut*ary, *dilap*idate, *itiner*ary. So valuable is this association that the practice of giving (or writing) an English derivative after the genitive singular is strongly recommended.[11]

---

[10] See Mason D. Gray, *Pupils' Companion to the Study of High School Latin,* Board of Education, Rochester, N. Y., Parts II and III, pp. 180-184, 202-203.

[11] *Ibid.,* pp. 198-199.

2. English words showing the participial stem of verbs.

a. Most of the important verbs of the first conjugation have English derivatives in -ation (or -ator or both) showing that the Latin verb belongs to the first conjugation; as *vocat*ion, *importa*tion, *curat*or, *spectat*or, *demonstrat*ion, *exclamat*ion, *habitat*ion, *elaborat*ion, *narrat*ion, *interrogat*ion, *stat*ion, *probat*ion, *affecta*tion, *excitat*ion, *locat*ion, *liberat*ion, *occupat*ion, *preservat*ion, desperation, *devastat*ion, *negat*ion, *orat*ion, *temptat*ion, *creat*ion, *privat*ion. Even irregularities are indicated as sec*ant* and *sect*ion.

b. The last principal parts of almost all important verbs of the second, third, and fourth conjugations are represented by English derivatives; as,[12]

2	3		
*mans*ion	*act*ion	*petit*ion	*solut*ion
*auct*ion	*occas*ion	*press*ure	*posit*ion
*doct*or	*capt*or	dere*lict*ion	con*sumpt*ion
ad*monit*ion	*claus*e	*erupt*ion	re*puls*ion
*mot*ion	*exclus*ion	*statut*e	*vict*uals
*vis*ion	excursion	*constitut*ion	con*tribut*ion
re*spons*e	*defens*e	contact	*intellect*ual
de*ris*ion	*dict*ion	*tract*or	*junct*ion
*sess*ion	con*duct*or	in*vas*ion	e*lus*ive
habit	*ascens*ion	*vers*ion	
debit	*fact*ory	*vict*or	4
*delet*ion	re*flex*ive	re*volut*ion	
*obsess*ion	in*flux*	*pens*ion	*audit*orium
*retent*ion	*fract*ion	*direct*ion	*dormit*ory
de*vot*ion	*fus*ion	de*script*ion	*munit*ion
	con*gest*ion	in*quisit*ion	in*vent*ion
	*miss*ion		*convent*ion

3. English words preserving irregular comparatives and superlatives; as,[13]

boon (adj.)	minority
malady	optimist
magnify	pessimist
ameliorate	maximum
impair	minimum
majority	

4. English words preserving special case or verb forms. These are not especially valuable as an aid in learning or retaining in-

---

[12] *Ibid.*, pp. 249-257.   [13] *Ibid.*, pp. 209, 211.

flections, but they have an inherent interest. Illustrations: [14] *No.,
omnibus, ignoramus, fiat.*

Importance of absolute mastery of forms. Whatever
methods are employed in mastering forms, the emphasis
should be placed throughout the four years upon the ability
to recognize individual forms and their functions. Drill in
selected words comprising typical forms, those of most frequent occurrence, those found in initial groups, those
having the largest number of possibilities, and those likely
to be confused should be a regular part of the daily program. Nothing short of constant drills of this type to
supplement the use of paradigms will produce the ability
to recognize instantaneously the form and function of words
as they are met in reading. Failure to recognize a form is
frequently due to unconscious confusion with a similar
form. It is the business of the teacher to explicate these
underlying confusions, since such forms do not usually
occur conveniently juxtaposed in the text.

The problem confronting the pupil in reading Latin according
to the methods recommended involves the prompt recognition of
the several possibilities of a given form, and the contemporaneous
recognition of all the grammatical ideas which up to that time
the pupil has actually learned to associate with that form. It is
more important, in our judgment, that a pupil should be able, for
example, to recognize promptly the four possibilities of form and
idea contained in a first declensional word ending in *-ae,* than to
be able formally to decline the word.[15]

For a detailed analysis of the knowledge, skills, abilities,
habits, attitudes, and ideas which are involved in the
mastery of inflections, see the author's chapter in *Supervision of Secondary Subjects.*[16]

---

[14] *Ibid., passim.*

[15] *The Classical Investigation* (Part I): *General Report* (Princeton
University Press, 1924), p. 229.

[16] W. L. Uhl, and Others, *The Supervision of Secondary Subjects*
(D. Appleton & Co., 1929), pp. 122-172.

CHAPTER VIII

THE IMMEDIATE OBJECTIVES: SYNTAX

CONTENT

In its recommendations regarding the syntax content of the Latin course and its distribution, the report of the Classical Investigation [1] makes the first adequate provision for relieving the long recognized congestion in the work of the first year.

Summary of results in syntax. The data derived from the tests on syntax, given in the classical report,[2] reflect accurately the results produced by the congestion of the traditional course, the inherent difficulty of developing a functional knowledge of syntax, and the consequent half-learning of syntactical principles. Thus in the Pressey Test on noun syntax, *place to which*, the most familiar principle represented on the test, was understood by 71 per cent of the pupils at the end of the second semester; the ablative absolute by 37 per cent; the dative with special verbs by 26 per cent; the ablative with *utor* by 25 per cent. These percentages include a gift of 25 per cent due to the multiple-choice character of the test. Not until the seventh semester is an average of 65 per cent secured in certain syntactical principles supposed to have been taught the first year. Similarly, in the Godsey test the subjunctive of purpose was understood by 30 per cent of the pupils, in a

---

[1] *The Classical Investigation* (Part I): *General Report* (Princeton University Press, 1924), pp 157-160.

[2] *Ibid.*, pp. 92, 137-138.

clause of fear by 16 per cent, in an indirect question by 4 per cent. When it is recognized that in this test, also, pupils should receive an average of 25 per cent by simply guessing, the futility of the traditional course in syntax seems obvious. The attempt to explain this situation on the grounds of poor teaching is utterly untenable in view of the acknowledged general superiority of teachers of Latin in ability and training.

There thus appears to be abundant justification for the recommendations of the classical report "that the principles of syntax taught during the first semester should be limited to a very few repeatedly occurring noun, verb, and adjective constructions, including the general principles of agreement and the commoner uses of the accusative and ablative cases with prepositions; that the many noun and verb constructions now commonly included in the work of the first year be distributed over the work of later semesters; and that, in particular, the teaching of the uses of the subjunctive should not be undertaken before the third semester." [3] Some of the details of the distribution recommended were discussed in the preceding chapter.

Definition of aim. The objective involved in the study of syntax may be defined as a functional knowledge of the most important grammatical ideas expressed by the forms of inflected words.

Two problems of syntax. It should be carefully observed that implicit in this definition of the objective are two quite distinct problems involving fundamentally different mental operations. One is the understanding of the grammatical idea expressed, and the other is the knowledge of the way in which that idea is expressed in Latin. This distinction is of fundamental importance, whether the specific task is that of comprehending a Latin sentence or of

---

[3] *Ibid.*, p. 140.

translating an English sentence into Latin. In the first
process the form must first be recognized as potentially able
to express certain ideas, and these ideas must be fully
understood as a basis for selecting the one required by the
context. In the second process, the idea expressed in English
must first be fully understood, and this step followed by
application of knowledge of how that idea is expressed in
Latin. Much emphasis is placed in the recommendations of
the classical report

upon the desirability of making an explicit distinction between
the underlying *idea* expressed in a given word, phrase, or clause,
and the *method of expressing* that idea. A clear recognition on the
part of the pupil of the distinction between these two is important
for several reasons. It permits of a discriminating attack by
teacher and pupil upon each of the two problems, by methods
appropriate to each. The grammatical idea is the underlying
logical relationship found in a given word, phrase, or clause, and
the approach to the problem may, therefore, be made on a logical
basis (that is, by determining and stating *what the word, phrase,
or clause tells* about the rest of the sentence). The method of
expressing an idea is, on the other hand, a matter of accepted
usage in a given language.[4]

Grammatical ideas, being logical, are universal, and an
understanding of them is not only indispensable for reading Latin, but is the basis for understanding general language concepts. On the other hand, similarities in the modes
of expressing ideas between Latin and English furnish an
object lesson in the development of the Aryan languages
from a common parent speech.

Differences between Latin and English. The difference
between the problems of syntax in Latin and English lies,
not in the grammatical ideas expressed, which are necessarily identical in the two languages, but in the methods
of expressing these ideas, which are in most instances radically different.

---

[4] *Ibid.,* pp. 220-221.

Source of difficulty in Latin. Attention has been called in the chapter on Inflections (pp. 91) to the fact that it is the difficulty of actually mastering functionally the principles of syntax, expressed synthetically through endings, that conditions the rate of progress in the study of inflections. It is not that the syntactical principles are inherently difficult in themselves, although their apprehension demands the exercise of keen analytical powers; the essential difficulty lies in recognizing and understanding principles when embodied in the forms and endings of words. Failure to make an immediate association between the form of a word and the possible grammatical ideas which it may express continues throughout the study of Latin to be the most persistent source of error. Ignoring the endings of Latin words is the most prolific cause of misinterpretations. This is due to the fact that the pupil's experience with English has not only failed to provide him with any important apperceptive material for understanding the genius of Latin in this respect, but it has inevitably trained him to depend in taking in the thought not on the endings of words, but only on their meanings and order.

Strong motivation for the study of syntax necessary. An intelligent understanding of the difference in the genius of the two languages, developing gradually and progressively into a conscious appreciation, will assist in securing the ability desired by defining the difficulty, and thus providing a motive for the study of syntax in relation to form not operative in the study of syntax in English. The chief argument against a thorough course in syntax in English is that it has limited functional outcomes. The pupils have sensed this, and the study of syntax in English appears to them as futile and boresome drudgery. This point of view regarding syntax, which the pupil is likely to bring with him to his study of Latin, must be carefully corrected. This can be done only by stressing the factor which makes a knowledge of syntax essential in Latin, and by showing the pupil that he cannot understand the thought of Latin sentences, as he can of English sentences, without a knowledge of syntax, and particularly without the ability, little used in English, to connect syntax with forms. It cannot be too strongly emphasized that it is not an understanding of syntactical principles which is the main problem. A pupil can, if desired, be brought to understand thoroughly the same principles in English without their contributing much to his ability to read Latin. The crucial problem is the development of an automatic association of function with form.

Analytical and synthetical languages. It is, therefore, highly desirable that pupils should, by simple stages, arrive at an intellectual understanding of the difference between analytical and synthetical methods of expressing ideas. It is not important that the difference be defined by technical terms, although, when the ideas back of them are understood, the use of the distinguishing terms will not cause much difficulty. Fortunately, English possesses side by side with its normal analytical types of expression, which show relations by the use of *separate words,* survivals of the older synthetical method inherited from the parent Aryan speech which show relations by the use of *endings.* Some of the latter type are in common use and make it possible for the teacher to exhibit through English the characteristic features of the two methods, one of which is the normal type in English while the other illustrates what may be anticipated as the normal type in Latin. Following are some of the most important illustrations, the significance of which should be thoroughly developed either on the presentation of the syntactical principle involved, or in connection with problems of translation.

Possession: analytical, *of the boy*
synthetical (like Latin), *boy's*

Indirect object: analytical, I gave a book *to him*
    synthetical, I gave *him* a book
With adjectives: analytical, you are similar *to him*
    synthetical, you are like *him* (dative)
Time how long: analytical, he stayed *for two days*
    synthetical, he stayed *two days*
Person and number in verbs: analytical, *I call*
    synthetical, (he) *calls* (in which
    the person and number are
    indicated by the ending *-s*)
Tense: analytical, he *will call*
    synthetical, he *called*
Comparison: analytical, *more beautiful*
    synthetical, *braver*

It will be granted that this intellectual grasp of the
fundamental difference between the mode of expressing
ideas that employs separate words to show relations (analytical), and that which uses endings to show relations
(synthetical) will not contribute directly to the ability to
associate function with form, but it provides a unifying
rationalization of the difficulties encountered and supplies
a motive for attacking them.

General language. Such a grasp of language structure
is, furthermore, a product reasonably to be expected of a
study which sets up the understanding of general language
concepts as one of its objectives. It provides, also, the basis
for explaining interesting crystallized survivals of older
constructions. Thus, *if you please* preserves the old imper-
sonal use of verbs without *it;* the dative, *you,* with the
verb *please* preceding the verb, and the subjunctive form
please. The expression meant originally *if it please you.*

METHOD

Regarding methods of apprehending new syntactical
principles the classical report [5] recommends "that all syn-

---

[5] *Ibid.,* p. 217.

what does teacher do about rules — Do learn then or try to apply them or what?

tactical constructions should first be met by the pupils in an appropriate context, preferably that supplied by a continuous narrative, and that pupils should be trained to discover first the grammatical idea and next the way in which the idea is expressed."

The development method in the study of syntax. It is safe to say that the presentation of new principles of syntax inductively or, as the procedure is more generally named, by the development method, is the common practice among Latin teachers. The only new element proposed by the report of the Classical Investigation is the earlier introduction of connected readings, and the use of this continuous narrative as a more effective instrument for developing new principles than detached, isolated sentences. In continuous narrative the necessity of understanding the new principle in order to understand the story supplies a more powerful motive than does the occurrence of the principle in an isolated sentence. Consciousness of the actual need for knowledge furnishes the best incentive for its acquisition and this consciousness is keener in reading connected thought.

The syntactical constructions occurring in the material read at any stage need not be limited to those principles which have been formally taught. . . . With the careful guidance of the teacher in an observant use of the context the pupil can in many cases see how to solve the difficulties presented by an unfamiliar case or mood construction, and in such sentences the progress of the pupil through the Latin sentence is apt to be hindered rather than aided by an interruption of the current thought for the sake of syntactical analysis.[6]

In other words, items frequently occur which will not worry the pupil unless the teacher worries him, and which will not hinder an understanding of the thought unless the teacher insists that they shall.

---

[6] *Ibid.*, p. 136.

Comparison with the so-called inductive method.
Teachers should not be misled by the fear that the classical
report resurrects the discredited inductive method [7] which
was a totally different conception from that involved in
the almost universal practice of developing syntactical
principles inductively. The inductive method, as embodied
in a Latin textbook of that name, introduced beginning
pupils at once to the first chapter of Cæsar, and attempted
on this narrow and tenuous basis to develop all the forms
and principles illustrated in the chapter. The report of the
Classical Investigation, on the contrary, urges a very
gradual introduction of syntactical principles, and an extensive reading experience with each new principle before
another is introduced. So far from proposing that Cæsar
be used as a basis for beginning Latin, the report recommends the postponement of Cæsar until the fourth semester.
The very title *Inductive Method* indicated that the object
was not to train pupils to read Latin, but to train them in
the use of a certain method to which the solution of every
problem must be made to conform. It is a characteristic
feature of the classical report that in connection with each
activity the particular method recommended is one
that develops logically from the nature of the particular
activity or problem. Much importance is attached to
methods appropriate to particular problems, but not to *a*
method.

It is unfortunate that the term *inductive*, as descriptive
of a method the soundness of which is universally accepted,
should apparently have become indissoluably associated
in the minds of some Latin teachers with one particularly
fantastic and extravagant embodiment of it.

Grammatical principles in English. Grammatical principles already familiar in English should be either defi-

[7] *See* Bennett and Bristol, *The Teaching of Latin and Greek*
(Longmans, Green & Co., 1899), pp. 80-84.

nitely reviewed in English and applied to Latin, or used immediately to illustrate the new principle, if it is developed first in Latin. Great importance should be attached to the conscious recognition of identical principles in the two languages.

Uniform terminology desirable. Differences in grammatical terminology in Latin, English, and other languages studied by pupils, undoubtedly often makes difficult the recognition of the identity of grammatical principles. The continued persistence of these differences despite the recommendations of national joint committees for uniform terminology is another indication of the wasteful "compartmentalism" characteristic of our secondary schools. As a practical means of assisting pupils to identify identical phenomena and of promoting actual correlation, teachers of Latin should not hesitate to take the initiative in urging their schools to adopt and use a uniform grammatical terminology in all language classes. The best basis thus far proposed is that contained in the report of the Joint Committee on Grammatical Nomenclature of the National Education Association.[8]

Desirable as a uniform terminology is, however, it should not be assumed that the ability to apply correctly a uniform label necessarily involves an understanding of the idea expressed. It is more important that the identity of an idea in two languages should be recognized, although defined by different words, than that a uniform technical term should be correctly used without any connotation of genuine meaning.

Provision for absolute mastery of important principles. The problem of securing actual mastery of new principles is one for which wholly inadequate provision is commonly made. Teachers are deceived by the ease with which most

---

[8] Copies of this report can be secured from the central office of the National Education Association, Washington, D. C.

pupils can be led to understand a new principle, and fail to recognize that it is a long road from the first understanding of a new principle to its permanent mastery. The repeated disclosures in later work that principles supposed to have been learned have been entirely forgotten has frequently led teachers into a critical attitude toward the pupils, instead of convincing them that the fault lay with a totally inadequate conception of the immense number of recalls, reviews, and conscious repetitions in differing environments that a new principle requires to produce mastery. Variety is an important requisite in such repetitions. Not until a principle can be recognized, no matter from what angle it is approached, can it be said to be *mastered*. The following methods are considered by experienced teachers as most effective:

1. Repeated occurrences in the reading and conscious recall of the principle before translation, with a procedure adapted to securing direct recall of the principle on the appearance of an appropriate ending.

2. Systematic recall through oral or written translation of English sentences into Latin, accompanied by conscious recognition of the principle. There appears to be little value in writing Latin correctly unless the pupil knows why it is correct and is conscious of the principle involved.

3. Type sentences illustrating each principle and reviewed intensively. This device does not guarantee that pupils can apply the principle elsewhere, but if they cannot master one application thoroughly, it is safe to assume that they cannot apply it elsewhere.

4. Application of the principle to the correction of an error in English speech which involves a violation of the principle. Since this involves the process of dissociation of the principle from any particular language, and its use as a free agent, this type of problem is especially potent in mastering the principle.

Use of technical terms. The report of the Classical Investigation urges less emphasis upon the use of technical terms and more upon the understanding of the idea. It is, of course, not the use of technical terms as such to which the report objects. If an idea is thoroughly understood, the use of a technical term to define it contributes both to clarity and to economy. The protest against the excessive use of technical terms rests on two grounds:

1. A syntactical principle is first of all a definition of a relationship existing between parts of a sentence. A given word, phrase, or clause embodies a grammatical principle not by virtue of anything in itself, but by virtue of its relation to the rest of the sentence. Any practice which obscures the idea of relationship in syntax interferes with a real understanding of the principle. Now every experienced teacher knows that the capacity of technical terms to become meaningless is almost limitless, and that their correct use frequently conceals a complete ignorance of the idea supposed to be briefly conveyed by it. The use of technical terms facilitates correct "pigeonholing" rather than the correct perception of relations. Emphasis upon the untested and inevitably meaningless use of technical terms has been encouraged by the fact that questions on syntax on examinations rarely require evidence of an understanding of the idea, but simply the correct use of technical terms. The correct choice of the technical term frequently rests upon the recognition of some fortuitous and external circumstance, rather than the recognition of the principle illustrated.

2. The report emphasizes the functional aspect of syntax. That is, it urges the mastery of grammatical principles as a means of getting the thought and not as a means of classifying thought after it has been comprehended. In practice the excessive use of technical terms deplored in the report is connected with an activity which all too frequently follows even the correct rendering of a Latin passage, questions on the syntax of the passage. Such questions embody simply a classifying process, unless asked for the purpose of pointing out an error.[9]

---

[9] "We believe that no improvement proposed in this report is more imperative than the elimination of the excessive attention commonly given to formal syntactical analysis especially when this analysis follows the translation. If the thought of the passage has been correctly expressed in the translation, syntactical analysis of

It is, accordingly, the misuse of technical terms as substitutes for an understanding of thought relations, and as a means of classifying thought instead of apprehending it, that the report criticizes. Technical terms are valuable classroom tools, provided (1) they are employed only after the principle involved has been thoroughly understood, and (2) their use thereafter is constantly tested to insure the presence of the fundamental idea of relationship. A technical term should be simply a shorthand way of stating what the word, phrase, or clause under discussion tells about the rest of the sentence, but unless the teacher is continually prodding beneath the surface, technical terms inevitably become purely mechanical. The capacity of the human mind to substitute words for thoughts is well-nigh infinite, and at no point is the danger greater than in the use of technical terms in Latin.

---

the passage is a wholly gratuitous exercise and an unjustifiable interruption of the story. If, on the other hand, the thought of the passage has been incorrectly interpreted or translated as a result of the pupil's failure to understand syntactical relations, it is the function of the teacher to have anticipated and removed the difficulty by preliminary questions, or by encouraging the pupil in advance to ask questions in regard to his own difficulties." *The Classical Investigation* (Part I): *General Report* (Princeton University Press, 1924), pp. 224-225.

CHAPTER IX

THE ULTIMATE OR EDUCATIONAL OBJECTIVES: INSTRU-
MENTAL AND APPLICATION

CONTENT AND METHOD

In the list of educational objectives of Latin given in Chapter III (page 33), the first three involve either "the direct use of the ability to read and understand Latin" (instrumental objectives), or "the application of facts or processes acquired in the study of Latin in the acquisition of other facts in the linguistic experience of the pupil outside the immediate field of Latin" (application objectives).

Classification of ultimate objectives. For the purpose of defining more concretely the relation of the activities involved in the study of Latin to the attainment of these objectives, and for the purpose of ascertaining more exactly the content and method necessary for their better realization, these three general objectives were divided in the report of the Classical Investigation into nine more specific objectives.[1] Each of these nine objectives, with one important exception mentioned on pages 117 and 118, will be considered separately in this and the two following chapters.

Realization of values not automatic. Several general considerations may profitably be noted at this point. In the first place, we shall need to remind ourselves constantly that in the case of none of these objectives can any marked degree of attainment be expected, unless the teacher makes

---

[1] *The Classical Investigation* (Part I): *General Report* (Princeton University Press, 1924), pp. 33-34.

it the object of systematic effort through the conscious choice of appropriate content and method. Only through the continuous, concurrent, and interdependent development of the immediate and ultimate objectives has the teacher a right to expect that educational results justifying the study of Latin will be secured.

Equipment demanded of the teacher. In the second place, if the ultimate educational objectives discussed in this chapter are to be attained the teacher must have an equipment comparable to that universally regarded as essential in the field of immediate objectives. On the basis of the usual college courses in Latin, teachers of Latin can usually ask (and answer) an almost limitless number of questions on the forms and syntax, but the number of questions which they can ask (and answer) on the application of the facts learned in Latin to experiences outside the Latin class will be far smaller and will probably be limited to the more superficial and less valuable types. For example, the derivative *viaduct* comes easily to a teacher's mind when *via* appears; less likely to occur to the teacher are the more significant and interesting derivatives *impervious, devious, previous, obvious, trivial.* In fact, immediately available knowledge of derivatives is likely to be limited to those beginning with the same letter or made by combining commonly used prefixes with roots. Teachers should have abundant resources in this field, and these can be secured only by intensive study. Not all of these resources will be used every day, but a wide margin of exact knowledge is as important in the field of the ultimate educational objectives of Latin as in the field of immediate objectives, both to reveal to the pupil appropriate opportunities for application, and to inspire confidence.

Application of Latin to foreign languages. The same situation exists with respect to the values of Latin as applied to learning other foreign languages. It is useless to expect pupils to appreciate any but the most obvious of identical elements in Latin and French, if, for example, the teacher is not familiar with such significant items as the correspondence in gender of Latin and French nouns. Here again it is essential that the teacher possess definite knowledge in the field of application.

For these reasons, in the discussion of each of the application objectives, considerable attention will be given to the sources of information available.

The dilemma confronting teachers of Latin. If systematic attention needs to be given to these objectives, the question naturally arises as to whether adequate time can be found for the contemporaneous development of the educational objectives of Latin and progress in Latin itself. While the writer does not believe that any serious difficulty exists, yet if the nature of Latin is such that progress in it entails the sacrifice of its potential educational values on the ground that there is not time enough, it is difficult to understand on what grounds Latin can be defended as an instrument of education in the secondary school. Those who argue that the development of the educational values of Latin involves an unjustifiable sacrifice of progress in Latin are really maintaining that Latin should be studied as an end in itself and only by those few pupils for whom a knowledge of Latin will be of direct value, and who will presumably continue the subject in college. One cannot carry water on both shoulders. One must advocate either that only about five out of every hundred pupils who now study Latin should be permitted to do so, and that those five study Latin for its direct value, or that the course be so organized that the ninety-five shall receive educational returns *as they progress* commensurate with the time spent.

However, no such dilemma is in fact created by the necessity of giving systematic attention to the educational objectives of Latin; for the five pupils out of one hundred who will continue Latin in college will find that the mastery of Latin itself has been promoted, and not retarded, by systematic attention to the development of educational values.

Application contributory to mastery of Latin. In the first place, every application outside Latin of a fact or process acquired in Latin is as valuable a review of that fact or process as another experience with that fact in Latin would be. Indeed, since such applications involve dissociation, it is probably a more economical method of mastering the fact for free use than is mere repetition in Latin. In other words, every application of Latin involves an activity which contributes to the mastery of Latin. The importance of this fact cannot easily be overestimated. Applications of Latin inevitably contribute to the mastery of Latin, provided always that they spring out of the Latin and are not developed merely as parallel or tangential activities. The central unifying *motive* is consciousness of growth in the ability to read and understand Latin. About this should center, from the beginning, all the activities involved in learning Latin, and from it should develop all its educational values.

Systematic consideration, not daily exercise, essential. It should, furthermore, be noted that a systematic attack upon these various objectives does not imply daily exercise devoted to their attainment. A proper standard of English in translation will naturally be insisted upon whenever translation is required. Probably the only application objective sufficiently important and extensive in character to require practically daily emphasis is the understanding of English derivatives. The essential factor in the case of the other application objectives is that they be given systematic consideration and not be left to chance. When the barriers between related experiences have been broken down, and the habit of making associations consciously created, we may reasonably expect pupils to continue the practice independently. Just how many conscious experiences are necessary to establish a given habit cannot be determined in advance. An outline, wholly tentative in character, suggesting the type of distribution needed is given in the Appendix (page 191).

Is ability to read Latin a valid ultimate objective? Before discussing the eight instrumental and application objectives which we consider valid, it will be desirable to call attention to an instrumental objective traditionally regarded as valid, which is rejected in the report of the Classical Investigation, that is, "ability to read Latin after the study of the language in school or college has ceased." [2]

It has been thought that the rejection of this objective is inconsistent with the striking amount of attention given throughout the report to the development of the power to read Latin. There is, however, no inconsistency in these positions. In fact it may be regarded as one of the notable features of the report that, on the basis of strict intellectual honesty, it provides for a synthesis of the aims commonly accepted as valid.

Ability to read Latin the supreme immediate objective. The data presented in the classical report demonstrate what every teacher has known well, that for the great majority of Latin pupils the last assigned lesson in the Latin class will be their last experience with the language as such. Bennett [3] goes much further and states that, even if the ability to read Latin were secured, and even if the desire to continue that reading were present, the field of Latin literature actually available and fruitful is too limited to warrant making that ability of major importance. The acceptance of the incontestable fact that few pupils will, in later life, read Latin does not, however,

---

[2] *Ibid.*, pp. 38-40.

[3] Bennett and Bristol, *The Teaching of Latin and Greek* (Longmans, Green & Co., 1899), pp. 92-95.

imply any reduction of emphasis upon the development of progressive ability to read Latin, as long as the study of it continues. It constitutes the one most powerful and legitimate *motivation* for the study of Latin, and upon it depends the satisfactory attainment of most of its educational objectives. A frank recognition of the facts with reference to the later use of Latin as such, with the corresponding changes in the course necessitated by them, will provide more favorable conditions for development of real power to read Latin. It may be asserted that the congestion and overloading of the traditional course, and in particular the excessive amounts of material from classical authors included in the traditional course, were in the main due to the conscious or unconscious attempt to attain the very objective rejected by the report as not valid. Pupils were thought to be studying Latin mainly in order to read more Latin. "We have only four years," so ran the argument, consciously or unconsciously, "in which to develop that ability for which other countries assign twice the length of time; therefore, a large amount of material must be compressed into the four years in order to secure this ability." The clarification of the situation produced by the data of the report not only makes possible the acceptance of objectives that are valid, but removes the inhibitive inheritances of the old traditional course in secondary Latin, which by its excessive demands fostered the "covering of ground" by methods which defeated the avowed purpose of securing an ability to read Latin.

Discussion of Individual Objectives

1. *Increased ability to understand Latin words, phrases, abbreviations, and quotations occurring in English.*[4]

---

[4] *The Classical Investigation* (Part I): *General Report* (Princeton University Press, 1924), pp. 41, 42.

This objective, while comparatively unimportant, gains significance from the fact that it involves a more or less direct use of Latin. Certainly the least that may reasonably be expected of pupils who have studied Latin from one to four years is that they shall be able to interpret the actual Latin occurring in their environment to a markedly higher degree than pupils who have not studied Latin. While the results of tests indicated that Latin pupils are distinctly superior to non-Latin pupils, the absolute results of four years of Latin were highly disappointing, and Dr. Hemmon's report [5] constitutes a severe indictment of the inability of Latin pupils to interpret common and comparatively easy Latin phrases.

Recommendation for improvement. The better realization of this value depends upon: (1) An intimate knowledge on the part of the teacher of the words and phrases which most commonly occur. A list of reference books is given in the Appendix (p. 193). (2) A definite plan for bringing such words and phrases to the attention of the pupils at appropriate times.

a. This may be accomplished, by encouraging pupils to discover these phrases for themselves in their English reading. Such discoveries may be listed and reported to the class, where any necessary help in interpretation may be supplied by the teacher. This is a desirable procedure because it fosters that intimate association between Latin and the outside environment of the pupil upon which other application values largely depend. It also emphasizes the use of such expressions in natural contexts.

b. Particular phrases may be introduced by the teacher upon the occurrence in the lesson of the central word of the phrase. Most books contain lists of Latin words and phrases in the Appendix, where they usually remain undisturbed. The expressions to be taught should be distributed by the teacher through the lessons at appropriate points indicated by specific annotations. The teacher should place little dependence on sudden inspiration.

---

[5] *Ibid.,* p. 41.

> **2.** *Increased ability to understand the exact meaning of English words derived directly or indirectly from Latin, and increased accuracy in their use.*[6] *Dictionaries*

This objective is rightly regarded by the majority of teachers as one of the most important in the list, and tests and experiments show that pupils can attain it in very satisfactory measure if there is proper organization of content and method. A wide margin of knowledge on the part of the teacher in this field is the first essential. For reference, the *New English Oxford Dictionary,* now completed, is the final authority. Skeat's *Etymological Dictionary* is a convenient, authoritative, and comprehensive treatment of derivation which should be in the possession of every teacher of Latin. *Words and Their Ways in English Speech,* by Greenough and Kittredge, contains a mass of material on derivation told in an interesting way. It is the lineal successor of *The Study of Words* by Trench, a pioneer in the exploration of the original meanings of derivatives. Gray's *Pupils' Companion, Part II,* contains a large amount of material conveniently arranged for systematic study by teachers. Some pages of this book are reprinted in the Appendix (pp. 194-202).

Material in textbook necessary. The second essential is that the textbooks in Latin for the first and second years, should contain systematically arranged material on the application of the growing knowledge of Latin to the interpretation of unfamiliar English derivatives. The attainment of this objective should not be treated as a by-product, but as one of the fundamental aims of the work for the first two years.

Familiar vs. **unfamiliar English derivatives.** It is important both in theory and in practice to make a

---

[6] *Ibid.,* pp. 42-44, 210-213.

clear distinction between English derivatives presumably familiar and those presumably unfamiliar. The former provide an apperceptive tool valuable for the acquisition of Latin vocabulary; the latter provide opportunity for the application of newly acquired Latin vocabulary. In the first instance, a known English word furnishes a clue to the meaning of an unfamiliar Latin word. In the latter instance the known Latin word is used in the interpretation of an unfamiliar English word. While no absolute line can be drawn between the two types, since knowledge of English vocabulary varies with individual pupils, most words can be assigned to one group or the other with sufficient accuracy for practical purposes. Thorndike's *Teacher's Word Book* will be found very helpful on this point.

Definition of aim. The treatment of English derivatives should be guided by the object in view. This can be defined as *the development of a permanent habit of using Latin words as a basis for interpreting unfamiliar English derivatives.* We desire this ability to function in the life of the pupil after the study of Latin has ceased. If this is to be expected, pupils must be appropriately trained. It is possible to treat derivation in such a way as to tend to restrict the total outcome to the material actually discussed in class. This is especially likely to be true unless meaning is stressed, rather than formation. Excessive attention to mere etymological analysis alone will not prove very fruitful.

Type of training desirable. It should also be borne in mind that the particular experience in which a knowledge of derivation will operate in later life will, for most pupils, be in connection with reading in English. They will rarely, if ever, have occasion to form for themselves derivatives from Latin words or roots. In all normal experiences the pupil will have the context as well as the derivation of the word as a basis for understanding the word, and context is as essential for the understanding of the meaning of an English as for a Latin word. We should, therefore, by the systematic study of derivatives occurring in natural English contexts, train the pupil for the actual use to which he will put his knowledge of derivation. Exclusive attention to the interpretation of words isolated from context obscures their essential function of expressing *meaning*.

Etymological analysis. Finally, while the ability to analyze words into their elements is indispensable, it is equally desirable that pupils should be able to recognize instantaneously, without formal analysis, the meaning of a word through derivation. For this, also, provision needs to be made. The distinction is analogous to that made between the slow conscious attack upon a Latin sentence, and the rapid unconscious acceptance of the thought.

Variety of application desirable. Thus, variety, which is essential in the study of derivatives from the point of view of interest, is also desirable in order to provide the different kinds of training necessary.

Accordingly, the activities recommended to secure the permanent habit aimed at are:

1. A certain amount of systematic and careful analysis of English derivatives, to provide pupils with accurate knowledge of the important constituent elements, namely, prefix, root, and suffix, and a thorough mastery of the significance of each element. At least some of the words discussed should be presented in context.

2. A larger amount of material, preferably presented in natural contexts, for rapid interpretation without formal analysis.

3. Systematic encouragement of the pupils to discover in their English reading occurrences of the derivatives discussed, and particularly occurrences of new derivatives from known Latin words.

Forming derivatives from Latin roots. The assembling of English derivatives from a given Latin root, especially with the aid of prefixes, is of value as an occasional exercise in giving pupils an impressive object lesson of the extent to which Latin roots pervade English, but this type of drill contributes little to an understanding of the meaning of the derivatives. A more desirable treatment is the explanation by the teacher or the textbook of the meaning of English words derived from a common Latin root, or their discovery by the pupil in context.

Prefixes especially important. For the understanding both of Latin and English compounds and derivatives, it will be found that a thorough knowledge of the prefixes is especially important. Only a few of the suffixes, notably *-tor, -tas, -tudo, -tio, -ulum (dimin), -bilis, -osus, -lentus, -alis, -tura, -idus,* are sufficiently distinctive in form and meaning, or occur with sufficient frequency in Latin and English, to warrant thorough mastery.

Stories of words. Especially important from the point of view of inherent interest are the fascinating histories of many English derivatives. The appeal of this type of work is almost universal. Material should be provided by the teacher or the textbook.[7]

The practice of requiring pupils merely to associate English words with Latin words does not appear to be of any great pedagogical value. It focuses the attention upon form only.

Writing English sentences containing derivatives objectionable. The practice sometimes recommended of requiring pupils to use in sentences derivatives discussed in class, is likewise open to criticism. It tends to put the emphasis upon words rather than meanings. It is desirable that a word be available for use when a thought arises which naturally requires it, but the attempt artificially to create a thought into which a word will fit is a reversal of the proper relations of words and thoughts. If teachers will at-

---

[7] A list of some of the most significant will be found in Mason D. Gray, *Pupils' Companion* (Board of Education, Rochester, N. Y., 1927), Part II, pp. 130-135.

tempt it themselves, they will understand why illustrative sentences manufactured by pupils are usually very wooden and unconvincing, and often contain incorrect uses of the word.

3. *Increased ability to read English with correct understanding.*[8]

It is this objective which justifies the great importance attached to the preceding objective. The systematic study of derivatives, especially if closely associated with natural contexts, should make a large contribution to the pupil's passive or reading vocabulary.

Value of intimate association with environment.   Data derived from experiments show clearly that, if in the early stages of the study of Latin pupils are directed constantly to their English environment, both for apperceptive material bearing on Latin itself and for opportunities to apply Latin, and if a type of English reading is recommended for this purpose which will provide the largest contributions, the resulting intensiveness with which pupils read English of the type prescribed will produce a marked improvement in the ability to comprehend English. One Latin class, so taught as to make intimate association with English the dominating note of the first few weeks, made during the first semester a gain in ability to read English, as measured by the Thorndike-McCall test, more than double that made by a non-Latin class of equal initial ability. If pupils are early set vigorously to work, for example, to cull from their English reading all the Latin words, phrases, etc., they find in actual use, and to search for good illustrations in actual English contexts, of derivatives discussed in class, a marked gain in the ability to read English with understanding may be anticipated.

---

[8] *The Classical Investigation* (Part I): *General Report* (Princeton University Press, 1924), pp. 44, 45.

4. *Increased ability to speak and write correct and effective English through training in adequate translation, and consequently, improved efficiency in the use of the mother-tongue as an instrument of thinking.*[9]

Insistence upon a high quality of translation becomes of paramount importance when it is understood that its function includes not only improvement in the ability to express thought effectively, but also improved efficiency in thinking itself. The desirability of using other methods besides translation as a means of testing the comprehension of a Latin sentence or paragraph, has already been urged both for the purpose of emphasizing in the minds of pupils that the primary object of reading Latin is to comprehend it, rather than to translate it, and for the purpose of discouraging the frequent use of translation as a means of comprehension, or even as a substitute for it.

Desirable limitation of amount translated. The reduction in the amount of Latin to be *translated* is also imperative in order to provide the time necessary to secure a standard of English that may reasonably be regarded as contributing to the objective under discussion.

Bennett, in his masterly analysis of the opportunities for improvement in English expression through translation, made the assertion that "no one will undertake to deny that the results here claimed are actual." [10] Unfortunately, it is precisely this claim that, in the light of the overwhelming evidence of data now available, must be denied so far as it assumes these results to be normal products of the traditional course in Latin.

Data regarding quality of translation. The significant data summarized in the report of the Classical Investigation, pages 47-48, have been supplemented by other studies,

[9] *Ibid.*, pp. 45-48. [10] Bennett and Bristol, *op. cit.*, p. 11.

notably that of Miss Woodring,[11] which she based upon an analysis of the English used by pupils who had studied Latin for four years in secondary schools, in translating the Latin on the entrance examination of the College Entrance Examination Board, and the joint study of Thompson, Price, and Richards,[12] based upon the English used by pupils taking the Regents' examination. Both documents deserve careful study by teachers of Latin. Miss Woodring's conclusions, based, it should be remembered, upon the work of a highly selected group, are that the English used exhibits characteristics quite the opposite of those claimed by Bennett, and that lack of variety in the choice of words, poor sentence structure, and "translation English" are the rule. The other study mentioned above shows that only 7 per cent of the pupils used acceptable English.

Abundant time needed for adequate translation. The explanation of this situation seems simple enough and the remedy equally obvious. Bennett was not under any delusion that the desired results came automatically; he undoubtedly realized they must be striven for persistently and conscientiously. But Bennett and others, who have emphasized the value of translation for English, seem to have had little appreciation of the amount of time it takes the average pupil to translate a page of Latin into natural idiomatic English. So long as the main emphasis was put upon the amount of ground covered and not upon the standard of English employed, just so long was it inevitable that, to facilitate "covering the ground," translation English would be the usual standard in translating. The reduction in the total amount of classical Latin to be *covered* in the course, now made possible by the changes in college en-

---

[11] M. N. Woodring, "A Study of the Quality of English in Latin Translations" (Columbia University, Bureau of Publications, 1925).

[12] William R. Price, H. G. Thompson, and E. B. Richards, "Translation English," *School and Society,* Vol. 23, No. 576 (Jan. 9, 1926).

trance requirements, and the still further reduction in the amount to be translated through the introduction of other means of testing comprehension, should make possible an immediate reform throughout the country in the standard of English uncompromisingly insisted upon for those passages which the pupils are required to translate.

Illustrations of proper standard of translation. Despite the importance of the subject, little attention has thus far been given to the task of providing teachers with systematic analyses of the chief problems met in translating Latin into idiomatic English. Most textbooks of the first and second years contain "Hints on Translation" which are valuable as far as they go. What is needed is an intensive study of the actual problems arising in the secondary course, and their reduction to principles with appropriate illustrations. The following brief list of "Do's" and "Don't's" will illustrate what the writer has in mind:

1. Do not translate a word by its English derivative. Derivatives are rarely the best translation, and their frequent use deadens effort and impoverishes vocabulary.

2. Do not translate literally unless the literal translation is also a good English translation. Literal translations are sometimes necessary *after* a good English translation to test a pupil's grasp of the syntax. Such translation should *follow,* not precede the good English translation. It is the idiomatic translation that indicates whether a pupil has grasped the thought.

3. Do not translate *magnus* by 'great,' *res* by 'thing,' *locus* by 'place.' English is far richer in words than Latin, and the habit of invariably rendering a particular Latin word by a particular English word should be avoided. This practice tends to impoverish vocabulary. *Locus* should be translated by *site, position, situation,* etc., as the context suggests.

4. Do not translate the ablative absolute by the nominative absolute. The nominative absolute is relatively of far less frequent occurrence than the ablative absolute, and its excessive use in translations tends to Latinize the pupil's English.

5. Do not translate the genitive invariably by the preposition 'of.' Use greater variety.

The essential first step is for each teacher to resolve that nothing but idiomatic English shall be accepted, and then he must insist that variety, flexibility, and accurate contextual usage shall characterize the choice of words, and that the genius of the English language shall control the sentence structure.

Teachers should be especially on their guard against those stereotyped phrases of translation English that have been heard so often that they appear to represent normal usage. The Latin class is probably the only place, for example, where people still "wage war."

5. *Increased ability to spell English words of Latin derivation.*[13]

The essential element is a thorough familiarity on the part of the teacher with the various fields in which this objective is of value. While there are many sporadic illustrations of relations in spelling between English and Latin words which cannot be classified, the great majority conform to a small number of well defined principles. These should be at the instant command of the teacher. A list of these principles is given in the Appendix (page 203).

It will also be found desirable gradually to acquaint the pupils with these principles. Familiarity with them will encourage the discovery of opportunities for application, and prevent errors arising from resemblances in words between which there is no real connection.

6. *Increased knowledge of the principles of English grammar and a consequently increased ability to speak and write grammatically correct English.*[14]

[13] *The Classical Investigation* (Part I): *General Report* (Princeton University Press, 1924), pp. 48-49, 213.

[14] *Ibid.,* pp. 49-51, 226-227.

The aim is the formation of a permanent habit of applying principles learned or emphasized through the study of Latin to problems of correct English speaking and writing.

There is probably no other application objective in which there can be so little ground for anticipating automatic transfer as in the case of the objective under discussion. The teaching of English grammar itself has of late years been attacked on the ground that a knowledge of it does not assist pupils to speak or write with greater grammatical correctness.

Automatic transfer not to be expected. English grammar is now taught with increasing emphasis upon the functional side, that is, principles are discussed in direct connection with problems of correct expression and practice in selecting correct expressions. Still less may it be expected that principles taught in Latin, twice removed, so to speak, from their application to English, will function in English unless definite practice in such application is given. It is not enough that pupils discover that many principles, as such, are identical in Latin and English. The essential step is direct application to the correction* and prevention of errors violating the principle common to the two languages.

Equipment of the teacher. The element indispensable for the successful attainment of this objective is explicit knowledge on the part of the teacher of the specific grammatical principles a knowledge of which should assist pupils to speak and write with grammatical correctness.[15] This knowledge should include familiarity with the common types of errors in English speech which the application of the principles studied in Latin should enable pupils to avoid. The teacher should be supported by the textbook,

---

[15] M. N. Woodring, *op. cit.*, p. 64.

which should contain specific illustrations of the application of principles to English in a form which makes their remedial function evident.

Most important grammatical principles. The grammatical elements potentially most important in the correction of errors in English speech are the principles of agreement, case uses as applied to the pronouns, especially *who*, and the parts of speech of certain troublesome words. As these principles are taken up in Latin, they should be systematically applied to the correct choice of English forms through classroom practice, for example, in selecting from two or more choices the correct form in accordance with the principle. Pupils should be encouraged consciously to apply grammatical principles learned in Latin when in doubt as to the correct form, and to note violations of the principles in the speech or writing of others.

Application assists in the learning of Latin. Such application will serve two valuable purposes. In the first place, if the learning of the principle has involved application to problems of expression in Latin, it possesses an immediate functional purpose not always obvious in English, and its further application to English is merely an extension of that function. In the second place, the application of a grammatical principle studied in Latin to the correction of an error in English grammar is definitely a more valuable and potent exercise for the comprehension of the principle itself than a second application to Latin would be.

Special tests embodying this objective should occasionally be given, or appropriate questions included in the term or semester examinations. For a sample test see the Appendix (pages 205-208).

7. *Increased ability to learn the technical and*
semitechnical terms of Latin origin employed

in other school subjects and in the professions and vocations.[16]

While this objective is only a special aspect of the general aim of making the knowledge of Latin vocabulary function in English, it is worth stressing as providing another specific opportunity for cultivating in the pupils the general habit of discovering Latin in their environment. "There is no better intermediate step in training pupils to use, in the later activities of life, facts and processes acquired in the study of Latin than training them to use their Latin vocabulary in the solution of linguistic problems met in their other school subjects." [17]

Suggested procedure. At the beginning of each year's work, except the first, it is suggested that five minutes of a class period be spent in finding out what school subjects are being pursued contemporaneously in which technical terms derived from Latin are likely to be met. The sciences, mathematics, and commercial subjects afford the best opportunities, but Latin-derived terms occur also in music and the social studies. Pupils should be encouraged to watch for opportunities to use their Latin vocabulary in their study of these subjects.

Definite assignments desirable. From time to time definite assignments of particular terms occurring in other subjects should be made, followed by repeated encouragement to search for further illustrations. In such applications it is extremely important that the emphasis be placed upon the *meaning* of the technical term as used in the subject, and upon the relation of that meaning to the meaning of the Latin word. Mere recognition that a technical term is derived from Latin is not particularly helpful. For this

---

[16] *The Classical Investigation* (Part I): *General Report* (Princeton University Press, 1924), pp. 51-52.

[17] *Ibid.,* p. 214.

reason teachers need to be familiar with these technical meanings. They should be equipped with typical lists of these terms with their specialized meanings. A number of such lists are available.[18]

Encouragement of coöperation between departments. One of the serious defects of the secondary school organization is its compartmental character. The objective under discussion affords an opportunity to make a slight breach in the compartmental barriers. It is suggested that the effort be made to secure the coöperation of the teachers of other subjects in this objective. Even if this goes no further than to have these teachers remind pupils who are studying Latin that they will find their knowledge of Latin helpful in understanding the technical terms of other subjects, one favorable condition for transfer has been created. If conditions permit, it will be found profitable to have lists of technical terms on the various subjects, with explanations of their meanings in terms of their derivation printed or mimeographed and distributed to pupils. The objective character of such lists helps to impress pupils with the reality of the opportunity.

8. *Increased ability to learn other foreign languages.*[19]

Some of the resemblances between Latin and the Romance languages are so obvious that recognition may be expected automatically. They fall within the field of "applications so nearly identical that they are a matter of course." [20] Hence, Latin pupils may be expected to make more rapid progress in the initial stages of French or Span-

---

[18] Mason D. Gray, *op. cit.*, pp. 143-165.

[19] *The Classical Investigation* (Part I): *General Report* (Princeton University Press, 1924), pp. 52-54, 215, 227-228.

[20] *Ibid.*, p. 185.

ish than non-Latin pupils of equal initial ability. This is supported by the data. But the similarities that lie on the surface are soon exhausted, and without definite training in seeing the relations between Latin and a modern language the initial advantage is lost.[21] Not many pupils will, for example, see the relation existing between the gender of nouns in Latin and French without having it definitely called to their attention with illustrations.

Equipment of the teacher.   As in the case of other application objectives, the first essential element is knowledge on the part of the teacher. It does not require a great number of references throughout a semester to develop in the pupil the habit of discovering similarities in the two foreign languages, but these references should be made with authority, if they are to be convincing and stimulating. All work in relating the vocabularies of Latin and French, for example, should carefully avoid those French words which although derived from Latin resemble even more closely the borrowed English words. For example, French pupils will probably associate *admirer* with English *admire* rather than with Latin *admirari*.

Anticipation during the first year.   While in most schools there cannot be any systematic effort to associate Latin with modern languages until the second or third year of Latin, when Latin pupils will for the first time be studying a second foreign language, it will nevertheless be found worth while to bring occasional references into the work of the first year. Such questions as "What will *mur, sept, si,* mean in French?" serve to create in the pupil the attitude of expecting to use his knowledge of Latin when he begins French. At the same time these resemblances in vocabulary provide an appropriate medium for pointing out the historical relation between Latin and French and other Ro-

---

[21] *Ibid.,* p. 53.

mance languages. Care should be taken to distinguish between derived and cognate languages (page 170).

Specific training essential. It cannot be too strongly urged that, if pupils are to derive from the study of Latin a permanently increased ability to learn and retain a modern language, systematic, though limited, training in perceiving relations and making associations is essential. If teachers are to recognize appropriate opportunities for giving this training economically, their own familiarity with these relations should be accurate and reasonably thorough. Elementary material illustrating the relation of Latin to French in forms and vocabulary will be found in the Appendix (pages 209-214).

Coöperation of teachers of ancient and modern languages. This objective furnishes another opportunity to correct, in some slight degree, the normally impermeable compartmentalism of secondary-school subjects. It is one of the most serious criticisms of almost all high-school subjects that they are taught as if they were never expected to function outside the classrooms of the particular subjects. Any effort through correlation to suggest to pupils that they will be held responsible elsewhere for what is learned in a particular class is directed at a very serious evil. It is probable that comparatively few teachers of modern languages make any effort to find out what pupils are studying or have studied Latin, or to help them to make use of knowledge acquired there. It is incumbent upon the teachers who are claiming transfer values for their subject, to provide as favorable conditions as possible for such transfer. The least that teachers of Latin can do is to call the attention of teachers of modern languages to the desirability of their encouraging pupils to make the utmost use of apperceptive bases acquired in the study of Latin. If a sympathetic attitude toward this eminently sound pedagogical principle exists, lists of some of the most important Romance words derived from Latin may profitably be furnished to the teacher of Romance languages for distribution to his pupils. If it accomplishes nothing more, it furnishes pupils with a tangible reminder of the inherent relationship between Latin and the Romance languages.

Application Objectives —
· Direct quotations
· Exact English meanings
· Adequate understanding
" Translation
Accurate Spelling ·
" Grammar
Technical terms
(Other languages)

CHAPTER X

THE ULTIMATE OR EDUCATIONAL OBJECTIVES: (DISCIPLINARY OR GENERAL TRAINING

CONTENT AND METHOD

Definition of aim. By the disciplinary values and corresponding objectives of Latin are meant those potential improvements in general habits resulting from the spread or transfer to fields other than Latin of habits of mental work developed in Latin. In this category of objectives we are not concerned with such potential results as improved efficiency in thinking through practice in adequate translation or the ability to apply in the study of other languages either specific linguistic facts or specific processes such as the habit of solving new words through context and related words. The values just described do not involve a transfer of mental abilities, but the "development of improved efficiency in the use of the mother-tongue as related to the mental elements which can be grasped and retained only by means of its terms."[1] This transfer applies only to limited linguistic spheres, while the disciplinary values under discussion in this chapter are general in their application.

"Transfer" in its broadest sense. Yet in a broad sense all indirect values, including those discussed in the preceding chapter, involve the problem of transfer. The essential factor is the presence of one or more common elements in

---

[1] A. J. Inglis, *Principles of Secondary Education* (Houghton Mifflin Co., 1918), p. 467.

the original training field of Latin and in the field in which the fact, process, ability, habit, attitude, or ideal is expected to operate. Thus the practical problems of transfer confronting the teacher are wide in extent and highly varied in character. We may regard the various aspects of these problems as resulting from an almost infinite variation in the extent and tangibility of the common element. "When the common element is large in extent and objective in character, as in the case of the vocabulary element common to Latin and English, the easier it is to train pupils to make the transfer. In the case of the disciplinary and cultural values, the common element, while still present, is far more intangible and calls for a much higher type of generalization before the new habit, attitude, or ideal can be freely associated with activities other than those of the Latin classroom." [2]

In discussing the potential disciplinary values of Latin it is necessary at the outset to distinguish between general habits which Latin, in common with all cumulative subjects, is potentially capable of developing or improving, and those specific values which the study of Latin is peculiarly fitted to develop.

Habits developed from the study of Latin may be either good or bad. A second important factor in the situation to which sufficient consideration is rarely given is that if the study of Latin or of any other subject is potentially able to foster good mental habits, it is also potentially able to foster bad mental habits. Latin propagandists are prone to forget this necessary complement, and to assume that Latin possesses some innate quality through which its study by any method must produce beneficial results with immunity from any evil results of inappropriate methods.

---

[2] W. L. Uhl and Others, *The Supervision of Secondary Subjects* (D. Appleton & Co., 1929), p. 145.

The fact must be faced that, if the study of Latin by sound methods is capable of developing good habits, its study by unsound methods is equally capable of producing bad habits. Any opportunistic denial of the latter implies the abandonment of any basis of hope for the former. We are dealing with an instrument which cuts both ways.

Necessity of developing the desired habit in Latin. A third factor in the situation, so obvious that it seems almost axiomatic, is that a habit cannot be transferred from one field to another unless it is actually developed in the first field. If Latin pupils have at the end of the first year attained an average of only 47 per cent on the noun-syntax set for mastery, an average of only 51 per cent on the verb-forms set for mastery, and an average of only 66 per cent on the vocabulary set for mastery, on what grounds is it claimed that the study of Latin has assisted in developing "ideals of achievement, accuracy, and thoroughness." For, as indicated by the table given on page 92 of the report of the Classical Investigation, the great majority of pupils are passed into the work of the second year on this record. If any habits have been acquired and transferred to other fields by pupils who have made so poor a showing, it must be frankly admitted to be the habits of satisfaction with lack of thoroughness, of inaccuracy, and of failure to achieve.

Bad habits also susceptible to spread. If the average Latin pupil does not attain until the sixth semester a 75 per cent degree of mastery of the verb-forms supposed to be mastered at the end of the second semester, and not until the seventh semester a 75 per cent degree of mastery of the noun-syntax supposed to be mastered at the end of the second semester, and not until the eighth semester a 75 per cent degree of mastery of the verb-syntax supposed to be mastered at the end of the second semester, on what grounds can it be argued that his study of Latin has tended to produce anything but the opposites of the desirable habits of "sustained attention, orderly procedure, overcoming obstacles, perseverance, dissatisfaction with partial success?"

These conditions cannot be waved aside. The intellectual honesty of those who advance claims for the disciplinary values of Latin is brought under grave suspicion by any attempt to ignore them. It would seem that such persons are mainly interested in Latin as a "cause," to be defended by fair means or foul, and not as an educational instrument, to be justified by its results. It is not without significance that the strongest advocates of the disciplinary values of Latin have been at the same time the most obdurate supporters of the traditional course, despite its conspicuous failure to provide favorable conditions for the development *within the subject itself* of the desirable habits which were supposed to spread.

A Latin course which can be mastered indispensable. It seems obvious that the first prerequisite to any expectation that habits of accuracy and thoroughness may be formed through the study of Latin is to construct a Latin course which can be mastered semester by semester. No more severe indictment can be brought against the traditional course than that it precluded for so many pupils the development *within the subject* of good mental habits. Its actual effect, especially upon the large percentage of pupils who failed, has undoubtedly been detrimental. Latin teachers have themselves fostered the development of a course, the chief outcome of which has been the recognition of Latin as a powerful selective agent. Conversely, the recommendations of the classical report for a radical redistribution of the elements of the course, are precisely those which will provide the most favorable conditions for the development of good mental habits. Mastery, the indispensable factor, has now been made possible.

With these general considerations in mind, we shall discuss, first, the potential value of Latin, shared with other cumulative subjects, in developing certain general desirable habits; and second, a group of special habits for the development of which Latin appears to provide peculiarly favorable conditions when the methods used are appropriate to the objects in view.

> 1. *The development of certain desirable habits and ideals which are subject to spread, such as habits of sustained attention, orderly procedure, overcoming obstacles, perseverance; ideals of achievement, accuracy, and thoroughness; and the cultivation of certain general attitudes such as dissatisfaction with failure or with partial success.*[3]

From the foregoing discussion it will be seen that the essential conditions necessary for the development of these desirable habits *within the subject itself* are:

Such reduction in and distribution of the material set for mastery as to make mastery feasible

Uncompromising insistence upon absolute mastery of this material

The mediums in Latin for the development of these habits must, furthermore, consist of the normal activities involved in learning or applying Latin. There is no mysterious essence pervading Latin which guarantees results in some magical fashion. The general habits desired must spring from the methods by which Latin vocabulary, Latin syntax, Latin forms, and the comprehension and translation of the Latin sentence are studied and the resulting knowledge applied. It is of the utmost importance, there-

---

[3] *The Classical Investigation* (Part I): *General Report* (Princeton University Press, 1924), pp. 55-58.

fore, that the course prescribed for each semester should be such as can be mastered, and that the material assigned to each semester for mastery should be defined with the utmost clearness.

What mastery involves. Mastery itself needs to be clearly defined and fully understood by pupils. It was pointed out above (p. 89) that not even a 75 per cent degree of mastery was attained by the average pupil on the work of the first year until late in the course, and even a 75 per cent achievement does not represent genuine mastery. We assuredly do not propose to justify Latin on the ground that it develops the habit of 75 per cent accuracy or 75 per cent thoroughness. We should insist that the material set for mastery be mastered to a 100 per cent degree, and limit what is sought to be mastered in any given semester to what can be so mastered. There is and should be other material in the Latin work which is not to be so mastered, and hence the necessity of clear definition, semester by semester, of what is expected to be mastered.

Relative potential training capacity of cumulative and noncumulative subjects. That on the basis of the traditional course the study of Latin has not proved a medium for the development of desirable habits in any degree superior to other subjects, a conclusion to which its failure to develop these habits *within the subject itself* inevitably leads, is demonstrated by data derived from tests and experiments, the results of which confirm our *a priori* judgment.[4] Teachers of Latin should be neither surprised nor discouraged at these negative results. It may be affirmed without much risk of dispute that the actual progressive *mastery* of a cumulative subject like Latin, which makes a constantly increasing demand upon the powers of concen-

---

[4] E. L. Thorndike, "Mental Discipline in High School Studies," *Journal of Educational Psychology,* January, 1924, pp. 1-22, February, 1924, pp. 83-98.

trating an increasing number of resources upon each new problem, is potentially able to make a more significant contribution to the development of the highest types of thinking than is made by subjects essentially noncumulative, in which each day's problems are, in the main, sufficient unto themselves.

Results of Thorndike. The results reported by Thorndike, while of great significance in reflecting the situation fostered by the traditional course in Latin, and demonstrating the need of reform, possess no significance for the ultimate determination of the relative value of subjects for the development of desirable general habits. They probably reflect the leveling effect of the "half-learning" which, as Morrison [5] has so convincingly shown, is the most striking characteristic of American education. This half-learning effectually washes out any inherent potential differences.

Morrison's views. Morrison's volume should appeal strongly, as a whole, to teachers of Latin, although the specific theory advocated as the basis for teaching Latin cannot be accepted by the present writer, involving as it does the uncompromising repudiation of any function for consciousness. Morrison is doubtless justified in denying any but an inhibitory influence to purely formal grammar, but he is led to the equally untenable extreme of denying any place to grammar even when taught functionally. Pupils, according to Morrison, must acquire the ability to understand forms and functions *unconsciously* through repetition of experiences with them in reading; but the fallacy of this theory has already been pointed out. On the other hand, teachers of Latin will find in Morrison a strong confirmation of the wisdom of demanding a radical redistribution of the materials of Latin instruction. Morrison [6] has

[5] H. C. Morrison, *The Practice of Teaching in Secondary Schools* (University of Chicago Press, 1926), Ch. iii.
[6] *Ibid.*

well portrayed what is involved in the actual mastery of any given topic. Furthermore, his statement that "we are continually underrating the ability of children and over-estimating their experience" summarizes with force and brevity some of the most significant recommendations of the report on the Classical Investigation. Teachers who are sympathetic toward the idea of mastery which we have repeatedly emphasized in this discussion will find in Morrison a refreshing contrast to the ideal of superficiality deliberately advocated by such educationalists as Snedden.[7]

High standard of achievement essential. In conclusion, "whatever methods are adopted for fixing the vocabulary [and syntax and inflections as well] to be permanently retained, we believe that a degree of attainment should be achieved which will adequately justify the claim commonly made, that Latin is a peculiarly suitable vehicle for the development of habits of accuracy and thoroughness. Teachers should, therefore, point out the value of such accuracy and thoroughness, not only for the study of Latin but for the study of other school subjects and for all situations in everyday life in which an accurate grasp of details is necessary for success."[8]

Selection of methods adapted to producing desirable habits. While actual mastery appears to be the fundamental essential for the development of desirable general habits, it is clear that the particular methods followed to secure this mastery must also be carefully adapted to the ends in view. It might be quite possible, for example, to secure 100 per cent mastery of the elements of Latin without developing thereby the habit of orderly procedure. This should be exemplified by the procedure used in class and

---

[7] D. Snedden, *The Sociological Determination of Objectives in Secondary Education* (J. B. Lippincott Co., 1921), Ch. v.

[8] *The Classical Investigation* (Part I): *General Report* (Princeton University Press, 1924), p. 210.

encouraged in home study. The classical report [9] emphasizes the desirability of training pupils to follow some regular way of attacking the various problems which arise in the study of Latin, and makes the following appropriate suggestions:

Orderly procedure on the part of the teacher, that is, in preparing the daily lesson plan.

Careful assignments embodying the principle of orderly procedure. (Failure to do this is probably a prolific source of mental confusion.)

Supervised study with emphasis upon orderly procedure in attacking the problems involved.

Insistence upon grasping the thought of a Latin sentence in the Latin order.

Insistence upon the use of idiomatic English in translation.

Systematic organization of inflections.

Susceptibility to mastery a continuous criterion. Teachers, in their efforts to combat the overloading of the course, should be particularly on their guard against the fallacy that pupils must study some topic or other before they can do something else. This fallacy was particularly prevalent when Cæsar was commonly begun in the third semester. Everything had to be "covered" during the first year, for how, otherwise, could pupils be expected to read Cæsar? The fallacy is still prevalent, although not in so virulent a form. The introduction of any new item beyond the limits prescribed by the ability of pupils to master the subject is done at the expense of those topics which could otherwise have been actually mastered. No more striking proof exists of the interference with *any* real learning by the attempt to prepare prematurely for something else than the tables on pages 137 to 138, and 142 of the report of the Classical Investigation. It should, furthermore, be noted that all such efforts fail in their preparatory object;

[9] *Ibid.*, p. 176.

for these same tables and that on page 92 of the report show conclusively that many pupils not only began but completed Cæsar, Cicero, and even Vergil with a hazy knowledge of the forms supposedly indispensable for beginning Cæsar. Such hazy knowledge is valueless as preparation, as well as subversive of acquiring desirable habits of accuracy. With this forcible object lesson before them, teachers should have no difficulty in resisting the argument that something or other *should* be taught in a given semester as a preparation for something else. Not what *should be taught* but *what can actually be mastered* is the decisive factor, and what cannot be done to-day should be religiously postponed until to-morrow.

Conditions essential for transfer. The general principles underlying the theory of the transfer of training, with especial reference to the conditions under which transfer takes place, should be familiar to teachers. The discussions of Inglis [10] and Gates [11] are particularly recommended. The section of the classical report [12] dealing with this topic is probably the best available summary of the present views of psychologists. The essential elements of the present theory are:

1. Transfer is not automatic to any considerable degree. (This has already been discussed; see pages 26-29.)

2. The desired general habits must be developed first in the training field before they can be expected to transfer elsewhere. (This has been the main theme of this chapter.)

3. The pupil should be made aware that the skill he is acquiring in Latin is not limited to that field, but is applicable elsewhere.

---

[10] A. J. Inglis, *Principles of Secondary Education* (Houghton Mifflin Co., 1918), pp. 394-412, 459-462.

[11] A. I. Gates, *Psychology for Students of Education* (Macmillan Co., 1923), Ch. xv.

[12] *The Classical Investigation* (Part I): *General Report* (Princeton University Press, 1924), pp. 183-188.

4. There should be explicit training in the application, outside Latin, of skills acquired through Latin, and in the discovery of new applications. The report [13] makes the following suggestions to that end:

> Explanation of the value of such habits in everyday life.
> Illustrations of the use of such habits in everyday life.
> Creating in the pupils a desire for the possession of such habits.
> Identifying the procedure taught in Latin with that followed in other subjects.

5. "The spread appears at first to be largely conscious, but, as with other mental processes, tends to become automatic." "To use a homely figure, we believe that the ordinary pump has to be primed to insure a flow of water, but we do not believe that the extent of the flow will be limited to the amount used in priming." [14]

> **2.** *The development of correct habits of reflective thinking applicable to the mastery of other subjects of study and to the solution of analogous problems in daily life.*[15]

This objective embodies some of the values which the study of Latin is peculiarly adapted to develop. It will be convenient to discuss it in relation to the specific methods previously recommended in the attack upon the various elements of Latin.

Undue dependence of the traditional course upon memory. It may be fairly said that the only method recognized in the traditional course for the learning of vocabulary, syntax, and inflection was memorization. Pupils with little or no independent reflection committed to memory lists of Latin words and their English equivalents, committed paradigms to memory, committed the rules of syntax to memory. Even from the point of view of learning Latin, exclusive dependence upon an unreflecting memoriter method did not produce satisfactory results, while the only

---

[13] *Ibid.*, p. 177.   [14] *Ibid.*, p. 187.   [15] *Ibid.*, pp. 60-61.

possible outcome in general training was increased efficiency in memorizing vocabulary, inflections, and syntax.

Adaptation of method to the varying nature of different problems. The methods recommended by the report to be used in the acquisition of vocabulary, inflections, and syntax are based upon a discriminating analysis of the nature of the problems presented by these various activities. The specific methods recommended are those which, in the judgment of the committee, were permanently valid for the mastery of Latin itself *throughout the course*, and at the same time contributed to the development of valuable general habits.

Methods of study of supreme importance. The emphasis throughout the report is upon methods of *study* rather than methods of teaching. "The methods adopted by the teacher can be effective in developing the pupil's power to understand and read Latin, or in developing valuable general habits, just in so far as they create corresponding methods of study on the part of the pupil. Upon the development of sound habits of study, permanent and general in their effect, the utmost emphasis should be placed. Not simply what the pupil does under the direction or personal supervision of the teacher, but what he does by himself in his own study of assigned lessons is the final test which any sound method of teaching must successfully meet." [16]

This point of view is emphasized by the repetition of the following statement in connection with the discussion of each of the activities of the Latin classroom:

The method to be employed in the teaching of Latin vocabulary [or syntax, etc.] should be designed . . . to develop correct habits of independent study, to contribute both to the mastery of Latin vocabulary and to the attainment of the ultimate objectives which teachers consider valid for their pupils.[17]

[16] *Ibid.,* p. 181. See also pp. 182-183.
[17] *Ibid.,* p. 206.

It is particularly to be noted that the first criterion employed by the report in recommending methods is their superior suitability for the mastery of Latin itself, and second their superior suitability for developing desirable general habits.

a. In the Study of Vocabulary

The methods recommended for getting the meanings of new Latin words were discussed in Chapter VI. These methods are not only permanently valid throughout the course for the mastery of Latin vocabulary itself, but they indisputably provide for a higher type of thinking and reasoning than is involved in a memoriter method.

Training value of solving new words. The problem consists of deciding upon a meaning for the new word which will satisfy the demands of context and of the root meaning as indicated by related English and Latin words. Whenever a pupil has solved correctly the meaning of a new word, he has gone through a very valuable mental process. It is exactly the scientific method, which has for its main characteristic a series of assumptions which are tentatively adopted, tested on the basis of their ability to fit all the facts, and finally accepted or rejected. The whole process, while following an assumed deductive form, is a perfect embodiment of the inductive, scientific procedure to which we owe most of the great discoveries of the past. "The assumptions, in this case, are the different meanings for the new word suggested by its context and its similarity to known Latin or English words; the test applied to each assumption in turn is its capacity to make sense." [18] Even if the effort to solve a new word fails, the effort has not been in vain.

Training for transfer. It is not claimed that the habit thus formed of regarding each new word as a challenge to

[18] *Ibid.*, pp. 208-209.

one's powers of independent thinking will transfer automatically to other fields. It merely creates favorable conditions for such transfer. "When pupils have developed facility in solving problems of this kind in Latin, their attention should be specifically called, by means of appropriate
illustrations, to the identity of the method used with that
employed in all scientific research." [19] The steps necessary
for generalization are outlined above.

b. In Learning Syntax

Training value of recognizing grammatical ideas. We
have discussed above the importance of making a clear
distinction in the treatment of syntax between the fundamental grammatical idea expressed by a new construction,
and the method by which that idea is expressed. The essence of the grammatical idea is its logicality, and that
quality at once suggests the appropriate methods valid for
the mastery of the element itself and for general training.
To train the pupil to see for himself what a new construction tells about the rest of the sentence—which is all that
the grammatical idea usually involves—not only serves
best the immediate purpose of getting an understanding of
the idea for the sake of progress in Latin, but it assuredly
involves a more valuable exercise of the power of reasoning than memoriter learning.

Training value of association. For the complementary
problem of learning how the idea is expressed in Latin,
the report does not recommend the exclusive use of any
method. Association with identical principles already familiar in English involves a use of apperception which, if
cultivated as an independent habit, has potential value in
training the pupil to use all the resources in his possession
in the solution of a new problem anywhere.

---

[19] *Ibid.*, p. 209.

Value and limitations of the inductive method. The occurrence of each new syntactical idea first in a connected Latin narrative undoubtedly provides favorable conditions for an inductive development of the principle as a whole, including both the idea expressed and the method of expressing the idea in Latin. Two cautions are, however, pertinent. In the first place, the use of the inductive or development method is sometimes carried to a point where it becomes a fetish. Where a new principle can be developed naturally and economically by this method, it should undoubtedly be encouraged; when it requires an exorbitant amount of time, or becomes artificial, there should be no forcing of the method. In the second place, it should be fully recognized that the process is inductive in form only. The validity of the conclusion for the pupil rests upon the assumption that the particular instance is typical. Genuine induction involves the examination of all possible cases, or at least of a sufficiently large number to guarantee the accuracy of the conclusion. Nevertheless, the mental effort demanded is, even with this limitation, a more valuable exercise of thinking power than memoriter learning. It should be noted that the report, in order to guard against the potential danger of training pupils to "jump at conclusions," recommends that a given principle should not be formulated by pupils until several illustrations have been met and discussed informally.

c. In the Learning of Inflections

Training value of the study of inflections. The importance of insisting that individual forms and their functions be intimately associated has been pointed out in Chapter VII, but the actual mastering of the forms make the most nearly legitimate demand for sheer memorization of any of the activities involved in learning Latin. Yet even here there is opportunity for enlisting and cultivating valuable mental activities as an aid to the memory. After one declension or one verb paradigm has been mastered, pupils should be trained consciously to employ in learning new forms all the resources of analogy and of resemblances and differences between the new paradigm and the old. The learning of all new inflections should be preceded by the effort on the part of the pupil to discover for himself just what is already familiar and what is new. No one will deny the desirability of fostering this attitude whether the object is to learn and retain the new form in the shortest possible time or to cultivate good mental habits. There can, in the nature of things, be no conflict between the method best for the learning of Latin and the method best for the intellectual development of the pupil. The emphasis previously recommended upon general principles underlying apparently different inflectional forms is not only a valuable aid in learning and retaining the forms, but is a potential training in the desirable habit of seeing uniform elements in apparently diverse phenomena. The suggestions made previously that pupils in learning forms be trained to use all the latent associations with Latin and English are of such special value for general training that they will be given further consideration in the discussion of the next objective.

d. In Learning to Comprehend Latin

Training value of Latin word-order method. The Latin word-order method is recommended in the report of the Classical Investigation primarily on the ground that it provides the best basis for the development of the ability to read, comprehend, and translate Latin, but this method has also potential training value of great significance. "Reflective thinking," says Dewey,[20] "in short, means judgment

---

[20] John Dewey, *How We Think* (D. C. Heath & Co., 1910), p. 13.

suspended during further inquiry; . . . the most important factor in the training of good mental habits consists in acquiring the attitude of suspended conclusion, and in mastering the various methods of searching for new materials to corroborate or refute the first suggestions that occur." There could hardly be a more accurate description of the process aimed at in training pupils to follow the Latin word-order in accepting the thought of a Latin sentence. It preeminently involves constant practice in suspending judgment, in noting and defining the limits within which the final judgment must fall, in estimating the relative value of evidence as it accumulates in the progress through the sentence, and in developing a lively but none the less scientific imagination. We should, however, be under no misapprehension as to the extent to which this ability, if acquired in Latin, becomes automatically a general attitude toward problems outside of the Latin class. It can scarcely be claimed that teachers of Latin as a class are conspicuous for their ability to hold their judgment in suspense on doubtful matters pertaining to fields other than Latin. To guarantee transfer, the conditions necessary for the generalization of the habit must be met, namely, conscious training in application to other fields.

3. *Development of the habit of discovering identical elements in different situations and experiences, and of making true generalizations.*[21]

Training value of seeing relationship. This is not so much a separate objective as it is a value implicit in the methods described in connection with the preceding objective. The discussion of the methods there recommended

---

[21] *The Classical Investigation* (Part I): *General Report* (Princeton University Press, 1924), p. 59. *See also* for vocabulary, pp. 206-217; for syntax, pp. 217-221; for forms, pp. 228-233.

will have failed of its purpose if it has not brought out the fact that the seeing of relationships between apparently different experiences is a fundamental ingredient of those methods. The study of Latin offers uniquely favorable opportunities for the development of the general habit of seeing relationships, because of the number and variety of contacts it affords with the other linguistic experiences of the pupil. The development of the general habit results from these numerous specific trainings in recognizing and utilizing the elements common to Latin and to (1) the apperceptive bases recommended as instruments for the learning of Latin; and to (2) the experiences with which the various application objectives are concerned.

Relationship in vocabulary. In the study of vocabulary, for example, the pupil is trained to see and use relationships existing in Latin and English in the acquisition of vocabulary, and conversely is trained to see and use latent relationships for application of Latin vocabulary in Latin itself, in English, and in the Romance languages.

Relationship in syntax. Similarly, in the case of syntax, pupils are trained to recognize and use principles already familiar in English in the acquisition of syntax, and conversely to apply the principles learned not only to the immediate field of Latin, but to the correction of errors in English speech and in other foreign languages.

Relationship in inflections. Finally, the study of inflections affords a particularly valuable experience for the development of the general habit of seeing relationships. It is clear that the value of the habit of detecting identical elements is in inverse ratio to the obviousness of the relationships detected. These relationships are relatively obvious in vocabulary and in syntax. The effort to see and utilize the less obvious although practically valuable relationships between Latin inflections and the borrowed or cognate forms appearing in English is a correspondingly more valuable potential contribution to the general habit of seeing identical elements. Further, the partial substitution of a rational process for one likely to be wholly mnemonic adds one more justification to the claim that Latin rightly taught has potential training values of great significance. We have called it "partial substitution," for sheer memoriter drill must accompany and follow the use of rational methods in the mastery of inflectional forms.

Significance of the general habit of seeing relationships. The importance of this general habit lies in the fact that it gives unity, coherence, and an ultimate common goal to the various types of application and to the various learning processes which involve the use of common familiar elements.

Finally, it should be noted again that the habit sought is precisely that upon which all transfer to a large extent depends. It is the ability to recognize identical elements in different experiences, to dissociate the common element, and to make it a general notion that is commonly regarded as the indispensable factor in all transfer. Thus a habit shown to be desirable for its own sake is potentially able to make the study of Latin more fruitful in all its aspects.

CHAPTER XI

THE ULTIMATE OR EDUCATIONAL OBJECTIVES: HISTOR-
ICAL-CULTURAL

CONTENT AND METHOD

Definition of "cultural" objectives. "By the historical-cultural objectives [of Latin] are meant those concerned with increasing the pupil's fund of [historical] information, developing his capacity for appreciation, extending his intellectual horizon, and broadening his sympathies by direct contact through the study of their language and literature, with the mind of a people remote in time and place."[1]

Among the objectives listed in Chapter III, the last five belong to the category under discussion. For the purpose of making a more accurate study of the present degree of attainment, and more discriminating recommendations with reference to the means for improving results, they are discussed in the report[2] as eight specific objectives, and they will be so discussed in this chapter.

Internal and external "cultural" objectives. The historical-cultural objectives which the writer regards as valid may be divided into two groups: (1) those of an external, extensive, informational type appropriate to any year of the course, but especially important in the first and second years; and (2) the internal, intensive, appreciative type,

---

[1] *The Classical Investigation* (Part I): *General Report* (Princeton University Press, 1924), p. 62.
[2] *Ibid.*, pp. 62-72.

chiefly, although not exclusively, appropriate to the last two years of secondary Latin.

Need for improvement. With reference to both types, it may be affirmed that "the evidence from all sources indicates that the greatest need for reorganization of content is in the historical-cultural and appreciative fields." [3] The evidence will be found in the classical report.[4] It is very significant that the changes most frequently recommended for the Latin course by former students of Latin to whom questionnaires were sent involve more attention to the historical-cultural values of Latin.[5]

The writers of the report fully realized that better results could not be expected from merely calling attention to their desirability. "Entirely in harmony with this evidence is the general judgment of psychologists that automatic realization of the values implicit in Latin cannot be counted on to any large extent, and that time must be found for the introduction of appropriate material and the use of appropriate methods in order to secure the satisfactory attainment of any of the ultimate objectives." [6]

Inadequacy of the traditional course. It is difficult to understand on what grounds it could ever have been claimed that the content of the traditional course for the first two years in Latin provided favorable conditions for the development of any historical-cultural values. How could a year spent upon the bare elements of Latin in preparation for a second year, which is itself spent upon the details of a small and isolated fragment of Roman history,[7] produce an "his-

---

[3] *Ibid.*, p. 98.

[4] *Ibid.*, pp. 64-72 and especially pp. 98-100.

[5] *Ibid.*, pp. 180-181.

[6] *Ibid.*, p. 100.

[7] "With the exception of the few chapters on the customs of the Gauls, Germans, and Britons, all of Cæsar's commentaries on the Gallic War might easily be summed up in a few brief lines, to the effect that for seven years he waged unceasing war against the

torical perspective," or an "appreciation of the influence of
Roman civilization on the course of western civilization," or
"increased knowledge of the life, history, institutions, mythology, and religion of the Romans"? And this was the extent
of the opportunity afforded more than two-thirds of the
pupils who began Latin! The less than one-third who went
on into the third and fourth years of the course found
that the excessive amount of reading to be covered quite
effectually prohibited any genuine cultural development.
"The teachers of Vergil, whose pupils are devoting an
amount of time to the preparation of their lessons greater
than is given to any other subject in any year, while practically unanimous in their opinion that literary appreciation
is a valid and attainable objective in the fourth year of the
course, say that they cannot find sufficient time to devote
to the attainment of this objective." [8]

The need for reorganization is recognized throughout the
report of the Classical Investigation in the discussion of
almost every activity connected with the study of Latin,
but the need for a better adaptation of content and method
to the attainment of the historical-cultural objectives is
especially emphasized.

Source of "cultural values."   The view embodied in the
report is that the historical-cultural objectives should have

---

Gallic and German tribes, and finally subdued them all. This is
practically the substance of the historical knowledge acquired by
the student in reading Cæsar. Without doubt Cæsar's Gallic campaigns were profoundly significant. They had a motive, perhaps a
double motive. . . . But though this is true, yet it does not appear
in Cæsar's *Commentaries.* The *Commentaries* themselves, in all their
weary detail of battle, siege, and march, never suggest their own
connection with contemporary or future history. To all intents and
purposes they stand outside of the events of their own day. They
do not contain facts the knowledge of which is of value to the
average pupil or the average educated person of mature years."
C. E. Bennett, *The Teaching of Latin and Greek,* pp. 113-114.

[8] *The Classical Investigation* (Part I): *General Report* (Princeton
University Press, 1924), p. 98.

their source and inspiration in the Latin being read, whether
the objectives are of the informational type or the appreciative type. It is, therefore, urged that the Latin reading
material should from the beginning be a suitable medium
for the development of these objectives, whether it is the
easy "made" or adapted Latin recommended for the first
three semesters,[9] or Latin selected from classical authors;[10]
and that collateral reading in English, recognized by all
as an essential element in the course, should develop naturally from contacts established through the content of the
Latin reading material itself, either as background for an
understanding of the Latin narrative[11] or as an amplifica-
tion of the Latin content.

Understanding of thought content a sine qua non. There
is one element essential to the realization of any historical-
cultural values through the content of the Latin reading
material which might have profitably received even more
vigorous support than is given in the report, and that is the
necessity of uncompromising insistence upon the actual
understanding of the content of every selection or paragraph read. The habit of translating words instead of understanding the thought intended to be conveyed is one
which has been encouraged by the kind and amount of
reading required in the traditional course. Even when a
pupil has translated a given passage with apparent correctness and into reasonably good English, he has not necessarily taken in the meaning. This is often shown by his
inability to restate the thought in his own language. If the
recommendations made in Chapter V with reference to the
attack upon the Latin sentence are carried into effect, it
will be found that the potential content value of a passage
is much more likely to be realized. The perpetration of so-
called translations which could not possibly have any mean-

---

[9] *Ibid.*, pp. 128-129.   [10] *Ibid.*, pp. 130-132.   [11] *Ibid.*, p. 204.

ing has probably been fostered by the fact that other translations, no less meaningless from the pupil's point of view, have been accepted as satisfactory by the teacher, who himself understood the meaning of the passage and supposed the pupil did. In teaching Cicero, for example, it will scarcely be an extravagant precaution to require pupils to state the thought relation of almost every sentence of any length to the preceding sentence and to the progress of the argument.

Broad opportunities afforded by the study of Latin. The contributions which the study of Latin should make to the development of desirable historical-cultural conceptions are not, however, limited to the content of the Latin reading material and the collateral reading in English. Further potential contributions are suggested in the report of the Classical Investigation in the study of each of the elements of Latin.

"Cultural" products of the Latin word-order method. The desirability of the Latin word-order method is urged not only on pedagogical grounds but because it provides a tangible medium for the direct appreciation of the genius of the Roman mind. "A pupil who has learned to comprehend the thought of a Latin sentence in the Latin order has to that extent thought as a Roman, and has come into direct contact with the genius of the Roman mind in the medium which is the most perfect embodiment of that genius, the Latin language." [12] When a pupil has once thought as a Roman, he has for the moment entered into and shared the genius of the Roman people. Thereafter Roman history, life, and customs cannot fail to have a much more intimate significance for him than for one who has not studied Latin.

The study of Latin a speech experience. "The study of Latin is a genuine speech experience; and this is primarily

---

[12] *Ibid.,* p. 63.

a form of participation of the social inheritance. As reading English is sharing the experience of those who speak and write English, so reading Latin is sharing the experience of those who spoke and wrote Latin. . . . As control over the language grows, the pupil's interest should be increasingly directed to the larger meaning of what he reads. The pupil may enter, at least in some measure, into the spirit of the great people whose literature he reads. According to his ability and opportunity he may be a partaker in the heritage that this people has bequeathed." [13] That this intimate experience is facilitated by training in accepting thought as it was originally conceived and expressed seems indisputable.

Cultural contributions of the study of vocabulary. Again, in the methods previously recommended for the acquisition and application of vocabulary, certain cultural outcomes are implicit. The perception of language relations emphasized in both processes cannot fail to produce a higher respect for the dignity of language; and at the same time many specific opportunities are afforded in the interpretation of English derivatives for the development of the historical and appreciative sense. Thus, the history of such words as *poetry, athlete, judicial, crescendo,* objectifies the indebtedness of our civilization to the peoples from which the ideas as well as the words are derived. Derivatives such as *pecuniary, rival, calculate,* provide tangible pictures of stages in the development of the race. Derivatives such as *street, Rochester, pagan, rostrum,* are repositories of historical events. Derivatives like *abominate, inaugurate, candidate, delirium, salary, subjugate,* preserve for the initiated vivid pictures of Roman characteristics. Cognates like *pater* and *father* potentially embody the idea of a common parent

---

[13] From the (unpublished) report of the Committee on Ancient Languages of the Commission of the National Education Association for the Reorganization of Secondary Education.

language. Heteronyms like _cordial_ and _hearty_, _provide_ and _foresee_, _contradict_ and _gainsay_ are particularly important in suggesting the operation among widely separated peoples of common ways of thinking. Vocabulary taught with this object in mind may make a substantial contribution to the intellectual outlook and the cultural appreciations of the pupil.

Contributions of the study of syntax and inflections. In the study of syntax, the distinction drawn between the grammatical idea and the method of expressing that idea involves, on the one hand, the conception of the universality of thought relations and the suggestion of the ultimate solidarity of the human race, and on the other, constitutes a further illustration of the common ancestry of the Aryan languages.

In the study of inflections, emphasis upon cognate forms in Latin and English reinforces the conception of a parent language suggested by cognate words and syntax.

Demands made upon the teacher. It is obvious that the development of these ideas makes another demand upon the teacher for wide and definite knowledge regarding the history, life, institutions, and ideas of the Romans, and at least an elementary knowledge of comparative philology. If a class period is to be shot through with stimulating references and suggestions bearing on these larger outlooks, the teacher must have generous resources at his command. The textbook, of course, should help, but the quality desired in making such experiences profitable to the pupil is spontaneity rather than formal assignment. Even when appropriate material is provided by the textbook, the teacher will find it more profitable to present it himself.

Discussion of Specific Objectives

1. _Development of an historical perspective and of a general cultural background through an_

increased knowledge of facts relating to the life, history, institutions, mythology, and religion of the Romans; an increased appreciation of the influence of their civilization on the course of western civilization; and a broader understanding of social and political problems of to-day.[14]

Conditions indispensable for attainment of "cultural" objectives. The provisions essential for the satisfactory attainment of this objective are implicit in the foregoing discussion. They are:

1. The presence of these topics in the Latin reading material from the beginning of the course.

2. Sufficient knowledge on the part of the teacher to develop the implications of the contacts established through the Latin reading material.

3. Collateral reading in English supplied both by the textbook and by supplementary books. This reading should have two distinct objects: (1) to furnish the background and setting necessary for a full understanding of the Latin reading material, and (2) to encourage wide supplementary reading and consequent "familiarity with such phases of Roman life, history and thought as are adapted to the maturity, interest, and capacity of pupils, and as grow naturally out of the Latin reading."[15]

4. Definite responsibility on the part of pupils for a satisfactory degree of attainment of this objective, secured through special tests on appropriate topics or by adequate representation of these topics in term or semester examinations.

Purposes of collateral reading in English. It will be found helpful to think of the collateral reading in English with reference to the two purposes suggested:[16]

1. Background knowledge, prerequisite for an understanding of the Latin texts read.

2. Wide reading on topics which prove of special interest.

---

[14] *The Classical Investigation* (Part I): *General Report* (Princeton University Press, 1924), p. 62.

[15] *Ibid.*, p. 205. [16] *Ibid.*, pp. 204, 205-206.

For both purposes definite material is necessary in the form of lists of books appropriate to each year of Latin. For the background knowledge desired of all pupils, such lists may profitably be accompanied by lists of topics and questions with specific references to sources of information.

In the Appendix (pages 215-217) will be found a list of books for general reading appropriate for the first two years of the course. Here also (pages 187-189) will be found reference material for more intensive background studies preliminary to the reading of certain Latin authors.

The general reading encouraged throughout the course will naturally differ widely among individual pupils in accordance with their divergent interests. Teachers who desire to have some kind of check upon the general reading of their pupils will find it helpful to use some such device as that reproduced (page 218) in the Appendix.

In the Appendix sample tests on this objective will also be found (pages 219-223), one testing the results of general reading pertaining to early Rome, and another the extent to which pupils secure definite ideas of the similarities and differences between Roman civilization and our own. "In the treatment of all topics bearing on the historical-cultural objectives marked emphasis should be placed upon comparison with present-day events and situations, such as survivals of Roman governmental policies, laws, and customs, Rome's contribution to the solution of present social and political problems, and allusions to Roman customs as they appear in the English reading of pupils, or as they are reflected in English words." [17]

>   2. *Increased ability to understand and appreciate references and allusions to the mythology, traditions, and history of the Greeks and Romans.*[18]

---

[17] *Ibid.*, p. 206.　　　　　　　[18] *Ibid.*, pp. 66-67.

Desirable conditions. The means necessary to secure attainment of this objective through the study of Latin are:

1. *Latin reading material on these topics.* Roman background, in the opinion of the writer, is the most appropriate theme to be stressed during the first year, and mythology should then receive special treatment during the third or fourth semesters.

2. *Familiarity of the teacher with the myths and legends of Greece and Rome.* This general knowledge should be supplemented by accurate information regarding the references and allusions most frequently met in English reading. A suggestive list will be found in the Appendix (pages 224-227).

3. *Collateral reading in English* to provide the setting for stories told in Latin, and the opportunity for wide reading in English inspired by the Latin reading. A list of reference books on mythology will be found in the Appendix (pages 184-185).

4. *Special tests on this objective,* or the inclusion of appropriate questions in term or semester examinations. For a sample test on mythology see the Appendix (pages 228-229).

5. *"Laboratory" work.* Since the purpose of this objective is to enable pupils to understand references met in their English reading, the discovery of such references should be systematically and vigorously encouraged. This activity provides a strong motive for discussion in class and for keeping a notebook. Intimate association with the normal environment of the pupil should be stressed at every opportunity.

3. *The development of right attitudes toward social situations.*[19]

Original purpose of the Roman legends. Latin is under the common obligations resting upon all subjects to contribute to the development of sound social ideals and attitudes. The material available in Latin has long met the test of successful use for this purpose; for the stories of the early Romans, especially those revealing the characteristic Roman virtues of patriotism, honor in keeping one's word, self-sacrifice, integrity in public life, sternness of discipline, frugality and simplicity, respect for the gods,

---

[19] *Ibid.,* pp. 67, 153-155.

respect for authority, pride in worthy achievement were taught to Roman children by their elders for the very purpose of inculcating right standards of conduct for the individual in relation to his family, his country, and his gods. In the elementary Latin books of the older type little use was made of this wealth of material supplied by Livy, Valerius Maximus, Aulus Gellius, and others, because pupils were too busy preparing to read Cæsar. The reorganization of the course, and especially the use of connected Latin from the beginning of the course, now makes possible the use of this material for its original purpose once more, that is, the setting before young people in narrative or dramatic form of models worthy of emulation.

Romans embodying desirable social qualities. The use of such material is particularly desirable in the first year, when pupils are still addicted to hero worship. The names of Curtius, Decius, Horatius, Scævola, Regulus, Fabricius, Cato, Brutus, Lucretia, Titus Manlius, the Fabii, Paulus, Marcellus should symbolize in the mind of the pupils not so many pages of Latin translated, but dramatic episodes illustrating the noblest of human qualities.

> 4. *A better acquaintance through the study of their writings with some of the chief personal characteristics of the authors read.*[20]

In the opinion of the writer this is the least important of the objectives here being discussed. It has been pointed out above that pupils cannot be expected, at the high-school age, to be greatly interested in authors as such. If the narrative of Cæsar, the arguments of Cicero, and the story of Vergil are really understood and appreciated, this is about all that can reasonably be expected. We are content if pupils reading *Ivanhoe* or *The Idylls of the King*

---

[20] *Ibid.*, pp. 67-78.

understand the content with its setting. We do not expect them to draw conclusions regarding the personal characteristics of Scott or Tennyson.

Teachers, however, should themselves fully appreciate the occasional revelations of character which Cæsar and Cicero made, and there can assuredly be no harm in calling the attention of pupils informally to the most striking instances. Thus, we may note Cæsar's swiftness of action (Bk. I, Chs. 10, 13; II, 3), his quickness of decision (VII, 85-87), his personal courage (I, 25; II, 25), his mildness of reproof (I, 22; IV, 21), his cruelty (I, 28), his unscrupulousness toward enemies (IV, 13-14), but any attempt to cull much more material of this sort from the text of Cæsar is likely to be artificial and unconvincing.

> 5. *The development of an appreciation of the literary qualities of the Latin authors read, and the development of a capacity for such appreciation in the literature of other languages.*[21]
>
> 6. *A greater appreciation of the elements of literary technique employed in prose and verse.*[22]
>
> 7. *Improvement in the literary quality of the pupil's written English.*[23]

These three objectives are discussed together because they represent simply different phases of the development of literary appreciation, the first involving unconscious appreciation, the second some understanding of the technique, and the third the ability to use the results of this appreciation and understanding in one's own writing. These three objectives are limited in their application certainly

---

[21] *Ibid.*, pp. 68-70.   [22] *Ibid.*, p. 70.   [23] *Ibid.*, pp. 70-71.

to the last two years, and for most pupils to the last year of the secondary course.

Limited degree of probable attainment. It should be observed that the classical report is exceedingly modest in its suggestions regarding the degree to which this group of objectives may be attained in the secondary schools. It considers the process of translating the means by which such appreciation may be developed indirectly, and regards as highly doubtful the prospect of securing for any considerable number of pupils direct appreciation or direct imitation of the original text. Latin teachers throughout the country have expressed their belief that such appreciation can be developed, were there time to devote to it. The desired reduction in the amount of ground to be covered during the third and fourth years is now practicable, and it should be accompanied by a serious attempt to develop a real appreciation of the literary qualities of Vergil.

Quality of translation. If it is granted that for most pupils their appreciation of Vergil will develop, if at all, from the effort to translate it adequately, a consideration of the results disclosed by Miss Woodring's thesis with reference to the rhetorical qualities exhibited in the translations of pupils who had just finished a year of Vergil, will indicate that we shall have a long road before us in the effort to reach the desired goal. Miss Woodring says: [24] "It was very evident from the beginning of the study to the end that pupils paid very little attention to style, diction, and rhetorical effectiveness in Latin translations. It was impossible to make a count of the rhetorical errors which occurred in the translations studied."

And again, Miss Woodring says [25] in regard to literary

---

[24] M. N. Woodring, *A Study of the Quality of English in Latin Translations* (Columbia University, Bureau of Publications, 1925), p. 64.   [25] *Ibid.*, p. 70.

appreciation: "This objective cannot be realized under the conditions found in this study."

Appeal of adequate translation. On the other hand, there is in most pupils studying Cicero and Vergil a real, if unconscious, capacity for appreciation within the limits indicated above. Pupils are quite able to distinguish between a translation which reflects the spirit and style of the original and one that does not. Every teacher has seen classes respond to some particularly happy rendering of a passage of Vergil or a period of Cicero. It is chiefly through this means, constantly stressed, that a development of the capacity for literary appreciation may be expected. It is consequently essential that, in addition to requiring a translation which shall be satisfactory from the point of view of correct English, a persistent effort be made to bring that translation into harmony with the spirit and literary style of the original.

A valuable practice is to have pupils write and present to the class translations of specially selected passages, and to ask the pupils themselves to decide which translation shows the best appreciation of the original. The teacher may profitably supplement this practice from time to time by reading from good translations of Cicero or Vergil, asking the pupils to select the one which in their judgment is the best, and inviting criticisms, especially as to losses involved in these translations. The translations recommended are: [26]

Billson, Charles J., *The Æneid of Virgil Translated* (Oxford, Basil Blackwell, 1923, new and revised edition).

Fairclough, H. R., *Translation of Vergil* (*Loeb Classical Library,* 1916).

McKail, J. W., *Vergil's Æneid* (prose) (Longmans, Green & Co., 1915).

---

[26] For other translations see the list in the Appendix, pages 188-189.

Equipment of the teacher. Naturally the teacher will need to be thoroughly familiar with the literary qualities characteristic of Cicero and Vergil. Especial stress should be placed upon those which assist pupils to comprehend the thought. These, in fact, provide the best introductions to the subject of style.

8. *An elementary knowledge of the simpler principles of language structure.*[27]

Various aspects of the study of Latin which may contribute to the attainment of this objective have been discussed in previous chapters. These are here recapitulated.

1. Appreciation of universality of grammatical principles. The grammatical idea expressed by a word, phrase, or clause embodies a logical relation universal in its application. Hence, when pupils become conscious through Latin of such grammatical functions, they are comprehending universal language concepts. This universality needs to be made explicit through comparisons between languages, especially between Latin and English. Any tendency toward provincialism should be carefully avoided. Otherwise, exclusive consideration of Latin in the discussion of *cum* clauses, for example, or of relative clauses, may easily lead to the unconscious notion that time clauses describing the situation under which another event occurs, or descriptive essential relative clauses (relative clauses of characteristic) express ideas peculiar to Latin. Parallel illustrations from English are at all times desirable.

The general principle should be emphasized, even in cases in which the methods of expressing the idea differ widely. Thus the absolute idea apparently meets an almost universal language-thought need, but it is expressed by the ablative in Latin, by the genitive in Greek, by the nom-

---

[27] *The Classical Investigation* (Part I): *General Report* (Princeton University Press, 1924), pp. 71-72, 221-222.

inative (originally the dative) in English, and by the dative in German.

2. Appreciation of analysis and synthesis in language.
If pupils are led to see the distinction between the analytical and synthetical modes of expressing ideas as recommended in Chapter VII, they will secure a most valuable insight into the structure of language and a genuine appreciation of the function of analysis and synthesis in language. From this conception inevitably springs increased appreciation of the nature of language and increased sense of its dignity.

3. Appreciation of language development. The recognition of similarities between Latin and English not due to borrowing should lead early in the course to the conception of a parent language from which Latin and the Anglo-Saxon element of English are derived. Some examples of these similarities are: Latin *mater* and English *mother* (German *Mutter*), the occurrence in English and Latin of the -*m* as the sign of the accusative (objective) case, and the use of the subjunctive mood in both languages to express volition. This extension of the pupil's linguistic horizon is a valuable cultural product as well as a fascinating topic. On this foundation may be built a simple explanation of the relation of the main branches of the Aryan or Indo-European family of languages, including Greek, Latin, Teutonic (German and Anglo-Saxon), Slavic, and Sanskrit. Care should be taken not to identify language descent with racial descent. The distinction should be gradually but clearly made between *derived* languages on the one hand, as French, Spanish, Italian derived from Latin, or *borrowed* elements, such as the Latin element in our English language, and *cognate* languages descended from a common parent speech, as Latin and Anglo-Saxon descended from the parent Aryan language.

It may be noted that English has *borrowed* from Latin

only in its vocabulary. The resemblances existing between Latin and English in forms and syntax are due to their cognate relationship. A possible exception is that English may have been influenced directly by Latin in the use of the infinitive with the subject in the objective case.

4. Appreciation of cognate words and forms. When the idea of a common parent language has once been established, the study of Latin furnishes abundant opportunities for illustrating and objectifying the common descent of Latin and English through cognate words, forms, and syntax. It is not here suggested that the course in Latin be converted into a premature course in comparative philology, but identification of simple and concrete results of cognate relationship is wholly appropriate to the secondary stage of education, and nowhere can these concrete evidences be seen so well as in the study of Latin in its relation to English. The pronouns *me* and *me, te* and *thee,* the numerals *tres* and *three, septem* and *seven,* the verbs *sto* and *stand, sedeo* and *sit,* the nouns *nomen,* and *name, ager* and *acre, mater* and *mother, pater* and *father* are so similar that an explanation of this similarity is not only appropriate but seems called for.

If the thread of cognate relationship is continued throughout the course, it will be found that pupils exhibit much interest and derive much intellectual satisfaction from detecting relations not at first so obvious. If *verbum* is cognate with *word, ventus* with *wind, vado* with *wade,* it is a simple inference that Latin *v* and English *w* correspond in cognates. If *pater* is cognate with *father, pes* with *foot, pabulum* with *food,* evidently English *f* and Latin *p* correspond. Similarly, Latin *f* and English *b* frequently correspond, as shown by *fero* and *bear, frater* and *brother, fui* and *be, frangere* and *break.*

Equipment of the teacher. Obviously, knowledge of these correspondences is an important part of the teacher's equipment. A mention of Grimm's Law in the Latin class-room would be highly inappropriate, but the main principles of the law should be familiar to all teachers of Latin. A summary of the most important points with illustrations will be found in the Appendix (pages 230-232), together with a list of some of the more important cognate forms.

APPENDIX

BIBLIOGRAPHY AND EQUIPMENT

Reference books and magazine articles appropriate for both pupils and teachers are included in the lists given below.

The rapidity with which new Latin texts and new books and articles on various phases of the teaching of Latin are appearing makes any bibliography incomplete within a short time after its appearance. It is of the utmost importance for progressive Latin teachers to establish and maintain connection with some agency by which they may be accurately, promptly, and continuously informed regarding new texts, new material, new equipment, new ideas. The most valuable agency for the purpose in this country is the Service Bureau for Classical Teachers, at Teachers College, Columbia University, New York, conducted by Frances E. Sabin. The activities of the Bureau consist in the publication of:

1. *Latin Notes*, a monthly magazine (eight issues), devoted to suggestions for the improvement of Latin teaching ($1.00 a year).
2. *Supplements to Latin Notes*, published at irregular intervals, devoted to a more elaborate treatment of special phases of Latin teaching (single copies $.10).
3. Hundreds of printed and mimeographed bulletins, pamphlets, handbooks, and other types of teaching material which are for sale or loan.

The Service Bureau is also a correspondence bureau with an affiliated group of specialists to insure a careful and competent consideration of questions submitted to it.

GENERAL BIBLIOGRAPHY FOR TEACHERS

The Teaching of Latin

ALEXANDER, RUTH, "Improvement Sheet for Teachers of First Year Latin," *Latin Notes,* Vol. 3, January, 1926, pp. 3-5.

BENNETT and BRISTOL, *The Teaching of Latin and Greek* (Longmans, Green & Co., 1899, *out of print*).

CARR, W. L., "The Teaching of Latin," a chapter in Vol. XII of *The Classroom Teacher* (The Classroom Teacher, Inc., Chicago, 1927).

——, "The Teaching of Latin in the Secondary School," *Latin Notes,* Vol. 4, May, 1927, pp. 1-2.

GAME, J. B., *Teaching High School Latin* (University of Chicago Press, 1925).

GRAY, M. D., "Pupil's Companion to the Study of High School Latin," Parts I-III, Rochester, N. Y., Board of Education, 1926.

——, "The Supervision of Latin," a chapter in Uhl and Others' *The Supervision of Secondary Subjects* (D. Appletone & Co., 1929).

HEADLAM, J. W., "The Teaching of Classics in the Secondary Schools of Germany," Board of Education, Special Reports, England, Vol. XX, 1910.

HECKER, E. A., *The Teaching of Latin in Secondary Schools* (Schoenhof Book Co., Boston, 1909, *out of print*).

NORTH and ALFORD, "The Teaching of High School Latin," *Maryland School Bulletin,* Vol. 3, No. 5 (September, 1921), State Department of Education, Baltimore, Md.

ROUSE and APPLETON, *Latin on the Direct Method* (University of London Press, 1925).

SABIN, FRANCES E., "The Relation of Latin to Practical Life," Service Bureau for Classical Teachers.

WOODRING, M. N., "An Analysis of a Teacher's Equipment," *Latin Notes,* Vol. 3, March, 1926, p. 3.

Dictionaries and General Reference Books

GOW, JAMES, *Companion to School Classics* (Macmillan Co., 1898).

JONES, J. S., *Companion to Roman History* (Oxford University Press, 1912).

LEWIS, C. T., *Elementary Latin Dictionary* (American Book Co., 1915).

——, and SHORT, CHARLES, *Harper's Latin Dictionary* (American Book Co., 1907).

MURRAY, J. A. H. (editor), *A New English Dictionary* (Oxford University Press). 24 Vols.

PECK, H. T., *Harper's Dictionary of Classical Literature and Antiquities* (American Book Co., 1897).

PETRIE, A., *An Introduction to Roman History, Literature and Antiquities* (Oxford University Press, 1918).

RICH, ANTHONY, *Dictionary of Antiquities* (Longmans, Green & Co., 1893, *out of print*).

SANDYS, J. E., *A Companion to Latin Studies* (Macmillan Co., 1921).

SEYFFERT, OSCAR, *Dictionary of Classical Antiquities, Mythology, Religion, Literature, and Art* (*revised by* NETTLESHIP *and* SANDYS) (Macmillan Co., 1908, *out of print*).

SKEAT, W. W., A *Concise Etymological Dictionary of the English Language* (Oxford University Press, 1901).

——, *An Etymological Dictionary of the English Language* (Oxford University Press, 1910).

SMITH, WILLIAM, *Dictionary of Greek and Roman Antiquities* (American Book Co., 1905).

——, *English-Latin Dictionary* (American Book Co., 1871).

WEEKLEY, ERNEST, *A Concise Etymological Dictionary of Modern English* (E. P. Dutton & Co., 1924).

WHITE, J. T., *English-Latin Dictionary* (Ginn and Co.).

——, *Latin-English Dictionary* (Ginn and Co.).

PERIODICALS

Classical Journal. Address W. L. Carr, University of Michigan, Ann Arbor, Mich., $2.50 a year.

Classical Weekly. Address Charles Knapp, Columbia University, New York, N. Y., $2.00 a year.

Latin Notes. Address Frances E. Sabin, Teachers College, Columbia University, New York, N. Y., $1.00 a year.

PICTURES

BRETSCHNEIDER, M., Reconstruction of Roman Buildings (10 x 7 inches). Address Via del Tritone 62, Rome, Italy. For a list see *Latin Notes*, Vol. 1, April, 1924, p. 2.

FORTI, E., 75 Pictures on Roman Life (9½ x 14½ inches, .50 each). Address Alinari, the Corso, Rome, Italy. Lists are obtainable from the Service Bureau for Classical Teachers.

GATTHESCHI, GIUSEPPE, 100 Restorations of Imperial Rome (150 *lire* a set). Address Libreria Spithoever, Piazza di Spagna, Rome, Italy.

SANFORD, EDITH, "Pictures for the Classical Teacher," *Bulletin II,* Service Bureau for Classical Teachers ($.30).

POST CARDS

Bell's Post Cards of Roman Life, in Colors (A. G. Seiler, $.75 a set).
Post Cards of British Museum: Set 29, "Greek and Roman Life"; Set 49, "Portraits of Roman Emperors"; Set 47, "Greek and Roman Reliefs" (Oxford University Press, $.80 a set).

Firms from Whom Catalogues and Pictures May Be Obtained

ALINARI, Corso Umberto, 137A, Rome, Italy.

ANDERSON, Via Salana, Rome, Italy.

BROWN & Co., GEORGE P., 38 Lovett Street, Beverly, Mass., catalogue $.04, half-tone prints, $.01-$.04.

COSMOS PICTURE Co., 119 West Twenty-Fifth St., New York, N. Y.

ELSON ART PUBLISHING Co., Belmont, Mass. (photogravures).

HILL, G. F., *Illustrations of School Classics* (Macmillan Co.).

PERRY PICTURE Co., Malden, Mass., catalogue $.15; half-tone prints $.01 and $.02.

SWAIN, GEORGE R., Ann Arbor, Mich., catalogue $.25; velox prints (3½ x 3½), $.05.

THOMPSON PICTURE Co., Syracuse, N. Y.

BRUDERHAUSEN, A., *Lists of Illustrative Material,* 47 W. Forty-Seventh St., New York, N. Y., $.10.

List of Photographs and Prints concerned with Classical Mythology, Latin Notes Supplement, No. 31, April, 1927, Service Bureau for Classical Teachers.

LANTERN SLIDES [1]

BOND SLIDE Co., 304 E. Lake Street, Chicago, Ill., $.50.

BRUDERHAUSEN, A., 47 West Forty-Seventh Street, New York, N. Y. 75 slides on the *Æneid,* $30.00 (may be rented).

EASTMAN ROMAN LIFE Co., Iowa City, Iowa (Address Extension Division, University of Iowa, Iowa City, Iowa).

KEYSTONE VIEW Co., Meadville, Pa., $.50.

STATE EDUCATION DEPARTMENT, Albany, N. Y. Visual Instruction Division Slides (lent to schools of the state without charge.)

SWAIN, GEORGE R., University of Michigan, Ann Arbor, Mich., $.50 special list for Cæsar).

UNIVERSITY OF MISSOURI, Columbia, Mo., Slides on classical subjects (lent to the teachers of the state for an annual fee of $2.00).

WALL MAPS

BREASTED, J. H., and HUTH, C. F., *History Wall Maps* (six on Rome: *Ancient World, Ancient Italy, Roman Power in Italy, Rome, Conquest of the Mediterranean, Cæsar's Gaul, Roman Empire,* 44 x 32 inches) (Denoyer-Geppert Co., $2.65-$7.60, according to mounting).

JOHNSTON, W., and A. K., *Ancient History Maps* (four on Rome: *Orbis Veteribus Notus, Orbis, Romanus, Italia Antiqua, Cæsar*

---

[1] For more extended lists see the *Classical Journal,* Vol. 17, January, 1922, pp. 230-231; Vol. 16, June, 1921, pp. 564-565.

de Bello Gallico, 52 x 44 inches) (A. J. Nystrom Co., $6.00-$9.50 each, according to mounting; set of any four maps, $28.00-$34.50).

KIEPERT, H., *Wall Maps* (three on Rome: *Ancient Italy,* 53 x 62 inches; *Ancient Latium,* 66 x 42 inches; *Ancient Gaul,* 69 x 55 inches; *Roman Empire,* 75 x 57 inches) (Denoyer-Geppert Co., $8.35-$21.40, according to map and mounting).

WEBSTER, KNOWLTON, and HAZEN, *European History Maps* (five on Rome: *The Ancient World, Ancient Italy, Development of the Roman Empire, Rome—Imperial and Republican, Roman Empire,* 50 x 38 inches) (A. J. Nystrom Co., $3.00-$7.00 each, according to mounting).

WESTERMANN, W. L., *Classical and Historical Maps* (three on Rome: *The Roman Republic, Cæsar's Campaigns in Gaul, The Roman Empire,* 60 x 46 inches) (Rand, McNally & Co., $8.75-$14.25 each, according to mounting).

ATLASES

Atlas of Ancient and Classical Geography (E. P. Dutton & Co., 1907, $1.00).

BREASTED-HUTH, *Ancient History Atlas* (Denoyer-Geppert Co., $.75).

GRUNDY, G. B., *Murray's Classical Atlas* (Oxford University Press, 1917, $2.50).

SCHREIBER, T., *Atlas of Classical Antiquity* (Macmillan Co., 1895, $10.00).

SHEPARD, W. R., *Historical Atlas* (Henry Holt and Co., 1911, $3.90).

CHARTS AND MODELS [2]

Cybulski Charts (23 pictures, 28 x 32 inches, $1.60 each) (A. J. Nystrom and Co.).

Gurlitt History Pictures (7 connected with Cæsar's Gallic War, 26 x 38 inches, $2.10 each) (A. J. Nystrom and Co.).

Lehmann Colored History Pictures (26 x 35 inches, $1.60-$6.75 each, according to mounting) (Denoyer-Geppert Co.).

THE INFLUENCE OF GREEK AND ROMAN CIVILIZATION UPON MODERN TIMES

BAILEY, CYRIL, *The Legacy of Rome* (Oxford University Press, 1923).

BLUNT, A. F. W., *The Ancient World and Its Legacy to Us* (Oxford University Press, 1928).

---

[2] For lists of models obtainable from Europe, address George E. Stechert Co., 31-33 East Tenth Street, New York, N. Y.

DeBurgh, W. G., *The Legacy of the Ancient World* (Macmillan Co., 1926).

Elson, Henry W., *Modern Times and the Living Past* (American Book Co., 1925).

Ferrero, G., *Ancient Rome and Modern America* (G. P. Putnams Sons, 1914, *out of print*).

Flannery, H. W., "Roman Women and the Vote," *Classical Journal*, Vol. 16, November, 1920, pp. 103-107.

Hadley, H. S., *Rome and the World To-day* (G. P. Putnams Sons, 1922).

Lewis, J. H., *Two Great Republics, Rome and the United States* (Rand, McNally Co., 1913, *out of print*).

Livingstone, R. W., *The Legacy of Greece* (Oxford University Press, 1921).

Mitchell, B. W., "Ariovistus and William II," *Classical Journal*, Vol. 14, February, 1919, pp. 295-307.

Osborn, E. B., *The Heritage of Greece and the Legacy of Rome* (George H. Doran Co., 1925).

Sabin, Frances E., "The Influence of the Classics on English Literature," *Bulletin VI*, Service Bureau for Classical Teachers.

History, Biography, and Political Institutions

Abbott, F. F., *The Common People of Ancient Rome* (Charles Scribner's Sons, 1911).

——, *Roman Political Institutions* (Ginn & Co., 1911).

——, *Roman Politics (Our Debt to Greece and Rome Series)* (Longmans, Green & Co., 1923).

——, *A Short History of Rome* (Scott, Foresman & Co., 1906).

——, *Society and Politics in Ancient Rome* (Charles Scribner's Sons, 1909).

Arnold, William Thomas, *Roman System of Provincial Administration to the Accession of Constantine the Great* (Blackwell, London, *new edition being prepared*).

Baker, G. P., *Sulla the Fortunate* (Dodd, Mead & Co., 1927).

Beesly, A. H., *Catiline, Clodius and Tiberius* (G. E. Stechert, 1924).

——, *The Gracchi, Marius and Sulla* (Charles Scribner's Sons, 1888).

Boak, A. E. R., *A History of Rome to 565 A.D.* (Macmillan Co., 1921).

Boissier, Gaston (Jones), *Cicero and His Friends* (G. P. Putnams Sons, 1907).

Botsford, G. W., *A Brief History of the World* (Macmillan Co., 1927).

——, *History of the Ancient World* (Macmillan Co., 1928).

——, *A History of Rome* (Macmillan Co., 1928).

BOTSFORD, G. W., and L. S., *Source Book of Ancient History* (Macmillan Co., 1927).

————, *The Story of Rome as the Greeks and Romans Tell It (source book)* (Macmillan Co., 1903).

BREASTED, J. H., *Ancient Times* (Ginn & Co., 1916).

————, *Survey of the Ancient World* (Ginn & Co., 1927).

CHURCH, A. J., *Roman Life in the Days of Cicero* (Dodd, Mead & Co., 1928).

————, *The Story of Carthage* (G. P. Putnams Sons, 1886).

DAVIDSON, J. L. S., *Cicero and the Fall of the Roman Republic* (G. P. Putnams Sons, 1906).

DAVIS, W. S., *Readings in Ancient History: Rome,* Vol. II (Allyn & Bacon Co., 1913).

DODGE, T. A., *Cæsar (Great Captains)* (Houghton Mifflin Co., 1892).

FERRERO, GUGLIELMO, *Characters and Events of Roman History* (G. P. Putnams Sons, 1909).

————, *Greatness and Decline of Rome* (G. P. Putnams Sons, 1907), 5 Vols.

————, *The Women of the Cæsars* (Century Co., 1911, *out of print*).

————, and BARBAGALLO, CORRADO, *A Short History of Rome* (G. P. Putnams Sons, 1918), 2 Vols.

FOWLER, W. WARDE, *The City State of the Greeks and Romans* (Macmillan Co., 1895).

————, *Julius Cæsar* (G. P. Putnams Sons, 1897).

————, *Rome* (Henry Holt & Co., 1912).

FRANK, TENNEY, *An Economic History of Rome* (Johns Hopkins Press, 1927).

————, *A History of Rome* (Henry Holt & Co., 1923).

————, *Roman Imperialism* (Macmillan Co., 1914).

FROUDE, J. A., *Cæsar: A Sketch* (Charles Scribner's Sons, 1895).

GOODSPEED, G. S., *A History of the Ancient World* (Charles Scribner's Sons, 1904).

GRANRUD, J. E., *Roman Constitutional History* (Allyn & Bacon Co., 1902).

GREENIDGE, A. H. J., *Roman Public Life* (Macmillan Co., 1901).

GREENWOOD, JOSEPHINE H., *Our Heritage from the Old World* (D. Appleton & Co., 1921).

GUERBER, H. A., *The Story of the Romans* (American Book Co., 1896).

HAAREN and POLAND, *Famous Men of Rome* (American Book Co., 1921).

HAMILTON, M. A., *Ancient Rome: The Lives of Great Men* (Oxford University Press, 1922).

————, *Outlines of Roman History* (Oxford University Press, 1915).

HARDING, C. H., and S. B., *The City of Seven Hills* (Scott, Foresman & Co., 1902).

HARDY, E. G., *Christianity and the Roman Government* (Macmillan Co., 1925).

HILL, IDA T., *Rome of the Kings* (E. P. Dutton & Co., 1925).

HOLMES, T. RICE, *Cæsar's Conquest of Gaul* (Macmillan Co., 1911).

———, *The Roman Republic* (Oxford University Press, 1923), Vols. I-III.

HOW, W. W. and LEIGH, H. D. A., *History of Rome to the Death of Cæsar* (Longmans, Green & Co., 1896).

HOYLAND, J. S., *A Brief History of Civilization* (Oxford University Press, 1925).

JEROME, THOMAS S., *Aspects of the Study of Roman History* (G. P. Putnam's Sons, 1923).

LEWIS, J. H., *Two Great Republics, Rome and the United States* (Rand, McNally & Co., 1913, *out of print*).

MACGREGOR, MARY, *The Story of Rome* (Thos. Nelson & Sons, 1913).

MARSH, F. B., *The Founding of the Roman Empire* (University of Texas, Austin, Texas, 1927).

MATHESON, P. E., *The Growth of Rome* (Oxford University Press, 1922).

MCCARTNEY, E. S., *Warfare by Land and Sea* (*Our Debt to Greece and Rome Series*) (Longmans, Green & Co., 1923).

MERIVALE, CHARLES, *General History of Rome* (American Book Co., 1877).

———, *The Roman Triumvirate* (Charles Scribner's Sons, 1889).

MILLS, DOROTHY, *Book of the Ancient Romans* (G. P. Putnams Sons, 1927).

MOMMSEN, THEODOR, *A History of Rome* (E. P. Dutton & Co., 1920, 1921), 4 Vols.

MOREY, W. C., *Outline of Roman History* (American Book Co., 1901).

MORRIS, CHARLES, *Historical Tales: Roman* (J. B. Lippincott Co., 1904), 15 Vols.

MUNRO, D. C., *Source Book of Roman History* (D. C. Heath & Co., 1904).

MYRES, J. L., *A History of Rome* (Rivington & Co., London, 1925).

NILSSON, M. P., *Imperial Rome* (Harcourt, Brace & Co., 1926).

OMAN, C. W. C., *Seven Roman Statesmen of the Late Republic* (Edward Arnold & Co., 1923).

PELHAM, H. F., *Outlines of Roman History* (G. P. Putnam's Sons, 1909).

PETERSSON, TORSTEN, *Cicero, A Biography* (University of California Press, 1920).

Plutarch's Lives (*Everyman's Library Series*) (E. P. Dutton Co., 1910), Vols. I-III.

ROLFE, J. C., *Cicero and his Influence* (*Our Debt to Greece and Rome Series*) (Longmans, Green & Co., 1923).

ROSTOVTZEFF, MICHAEL, *A History of the Ancient World* (Oxford University Press, 1927), Vol. I *Greece*, Vol. II *Rome*.

SEIGNOBOS, CHARLES (WILDE), *History of Ancient Civilization* (Charles Scribner's Sons, 1906).

SEIGNOBOS, CHARLES (FAIRLEY), *History of the Roman People* (Henry Holt & Co., 1912, *out of print*).

SELLAR, W. Y., *Vergil* (Oxford University Press, 1897).

SHOWERMAN, GRANT, *Eternal Rome* (Yale University Press, 1925).

SIHLER, E. G., *Annals of Cæsar* (G. E. Stechert & Co., 1911).

———, *Cicero of Arpinum, A Political and Literary Biography* (Yale University Press, 1914, *out of print*).

SMITH, R. B., *Rome and Carthage* (Charles Scribner's Sons, 1889).

TAPPAN, E. M., *The Story of the Roman People* (Houghton Mifflin Co., 1911).

TAYLOR, HANNIS, *Cicero, A Sketch of His Life and Works* (McClurg & Co., 1926).

TAYLOR, R. M., *A Constitutional and Political History of Rome* (Methuen and Co., 1899).

TIGHE, AMBROSE, *The Development of the Roman Constitution* (American Book Co., 1886).

TROLLOPE, ANTHONY, *Life of Cicero* (Harper & Bros., *out of print*).

VAN LOON, HENDRIK, *The Story of Mankind* (Macmillan Co., 1922).

WEST, W. M., *Ancient World* (Allyn & Bacon Co., 1913).

———, *The Story of Man's Early Progress* (Allyn & Bacon Co., 1920).

WESTERMANN, W. L., *The Story of the Ancient Nations* (D. Appleton & Co., 1912).

WHITE, E. L., *Why Rome Fell* (Harper & Bros., 1928).

WOLFSON, A. M., *Ancient Civilization* (American Book Co., 1916).

———, *Essentials in Ancient History* (American Book Co., 1902).

FICTION

ALLINSON, ANNE C., *Children of the Way* (Harcourt, Brace & Co., 1923).

———, *Roads from Rome* (Macmillan Co., 1913).

ANDERSON, PAUL, *With the Eagles* (D. Appleton & Co., 1929).

ATHERTON, GERTRUDE, *The Immortal Marriage* (Boni & Liveright, 1927).

AUSTIN, FREDERICK BRITTEN, *When Mankind was Young* (Doubleday, Page & Co., 1927, *out of print*).

BULWER-LYTTON, *The Last Days of Pompeii* (E. P. Dutton & Co., 1908).

CHURCH, A. J., *The Burning of Rome* (Macmillan Co., 1892, *out of print*).

———, *Lords of the World* (Charles Scribner's Sons, 1898).

CHURCH, A. J., *Lucius: The Adventures of a Roman Boy* (Dodd, Mead & Co., 1924).

———, *To the Lions* (G. P. Putnam's Sons, *out of print*).

CRAMP, WALTER S., *Psyche* (Little, Brown & Co., 1905).

DAVIS, W. S., *A Friend of Cæsar* (Macmillan Co., 1915).

———, *A Victor of Salamis* (Macmillan Co., 1916).

DOYLE, CONAN, *The Last Galley* (Doubleday, Page & Co., 1916, *out of print*).

ECKSTEIN, ERNST, *Prusias: A Romance of Ancient Rome under the Republic* (Gottsberger, 1882).

ERSKINE, JOHN, *The Private Life of Helen of Troy* (Grossett & Dunlap, 1925).

FENN, GEORGE M., *Marcus, the Young Centurion* (E. Nister, London, 1904).

FLAUBERT, GUSTAVE, *Salambo* (RAGOZIN, translator) (G. P. Putnam's Sons, 1862, *out of print*).

HALL, JENNIE, *Buried Cities* (Macmillan Co., 1923).

HANNAH, IAN C., *Voadica* (Longmans, Green & Co., 1928).

HAWTHORNE, NATHANIEL, *The Marble Faun* (E. P. Dutton & Co., 1910).

HENTY, GEORGE H., *Beric, The Briton* (Charles Scribner's Sons, 1924).

———, *The Young Carthaginian* (Charles Scribner's Sons, 1886).

HUBBARD, WILFRANC, *Shadows on the Palatine* (Minton, Balch & Co., 1925).

KIPLING, RUDYARD, *Puck of Pook's Hill* (Doubleday, Page & Co., 1913).

MACAULAY, T. B., *The Lays of Ancient Rome* (Longmans, Green & Co., 1887).

MITCHISON, NAOMI, *The Conquered* (Harcourt, Brace & Co., 1923).

———, *When the Bough Breaks* (Harcourt, Brace & Co., 1924).

ORCZY, BARONESS E., *Unto Cæsar* (A. L. Burt Co., 1914, *out of print*).

OSBORNE, DUFFIELD, *The Lion's Brood* (Doubleday, Page & Co., 1909).

PATER, WALTER, *Marius, The Epicurean* (Macmillan Co., 1911).

SHERER, J. A. B., *The Tree of Light* (T. Y. Crowell Co., 1921).

SIENKIEWICZ, HENRY, *Quo Vadis?* (Cromwell Publishing Co., 1921, *reprint*).

SNEDEKER, CAROLINE D., *The Perilous Seat* (Doubleday, Page & Co., 1923).

———, *The Spartan* (Doubleday, Page & Co., 1912).

———, *Theras and His Town* (Doubleday, Page & Co., 1924).

STODDARD, WILLIAM, *The Swordmaker's Son* (Century Co., 1903, *out of print*).

TAYLOR, C. B., *Nicanor, Teller of Tales* (McClurg & Co., 1906, *out of print*).

VAN SANTVOORD, SEYMOUR, *Octavia* (E. P. Dutton & Co., 1923).

WALLACE, LEW, *Ben Hur* (Harper & Bros., 1908).

WELLS, R. F., *On Land and Sea with Cæsar* (Lothrop, Lee & Shepard Co., 1926).

———, *With Cæsar's Legions* (Lothrop, Lee & Shepard Co., 1923).

WHITE, E. L., *Andivius Hedulio* (E. P. Dutton & Co., 1921).

———, *Helen* (George H. Doran Co., 1925).

———, *The Song of the Siren* (E. P. Dutton & Co., 1919, *out of print*).

———, *The Unwilling Vestal* (E. P. Dutton & Co., 1918).

WHITEHEAD, A. D., *The Standard Bearer* (American Book Co., 1914).

WHYTE-MELVILLE, G. J., *The Gladiators* (E. P. Dutton & Co., 1911).

SOCIAL CONDITIONS AND PRIVATE LIFE

ABBOTT, F. F., *Society and Politics in Ancient Rome* (Charles Scribner's Sons, 1909).

BAILEY, CYRIL, *The Legacy of Rome* (Oxford University Press, 1923).

BECKER, W. A., *Gallus* (Longmans, Green & Co., 1903).

CHARLESWORTH, M. P., *Trade Routes and Commerce of the Roman Empire* (Cambridge University Press, 1926).

DAVIS, W. S., *A Day in Old Rome* (Allyn & Bacon Co., 1924).

———, *The Influence of Wealth in Imperial Rome* (Macmillan Co., *out of print*).

DILL, SAMUEL, *Roman Society from Nero to Marcus Aurelius* (Macmillan Co., 1905).

FOWLER, W. W., *Social Life at Rome in the Age of Cicero* (Macmillan Co., 1909).

FRIEDLANDER, LUDWIG, *Roman Life and Manners under the Early Empire* (E. P. Dutton & Co., 1909), 4 Vols.

GUHL and KONER, *The Life of the Greeks and Romans* (Charles Scribner's Sons, 1896, *out of print*).

GWYNN, AUBREY, *Roman Education from Cicero to Quintilian* (Oxford University Press, 1926).

HALL, JENNIE, *Buried Cities* (Macmillan Co., 1928).

HILL, G. F., *Illustrations of School Classics* (Macmillan Co., 1903).

INGE, W. R., *Society in Rome under the Cæsars* (Charles Scribner's Sons, 1913, *out of print*).

JOHNSTON, H. W., *The Private Life of the Romans* (Scott, Foresman & Co., 1903).

MANN, EUPHEMIA, "Some Private Houses in Ancient Rome," *Classical Weekly,* Vol. 19, March 1, 1926, pp. 127-132.

McDANIEL, W. B., "Guide for the Study of English Books on Roman Private Life," *Bulletin III,* Service Bureau for Classical Teachers.

McDANIEL, W. B., *Roman Private Life and its Survivals (Our Debt to Greece and Rome Series)* (Longmans, Green & Co., 1924).

MOONEY, W. W., *Travel Among the Ancient Romans* (R. G. Badger, 1920, *out of print*).

PRESTON and DODGE, *Private Life of the Romans* (B. H. Sanborn & Co., 1893).

ROGERS and HARLEY, *The Life of Rome* (Oxford University Press, 1927).

SHUMWAY, E. S., *A Day in Ancient Rome* (D. C. Heath & Co., 1887).

TUCKER, T. G., *Life in the Roman World of Nero and St. Paul* (Macmillan Co., 1928).

WILKINS, A. S., *Roman Antiquities* (American Book Co., 1925).

———, *Roman Education* (Macmillan Co., 1914).

WILSON, LILLIAN M., *The Roman Toga* (Johns Hopkins Press, 1924).

MYTHOLOGY AND RELIGION

BAILEY, CAROLYN, *Wonder Stories* (Milton Bradley Co., 1924), pp. 74-83.

BAKER, E. K., *Stories of Old Greece and Rome* (Macmillan Co., 1927).

BALDWIN, JAMES, *The Story of the Golden Age* (Charles Scribner's Sons, 1904).

BENET, STEPHEN, "Winged Man" (a poem), *Latin Notes,* Vol. 4, December, 1926.

BLACK, JANE, *Mythology for Young People* (Charles Scribner's Sons, 1925).

BUCKLEY, ELSIE, *Children of the Dawn* (Macmillan Co., 1925).

BULFINCH, THOMAS, *Age of Fable* (E. P. Dutton & Co., 1926).

———, *Mythology (Everyman's Library Series)* (E. P. Dutton & Co., 1913).

———, *Stories of Gods and Heroes* (T. Y. Crowell Co., 1923).

CARTER, J. B., *The Religion of Numa* (Macmillan Co., 1906, *out of print*).

CHURCH, A. J., *Æneid for Boys and Girls* (Macmillan Co., 1927).

COLUM, PADRAIC, *The Golden Fleece* (Macmillan Co., 1912).

CUMONT, FRANZ, *After Life in Roman Paganism* (Yale University Press, 1923).

FAIRBANKS, ARTHUR, *The Mythology of Greece and Rome* (D. Appleton & Co., 1908).

FARJEON, ELEANOR, *Mighty Men* (D. Appleton & Co., 1926).

FOWLER, W. W., *The Religious Experience of the Roman People* (Macmillan Co., 1922).

———, *Roman Ideas of Deity* (Macmillan Co., 1914).

FOX, W. S., *Greek and Roman Mythology (Mythology of All Races,* Vol. I) (Marshall Jones Co., 1928).

GAYLEY, C. M., *Classic Myths in English Literature and Art* (Ginn & Co., 1911).

GUERBER, H. A., *Myths of Greece and Rome* (American Book Co., 1893).

HARDY, E. G., *Christianity and the Roman Government* (Macmillan Co., 1925).

HARRINGTON and TOLMAN, *Greek and Roman Mythology* (B. H. Sanborn & Co., 1897).

HARRISON, JANE E., *Mythology* (*Our Debt to Greece and Rome Series*) (Longmans, Green & Co., 1924).

HAWTHORNE, NATHANIEL, *Tanglewood Tales and Wonder Book* (Houghton Mifflin Co., 1881).

HUTCHINSON, W. M. L., *The Sunset of the Heroes: Last Adventures of the Takers of Troy* (E. P. Dutton & Co., 1911).

——, *The Muses Pageant: Myths and Legends of Ancient Greece Retold* (*Everyman's Library Series*) (E. P. Dutton & Co., 1912).

KINGSLEY, CHARLES, *The Heroes* (*King's Treasury of Literature*) (Macmillan Co., 1928).

KINNEY, MURIEL, *Stars and Their Stories* (D. Appleton & Co., 1926).

LANG, ANDREW, *Tales of Greece and Troy* (Longmans, Green & Co., 1912).

"Operas based upon the Greek Myths," *Latin Notes Supplement 22,* December, 1926, Service Bureau for Classical Teachers.

SABIN, FRANCES E., *Classical Myths that Live Today* (Silver, Burdett & Co., 1927).

TAPPAN, E. M., *Old World Hero Stories* (Houghton Mifflin Co., 1911).

The Children's Plutarch—Tales of the Romans (Harper & Bros., 1910).

WALSH, WILLIAM SHEPARD, *Heroes and Heroines of Fiction* (J. B. Lippincott & Co., 1915), Vol. I, *Modern Prose and Poetry,* Vol. II, *Classical, Mediæval and Legendary.*

WHITCOMB, I. P., *Heroes of History* (Charles E. Merrill Co., 1904).

ART, LITERATURE, AND LITERARY BACKGROUND

BAIKIE, JAMES, *Ancient Crete, The Sea Kings' Eyrie* (Blackwell, London, 1924).

——, *The Life of the Ancient East* (Macmillan Co., 1923).

——, *Sea Kings of Crete* (Macmillan Co., 1926).

BAILEY, CYRIL (editor), *The Mind of Rome* (Oxford University Press, 1926).

BOISSIER, GASTON, *The Country of Horace and Vergil* (G. E. Stechert & Co., 1923).

COMPARETTI, DOMENICO, *Virgil in the Middle Ages* (Macmillan Co., 1895, *out of print*).

CRUMP, M. M., *The Growth of the Æneid* (Blackwell, London, 1928, *new edition being prepared*).

CRUTTWELL, C. T. A., *A History of Roman Literature* (Charles Scribner's Sons, 1878, *out of print*).

DINSDALE, M. S., *A History of Latin Literature* (D. Appleton & Co., 1915).

DUFF, J. W., *A Literary History of Rome in the Golden Age* (Charles Scribner's Sons, 1927).

FRANK, TENNEY, *Vergil, A Biography* (Henry Holt & Co., 1922).

GARDNER, E. A., *Handbook of Greek Sculpture* (Macmillan Co., 1924).

GARDNER, HELEN, *Art through the Ages* (Harcourt, Brace & Co., 1926).

GLOVER, T. J., *Vergil* (Macmillan Co., 1912).

HAIGHT, ELIZABETH H., *Italy, Old and New* (E. P. Dutton & Co., 1923, *out of print*).

HILL, IDA T., *Rome of the Kings* (E. P. Dutton & Co., 1925).

MACKAIL, J. W., *Virgil and His Meaning to the World Today* (*Our Debt to Greece and Rome Series*) (Longmans, Green & Co:, 1922).

——, J. W., *Classical Studies* (Macmillan Co., 1926).

——, *Latin Literature* (Charles Scribner's Sons, 1895).

MASEFIELD, JOHN, *The Tragedy of Pompey the Great* (Macmillan Co., 1914).

McKINLEY, ARTHUR P., *Letters of a Roman Gentleman* (Houghton Mifflin Co., 1926).

MOSELY, N., *Characters and Epithets, A Study in Vergil's Æneid* (Yale University Press, 1926).

NETTLESHIP, HENRY, *Lectures and Essays* (Oxford University Press, 1885, *out of print*).

NITCHIE, ELIZABETH, *Vergil and the English Poets* (Columbia University Press, 1919).

PRESCOTT, HENRY W., *The Development of Virgil's Art* (University of Chicago Press, 1928).

RAND, EDWARD K., *Ovid and His Influence* (*Our Debt to Greece and Rome Series*) (Longmans, Green & Co., 1925).

REINACH, SOLOMAN, *Apollo, An Illustrated Manual of the History of Art* (Charles Scribner's Sons, 1924).

SABIN, FRANCES E., *Classical Associations of Places in Italy* (Service Bureau for Classical Teachers, 1927).

SELLAR, W. Y., *Virgil* (Oxford University Press, 1897).

SEYMOUR, T. D., *Life in the Homeric Age* (Macmillan Co., 1907, *out of print*).

SIKES, P. E. E., *Roman Poetry* (E. P. Dutton & Co., 1923).

SINCOX, C. A., *History of Latin Literature* (Harper & Bros., 1883, *out of print*), 2 Vols.

SLAUGHTER, M. S., *Roman Portraits* (*Lucretius, Vergil, Horace, Augustus, Cicero*) (Yale University Press, 1925).

SMITH, WILLIAM, *Rome and Carthage* (Charles Scribner's Sons, 1888).

TARBELL, F. B., *A History of Greek Art* (Macmillan Co., 1913).

TOLMAN and SCOGGIN, *Mycenean Troy* (American Book Co., 1903).

TYRRELL, R. Y., *Latin Poetry* (Houghton Mifflin Co., 1895, *out of print*).

ARTICLES ON THE BACKGROUND AND CONTENT OF CICERO

DONNELLY, FRANCIS P., "Cicero's Literary Style as a Basis for the Study of English Expression," *Latin Notes Supplement 13*, December, 1925.

HENRY, MARGARET Y., "Cicero and the Great Society," *Classical Weekly,* Vol. 17, December 10, 1923, pp. 67-72.

———, "The Ideal Element in the Politics of Cicero," *Classical Journal,* Vol. 18, October, 1922, pp. 26-32.

HUSBAND, R. W., "Election Laws in Republican Rome," *Classical Journal,* Vol. 11, June, 1916, p. 535.

LODGE, GONZALEZ, "Cæsar, Cicero, and Pompey," *Latin Notes Supplement 28*, February, 1927.

———, "Marcus Tullius Cicero—Citizen," *Latin Notes Supplement 28*, February, 1927.

———, "The Value of the Classics in Training for Citizenship," *Latin Notes Supplement 24*, January, 1927.

RADIN, MAX, "A Meeting of the Senate," *Latin Notes,* Vol. 2, January, 1925, pp. 1-3.

———, "A Simple Account of Legal Procedure in a Roman Court," *Latin Notes,* Vol. 1, December, 1923, p. 1.

RIESS, ERNST, "Then and Now: Social Problems in Cicero's Times," *Latin Notes,* Vol. 3, January, 1926, p. 7.

———, "Stylistic Devices in Cicero's Orations," *Latin Notes,* Vol. 2, March, 1925, pp. 1-3.

SHOWERMAN, GRANT, "On the Teaching of Cicero," *Classical Journal,* Vol. 3, May, 1908, pp. 261-270.

ARTICLES ON THE BACKGROUND AND CONTENT OF VERGIL

BURCHETT, BESSIE, "Remarks on Teaching Vergil," *Classical Weekly,* Vol. 21, May 21, 1928, pp. 214-216.

DREW, D. L., "Gray's Elegy and the Classics," *Classical Weekly,* Vol. 19, February 1, 1926, pp. 109-111.

KEITH, ARTHUR, "The Greatness of Rome as Seen in Book I of Vergil's Æneid," *Latin Notes,* Vol. 5, February, 1928, pp. 3-4.

MCCREA, NELSON, "Bibliography for the Study of Vergil," *Latin Notes Supplement 3*, April, 1924.

OGLE, MARBURY, "Vergil and Some Problems of the Present," *Classical Weekly,* Vol. 21, October 3, 1927, pp. 3-8.

SABIN, FRANCES E., "The English Pronunciation of Proper Names in the First Six Books of the Æneid," *Latin Notes Supplement 1,* June, 1926.

——, "Some Allusions in English Literature to Vergil's Æneid," *Latin Notes Supplement 2,* May, 1924.

SAUNDERS, CATHARINE, "The Present Trend in Vergilian Studies," *Classical Weekly,* Vol. 20, October 25, 1926, pp. 27-29.

SILLS, K. C. M., "Idea of Universal Peace in the Works of Vergil and Dante," *Classical Journal,* Vol. 9, January, 1914, pp. 139-153.

SLAUGHTER, M. S., "Vergil: An Interpretation," *Classical Journal,* Vol. 12, March, 1917, pp. 359-377.

TRANSLATIONS OF CLASSICAL AUTHORS

BILLSON, CHARLES J., *The Æneid of Virgil Translated* (Blackwell, London, 1924, new and revised edition) (Stechert, Importer).

BLAKENEY, E. H., *Pages from Latin Authors* (E. P. Dutton & Co., 1924).

BUTCHER and LAING, *Homer's Odyssey* (Macmillan Co., 1928).

CONINGTON-ALLISON, *Translation of the Æneid* (prose) (Scott, Foresman & Co., 1923).

FAIRCLOUGH, H. R., *Vergil, with an English Translation* (*Loeb Classical Library*) (G. P. Putnams Sons, 1916), Vol. I, *Æneid* 1-6, Vol. II, *Æneid* 7-12, and Minor Poems.

HOWE and HARRER, *Greek Literature in Translation* (Harper & Bros., 1924).

——, *Roman Literature in Translation* (Harper & Bros., 1924).

JACKSON, JOHN, *Translation of Vergil* (prose) (Oxford University Press, 1921).

LANG, LEAF, and MYERS, *Translation of the Iliad* (Macmillan Co., 1928).

MACKAIL, J. W., *Vergil's Æneid* (prose) (Macmillan Co., 1927).

MURRAY, GILBERT, *The Trojan Women* (Euripides) (Oxford University Press, 1915).

NORTON, C. E., *Translation of Dante's "The Divine Comedy"* (Houghton Mifflin Co., 1922), 3 Vols.

PALMER, HERBERT, *Translation of the Odyssey* (Houghton Mifflin Co., 1921).

PYM, DORA, *Readings from the Literature of Ancient Rome* (Harcourt, Brace & Co., 1923).

RHOADES, JAMES, *Translation of Vergil* (*World's Classics*) (Oxford University Press, 1921).

ROGERS and HARLEY, *The Life of Rome* (Oxford University Press, 1927).

SHOWERMAN, GRANT, *Century Readings in Ancient Classical and Modern European Literature* (Century Co., 1925), Vol. I.

TAYLOR, FAIRFAX, *Æneid in Spenserian Stanzas* (E. P. Dutton & Co., 1903).

WAY, A. S., *Translation of the Fall of Troy by Quintus of Smyrna* (*Loeb Classical Library*) (G. P. Putnams Sons, 1913).

WILLIAMS, T. C., *Vergil, The Æneid* (translated into blank verse) (Houghton Mifflin Co., 1910).

TOPOGRAPHY AND MONUMENTS

DENNIE, JOHN, *Rome of Today and Yesterday* (G. P. Putnam's Sons, 1914).

EMMONS and HUNTINGTON, *Traveler's Book of Verse* (Henry Holt & Co., 1928).

HALL, JENNIE, *Buried Cities* (Macmillan Co., 1922).

HALLAM, G. H., *Horace at Tibur and the Sabine Farm* (Harrow School Book Shop, 1927).

HAMMERTON, J. A., *Wonders of the Past* (G. P. Putnams Sons, 1923), Vols. I-IV.

HUELSEN, CHRISTIAN, *The Roman Forum and the Palatine* (Bruderhausen, 1928).

LANCIANI, RODOLFO, *Ancient and Modern Rome* (Longmans, Green & Co., 1927).

——, *Ancient Rome in the Light of Recent Discoveries* (Houghton Mifflin Co., 1895, *out of print*).

——, *New Tales of Old Rome* (Houghton Mifflin Co., 1901).

——, *The Ruins and Excavations of Ancient Rome* (Houghton Mifflin Co., 1897, *out of print*).

LOVELL, ISABEL, *Stories in Stone from the Roman Forum* (Macmillan Co., 1926).

MAGOFFIN, RALPH, "The Roman Forum," *Bulletin VII,* Service Bureau for Classical Teachers.

MANN, EUPHEMIA, "Some Private Houses in Ancient Rome," *Classical Weekly,* Vol. 19, No. 16 (March 1, 1926), pp. 127-132.

MASTERS, DAVID, *The Romance of Excavation* (Dodd, Mead & Co., 1923).

MAU-KELSEY, *Pompeii* (Macmillan Co., *new edition now preparing*).

PLATNER, S. B., *The Topography and Monuments of Ancient Rome* (Allyn & Bacon Co., 1911).

SABIN, FRANCES E., *Classical Associations of Places in Italy* (F. E. Sabin, New York, 1927).

SHUMWAY, E. S., *A Day in Ancient Rome* (D. C. Heath & Co., 1885).

STOBART, J. C., *The Grandeur That Was Rome* (J. B. Lippincott Co., 1925).

TYPICAL LATIN QUESTION WORDS AND PHRASES

1. **Quis, Quid:** *who, what?* and other forms of the interrogative pronoun
2. **Quālis:** *what sort of?*
3. **Quantus:** *how great? how much?*
4. **Quot:** *how many?*
5. **Quotiēns:** *how often?*
6. **Quō modō:** *in what manner? by what means?* also suggesting *ita, tam,* etc., followed by a result clause
7. **Quā rē:** *by what means?* (to distinguish means from manner)
8. **Quantō opere:** *how much?* suggesting an adverb of quantity
9. **Quō respectū:** *in what respect?*
10. **Quā dē causā:** suggesting an ablative of cause or reason
11. **Quandō:** *when* suggesting an ablative of time, or a temporal clause
12. **Ex quō tempore:** *since when?*
13. **Quoad:** *till when* suggesting a **dum** clause or **ad** and the accusative
14. **Quam diū:** *how long?* suggesting the accusative of duration of time
15. **Quam longē:** *how far?* suggesting the accusative of extent
16. **Ubi:** *where?* suggesting the ablative of place or **trāns.,** etc., with the accusative
17. **Unde:** *whence?* suggesting place from which, or source
18. **Quō:** *whither?* suggesting place to which
19. **Quam ob rem:** *on what account?* suggesting **propter** and the accusative
20. **Cūr:** *why?* suggesting a causal clause
21. **Quō consiliō:** *for what purpose?* suggesting a purpose clause
22. **Contrā quam rem:** suggesting an adversative or concessive clause
23. **Quā condiciōne:** suggesting a condition, attendant circumstance, or **cum** circumstantial clause
24. **Quid ex hīs rēbus efficiēbātur?** etc.: suggesting a substantive result clause
25. **Quam ad rem:** suggesting **ad** with the gerund or gerundive

A SUMMARY OF THE IMMEDIATE AND ULTIMATE OB-
JECTIVES WITH BRIEF INDICATIONS OF THE ESSENTIAL
PROBLEMS, AND WITH PARTICULAR ATTENTION TO THEIR
BEARING ON THE DAILY PROGRAM OF THE TEACHER.

Immediate Objectives

1. Comprehension of Latin (variety in methods of testing):
Daily work at sight: minimum 15 minutes daily in 9th grades of
junior high school; minimum 10 minutes daily in 8th grades.

2. Vocabulary: (*a*) methods of solving (regular distribution of
emphasis upon the three methods); *daily sight work;* (*b*) mastery
of: reviews; tests; make-up classes.

3. Inflections: (*a*) recognition of individual forms; board work:
2 or 3 minutes daily (maximum, 5); home work: (*b*) paradigms:
written home assignments (emphasis upon combinations); board
work in class; make-up classes; *oral requirements*. Object to get
the work well done with the least expenditure of class time.

4. Syntax: (*a*) development (inductively or by association with
English): as the topic arises (anticipation—intensive attack follow up). (*b*) mastery: sentences on board; written and oral
translation from English into Latin.

Ultimate Objectives

1. Increased ability to understand English derivatives: daily
assignment and class work (alternating full analysis and rapid
interpretation); required work; required discoveries; *independent
application*.

2. Increased ability to apply English grammatical principles
studied in Latin: two or three minutes every week on the occasion of a new development, a mistake in English, need for another
review, or *without motivation. Systematic* encouragement of *independent application*.

3. Increased ability to spell English words derived from Latin:
daily until all rules have been developed—then an effort to in-

clude spelling problems *systematically* among derivatives assigned. *Variety* essential. *Rules* once learned should be maintained. *Systematic* encouragement to make application *independently*.

4. Ability to learn other foreign languages: *once or twice a month systematically*. (In first year: an attitude of anticipated familiarity). *Systematic* encouragement of *independent* application.

5. Increased facility in English: *daily* through standard of translation. Suggested improvements by pupils should be a normal part of translation. *Systematic* insistence upon this element in prepared translation.

6. Ability to explain technical terms: *systematic* encouragement of *discovering applications* in textbooks or other subjects.

7. Historical background: (*a*) general; collateral reading sheets distributed and record sheets posted within first week; ask: "How many have read one book thus far? Two?" Kept up *throughout the term:* notebook. (*b*) specific; special sheets of references and questions for particular authors; covered *systematically* in class.

8. General language: *3 minutes every week* on the occasion of a grammatical development, a cognate form, a cognate word, a heteronym, or *without motivation*.

REFERENCES TO MATERIAL RELATING TO LATIN WORDS, PHRASES, ABBREVIATIONS AND QUOTATIONS OCCURRING IN ENGLISH

D'OOGE, *Elements of Latin* (Ginn & Co., 1921), p. 383.

Foreign Phrases in Daily Use (Funk & Wagnalls Co.).

GRAY, "Introductory Lessons in Latin and English," Board of Education, Rochester, N. Y. Part I, Lessons IV, XIII, XVI, XLII. Part II, Lessons X, XI, XII, XIX, and *passim.* Part III, *passim.*

———, "Pupils' Companion to the Study of High School Latin" (Board of Education, Rochester, N. Y., 1927), Part II, pp. 140-142.

Latin Course of Study for Senior and Junior High Schools (Department of Education, Baltimore, Md., 1924), pp. 40-43.

SMITH, *Elementary Latin* (Allyn & Bacon Co., 1920), pp. 276-281.

ULLMAN and HENRY, *Elementary Latin* (Macmillan Co., 1923). See index under "Latin phrases and quotations in English," and "loan words," both classified under "Word studies."

WYCKOFF, R. T., "Latin Mottoes," Bloomington, Ind., R.F.D. No. 5, Box 154 ($.25).

WALKER, LOUISA, "Latin in Current Periodicals and Newspapers," *Latin Notes,* Vol. 3, No. 8, p. 2.

"English Expressions from Roman History," *Latin Notes,* Vol. 1, No. 2, p. 3.

KRAEMER, CASPER, "Some Latinisms in English," *Classical Weekly,* Vol. 21, No. 8 (December 5, 1927), pp. 57-61.

ENGLISH-LATIN WORD STUDY

Review of Verbs

Directions: Give the Latin verbs from which are derived the English words in the first column below (or with which they are connected by derivation); give the meaning of each Latin verb; and explain the English derivative of that verb given in the fourth column:

English Derivative	Latin Word	Meaning of Latin Word	Derivative for Explanation
1. agent	agō	move, do	exigent
2. decadent	cadō	fall	deciduous
3. suicide	caedō	cut, slay	incision
4. capture	capiō	take	recipient
5. proceed	cēdō	go, yield	excessive
6. discern	cernō	separate, decide	discreet
7. exclamation	clāmō	shout	clamant
8. exclude	claudō	close, shut	preclude
9. recline	-clīnō	lean	declension
10. credulous	crēdō	believe, trust	incredible
11. current	currō	run	precursor
12. contradict	dīcō	say	valedictory
13. dative	dō	give, put	tradition
14. conductor	dūcō	lead	conducive
15. redeem	emō	take, buy	preëmpt
16. exit	eō	go	transitory
17. manufactory	faciō	make, do	efficient
18. defend	-fendō	strike	inoffensive
19. refer	ferō	bear, carry	translation
20. clarify	-ficō	make	amplify
21. suffix	fīgō	fasten	crucifixion
22. flexible	flectō	bend	reflective
23. confluence	fluō	flow	affluence
24. preface	for	speak	infant
25. fracture	frangō	break	irrefragable
26. fugitive	fugiō	flee	centrifugal
27. transfusion	fundō	pour	diffuse
28. congestion	gerō	bear, carry	indigestible

194

English Derivative	Latin Word	Meaning of Latin Word	Derivative for Explanation
29. progenitor	gignō	produce	congenital
30. progress	gradior	step	retrograde
31. habit	habeō	have	inhibition
32. adhere	haereō	stick	cohesion
33. eject	jaciō	throw	trajectory
34. judge	jūdicō	judge	adjudicate
35. junction	jungō	join	subjunctive
36. legible	legō (3)	read, gather	predilection
37. delegate	lēgō (1)	appoint	relegate
38. ligament	ligō	bind	obligatory
39. eloquent	loquor	speak	circumlocution
40. prelude	lūdō	play	disillusion
41. remit	mittō	send	intermittent
42. move	moveō	move	mobility
43. cognate	nāscor (-gnāscor)	be born	renaissance
44. recognition	nōscō (-gnōscō)	know	reconnaissance
45. note	notō	note, make out	notable
46. enunciation	nūntiō	report	denunciation
47. orator	ōrō	speak, beg	inexorable
48. prepare	parō	make ready	irreparable
49. patient	patior	suffer, endure	compassion
50. repel	pellō	drive	repulsive
51. appendix	pendeō	hang	independent
52. expend	pendō	weigh	compensation
53. petition	petō	seek	petulant
54. complete	-pleō	fill	expletive
55. complicate	plicō	fold	explicate
56. position	pōnō	place	deposition
57. portable	portō	carry	deportment
58. potential	possum	be able	plenipotentiary
59. comprehend	prehendō	seize	reprehensible
60. press	premō	press	irrepressible
61. approbation	probō	test, approve	reprobate
62. puncture	pungō	prick	compunction
63. dispute	putō	think, cut	compute
64. inquire	quaerō	seek, ask	prerequisite
65. rapacious	rapiō	seize	surreptitious
66. direct	regō	make go straight, rule	incorrigible
67. interrogative	rogō	ask	prerogative
68. disrupt	rumpō	break	incorruptible
69. resilient	saliō	leap	desultory

English Derivative	Latin Word	Meaning of Latin Word	Derivative for Explanation
70. ascend	scandō	climb	condescension
71. inscribe	scrībō	write	subscription
72. dissection	secō	cut	intersection
73. preside	sedeō	sit	supersede
74. consent	sentiō	feel	presentiment
75. sequel	sequor	follow	obsequious
76. conservation	servō	keep	reservation
77. absolve	solvō	loosen	dissolution
78. conspicuous	-spiciō	look	perspicacity
79. respiration	spīrō	breathe	conspirator
80. sponsor	spondeō	promise	correspondent
81. station	stō	stand	circumstance
82. resist	sistō	stand, set	inconsistent
83. constitution	statuō	set up	restitution
84. stringent	stringō	bind	restrictive
85. construct	struō	build	obstruction
86. absent	sum	be	essential
87. consume	sūmō	take	presumption
88. tangent	tangō	touch	contiguity
89. extend	tendō	stretch	attention
90. retain	teneō	hold	abstinence
91. contortion	torqueō	twist	retort
92. tractor	trahō	draw	protracted
93. attribute	tribuō	assign	retribution
94. utensil	ūtor	use	perusal
95. invalid	valeō	be strong	prevalent
96. convention	veniō	come	contravention
97. invert	vertō	turn	incontrovertible
98. vision	videō	see	providential
99. victor	vincō	conquer	invincible
100. revive	vīvō	live	survivor
101. vocation	vocō	call	irrevocable
102. benevolent	volō	wish	volunteer
103. revolve	volvō	roll	evolution

REVIEW OF NOUNS AND ADJECTIVES

Directions: Give the Latin noun, pronoun, adjective, or adverb from which is derived each of the English words in the first column below (or with which it is connected by derivation); give the meaning of each Latin word; and explain the English derivative of that word given in the fourth column.

English Derivative	Latin Word	Meaning of Latin Word	Derivative for Explanation
1. acrid	ācer, -ris, -e	sharp	exacerbate
2. equator	aequus, -a, -um	equal	iniquity
3. animated	anima, -ae	breath, life	inanimate
4. unanimous	animus, -ī	mind	equanimity
5. annual	annus, -ī	year	perennial
6. arms	arma, -ōrum	arms	armistice
7. art	ars, -artis	art	artificial
8. belligerent	bellum, -ī	war	bellicose
9. benefactor	bene	well	benison
10. bonbon	bonus, -a, -um	good	bounty
11. brevity	brevis, -e	short	abbreviate
12. cavalier	caballus, -ī	horse	chivalry
13. capital	caput, -itis	head	decapitate
14. chariot	carrus, -ī	wagon	caricature
15. cause	causa, -ae	cause	accusation
16. century	centum (indecl.)	a hundred	centipede
17. civic	cīvis, -is	citizen	civilian
18. citadel	cīvitās, tātis	state	city
19. contrary	contrā	against	encounter
20. cordial	cor, cordis	heart	accord
21. corpulent	corpus, -oris	body	corpuscle
22. crucify	crux, crucis	cross	excruciating
23. curator	cūra, -ae	care	sinecure
24. decimal	decem	ten	decimate
25. dental	dēns, dentis	tooth	indent
26. deity	deus, -ī	god	deify
27. diary	diēs, -ēī	day	dismal
28. dignify	dignus, -a, -um	worthy	condign
29. dominion	dominus, -ī	master	predominant
30. domicile	domus, -ūs	house	domesticate
31. dual	duo, -ae, -o	two	duplicity
32. exemplify	exemplum, -ī	example	exemplar
33. exterior	exterus, -a, -um	outer, foreign	extraneous
34. infamous	fāma, -ae	report, fame	defamation
35. fidelity	fidēs, eī	faith	perfidious
36. filial	fīlius, -ī	son	affiliate

English Derivative	Latin Word	Meaning of Latin Word	Derivative for Explanation
37. filament	fīlum, -ī	thread	profile
38. final	fīnis, -is	end, limit	infinity
39. firm	firmus, -a, -um	strong	infirmity
40. florist	flōs, flōris	flower	florid
41. foliage	folium, -ī	leaf	exfoliate
42. fortitude	fortis, -e	strong, brave	comfort
43. fortune	fortūna, -ae	chance, fortune	fortuitous
44. front	frōns, frontis	forehead, face	confront
45. gentile	gēns, gentis	tribe, nation	congenial
46. general	genus, -eris	kind	gender
47. gradual	gradus, -ūs	step	graduated
48. gracious	grātia, -ae	favor, thanks	ingratiate
49. gratify	grātus, -a, -um	pleasing,	ingratitude
50. gravity	gravis, -e	heavy	aggravate
51. congregate	grex, gregis	flock	segregate
52. homicide	homō, -inis	man	homage
53. hostile	hostis, -is	enemy	host
54. identical	īdem, ea-, i-	the same	identify
55. peninsula	īnsula, -ae	island	insulate
56. interior	intrā	within	intrinsic
57. judicial	jūdex, -icis	judge, juror	prejudice
58. justice	jūs, jūris	right, law	jurisdiction
59. latitude	lātus, -a, -um	wide	latitudinarian
60. lateral	latus, -eris	side	equilateral
61. legal	lēx, lēgis	law	legislate
62. library	liber, -rī	book	libretto
63. liberty	līber, -era, -erum	free	illiberal
64. literal	lītera, -ae	letter	obliterate
65. local	locus, -ī	place	dislocate
66. longitude	longus, -a, -um	long	longevity
67. lucid	lūx, lūcis	light	elucidate
68. magnify	magnus, -a, -um	great	magnanimous
69. malefactor	malus, -a, -um	bad	malevolent
70. manual	manus, -ūs	hand	manacles
71. marine	mare, -is	sea	submarine
72. maternal	māter, mātris	mother	matrimony
73. maximum	maximus, -a, -um	greatest	maxim
74. immediate	medius, -a, -um	middle	intermediate
75. ameliorate	melior, -ius	better	
76. memory	memoria, -ae	memory	commemorate
77. mental	mēns, mentis	mind	demented
78. military	mīles, -itis	soldier	militate
79. millennium	mīlle (indecl.)	thousand	mile
80. minimum	minimus, -a, -um	least	minimize

English Derivative	Latin Word	Meaning of Latin Word	Derivative for Explanation
81. minority	minor, -us	less	minuend
82. mode	modus, -ī	manner	modulate
83. mountainous	mōns, montis	mountain	promontory
84. mortal	mors, mortis	death	mortuary
85. demoralize	mōs, mōris	custom	demure
86. multitude	multus, -a, -um	much, many	multiply
87. remuneration	mūnus, -eris	task, gift	munificent
88. mural	mūrus, -ī	wall	immure
89. natural	nātūra, -ae	nature	naturalize
90. navy	nāvis, -is	ship	navigable
91. neutral	neuter, -tra, -trum	neither	neutralize
92. nobility	nōbilis, -e	noble	ignoble
93. nominate	nōmen, -inis	name	denomination
94. November	novem	nine	noon
95. novice	novus, -a, -um	new	renovate
96. nocturnal	nox, noctis	night	equinoctial
97. nullify	nūllus, -a, -um	no (adj.), none	annul
98. numeral	numerus, -ī	number	innumerable
99. announce	nūntius, -ī	messenger	annunciation
100. octette	octō	eight	October
101. omniscient	omnis, -e	all	omnibus
102. exonerate	onus, -eris	burden	onerous
103. coöperation	opus, -eris	work	inoperative
104. order	ōrdō, -inis	order, rank	inordinate
105. oral	ōs, -ōris	mouth	orifice
106. ossify	os, -ossis	bone	osseous
107. peninsula	paene	almost	penult
108. par	pār, paris	equal	disparity
109. impartial	pars, partis	part	participate
110. surpass	passus, -ūs	pace	compass
111. paternal	pater, patris	father	patron
112. expatriate	patria, -ae	country	repatriate
113. pacific	pāx, pācis	peace	pacifist
114. impair	pejor, -jus	worse	
115. quadruped	pēs, pedis	foot	centipede
116. pessimist	pessimus, -a, -um	worst	pessimism
117. expletive	plēnus, -a, -um	full	plenipotentiary
118. plural	plūs, plūris	more	pluperfect
119. penal	poena, -ae	punishment	subpœna
120. pontoon	pōns, pontis	bridge	pontifical
121. popular	populus, -ī	people	depopulate
122. portal	porta, -ae	gate, door	portière
123. posterity	posterus, -a, -um	following	preposterous

English Derivative	Latin Word	Meaning of Latin Word	Derivative for Explanation
124. primary	prīmus, -a, -um	first	primeval
125. priority	prior, -ius	former	
126. propinquity	prope	near	approximate
127. proper	proprius, -a, -um	one's own	appropriate
128. pugnacious	pugna, -ae	fight	repugnant
129. quartette	quārtus, -a, -um	fourth	quarto
130. quadrilateral	quattuor	four	quadrennial
131. quinquennial	quīnque	five	quintessence
132. rational	ratiō, -ōnis	reason	ratiocination
133. reality	rēs, -reī	thing	rebus
134. regal	rēx, rēgis	king	regicide
135. rotation	rota, -ae	wheel	rotary
136. consecrate	sacer, -cra, -crum	sacred	sacrilegious
137. salutary	salūs, -ūtis	health, safety	salubrious
138. satisfy	satis	enough	insatiable
139. secondary	secundus, -a, -um	second	second (of time)
140. September	septem	seven	septennial
141. sextette	sex	six	sexagenarian
142. sign	signum, -ī	sign, seal	resignation
143. similar	similis, -e	like	assimilate
144. society	socius, -ī	companion	associate
145. sole	sōlus, -a, -um	alone	soliloquy
146. specious	speciēs, -ēī	appearance	specify
147. sum	summa, -ae	total	consummate
148. superior	suprā	above	sovereign
149. tardy	tardus, -a, -um	slow	retard
150. temporal	tempus, -oris	time	contemporary
151. terminal	terminus, -ī	end	interminable
152. terrace	terra, -ae	earth	disinter
153. total	tōtus, -a, -um	whole, all	factotum
154. trio	trēs, tria	three	trinity
155. ulterior	ultrā	beyond	outrage
156. ultimate	ultimus, -a, -um	last	penult
157. unit	ūnus, -a, -um	one	unanimous
158. urban	urbs, urbis	city	urbanity
159. ventilate	ventus, -ī	wind	
160. verb	verbum, -ī	word	verbose
161. verify	vērus, -a, -um	true	veracious
162. viaduct	via, -ae	way	impervious
163. virile	vir, -ī	man	virago
164. vim	vīs (abl. vī)	strength	inviolable
165. vital	vīta, -ae	life	vitalize
166. revive	vīvus, -a, -um	living	vivisection
167. vocal	vōx, vōcis	voice	equivocal

LATIN-ENGLISH WORD STUDY

Directions: Study the English derivatives of the Latin words given below as they are assigned by your teacher and be prepared to explain their derivation.

1 *a.* Give the meaning of **ācer.**   "sharp," "fierce"

  b. Give three English words derived from **ācer.**   acrid, acrimonious, eager

  c. Explain briefly the meanings of the derivatives of **ācer** given above.

    acrid = having a **sharp** taste

    acrimonious = **sharp,** bitter, that is, "an acrimonious debate"

    eager = **sharply** inclined, that is, "eager spirits"

2 *a.* Give the meaning of **ager.**   "field"

  b. Give two English words derived from **ager.**   agrarian, pilgrim

  c. Explain briefly the meanings of the derivatives of **ager** given above.

    agrarian = pertaining to **fields** or farms, like, "agrarian laws"

    pilgrim = one who goes through (per) the **fields,** a traveler

3 *a.* Give the meaning of **alere.**   "to nourish"

  b. Give three English words derived from **alere.**   alimentary, alimony, alma mater

  c. Explain briefly the meanings of the derivatives of **alere** given above.

    alimentary (canal) = the **nourishing** (canal)

    alimony = money given to **support** a divorced wife

    alma mater = **nourishing** mother

4 *a.* Give the meaning of **alius.**   "another" (of any number)

  b. Give four English words derived from **alius.**   alien, alienate, alias, alibi

  c. Explain briefly the meanings of the derivatives of **alius** given above. (The English derivatives preserve the idea that **any** number of objects or ideas may be involved.)

    alien = **another,** foreign, that is, "There are many alien nations"

    alienate = to make **another's,** to estrange, to repel, as, "He alienated every one by his conceit"

    alias = at **another** time, that is, "Smith alias Simpson," then = an assumed name, as, "Smith gave several aliases" alibi = in **another** place, then = the fact of having been present at another place, that is, "He tried to prove an alibi"

5 *a*. Give the meaning of **alter**.   "the other" (of two)
  b. Give five English words de-   alternative, alternate, alter,
     rived from **alter**.

                                    altercation, altruism

  c. Explain briefly the meanings of the derivatives of **alter** given above.

(The English derivatives preserve the idea that only **two** objects or ideas can be involved.)

alternative = **the other** choice, (there can be only two alternatives) as, "He faced the alternatives of imprisonment or exile"

alternate = each following **the other** (of two only), as, "Two boys can preside alternately, three cannot"

alter = to make **other**, to change

altercation = speaking one after **the other**, hence = disputing, as, "An altercation arose between the brothers"

altruism = regard for **the other** fellow, as, "One was inspired with altruism, the other with egotism"

6 *a*. Give the meaning of **altus**.   "high"
  b. Give five English words de-   altitude, exalt, exaltation, alto,
     rived from **altus**.   altissimo

  c. Explain briefly the meanings of the derivatives of **altus** given above.

altitude = **height**

exalt = **lift** up (ex) on high, as, "to reach an exalted position"

exaltation = an **uplifting** of the spirit

alto = the voice so called from being originally **higher** than the tenor

altissimo = very **high**

7 *a*. Give the meaning of **ambu-**   "to walk"
     lāre.
  b. Give six English words de-   somnambulist, preamble, per-
     rived from **ambulāre**.   ambulate, perambulator, am-
                                    bulance, amble

  c. Explain briefly the meanings of the derivatives of **ambulāre** given above.

somnambulist = sleep **walker**

preamble = that which **walks** or goes before a resolution

perambulate = to **walk** through, or around

perambulator = carriage propelled by one who **walks** along behind, originally = the person who walks along

ambulance = a **walking** or moving hospital

amble = easy **gait** of a horse, slower than a trot, a brisk **walk**

Application of Latin to English Spelling

A. The Rules with Illustrations

1. **Original double consonants are regularly preserved in derivatives** (except at the ends of compounds). Terra has two r's. Therefore the derivative **terrestrial** has two r's.

2. **The "obscure" vowel follows the original Latin.** Tempore is spelled with an **o**. Therefore **temporal** is spelled with an **o**.

3. **Many original combinations whose pronunciation has changed are preserved in English.** Discipulus is spelled with **sc**. Therefore **disciple** preserves **sc**.

4. **When a prefix ending in a consonant** (ad, con, in, ex, ob, dis, sub) **is prefixed to a word beginning with a consonant,** the first consonant is assimilated, if possible, to the second, and **double consonants are produced in the derivative.** Affiliate is derived from the prefix **ad** and **filius**. Therefore **affiliate** is spelled with two ll's.

5. **Initial s after ex is lost.**
Exspecto has an s after ex. In the derivative **expect** the s is lost.

6. **Words in -ant (ance) and -ent (ence) are from present active particles and follow the original Latin. Words of the first conjugation end in -ant, all others in -ent; -io verbs end in -ient.** Porto belongs to the first conjugation. Therefore **important** is spelled **ant**.

   Exception: Some words which should end in **-ent** become nouns and are spelled **-ant.** When the original part of speech (that is, adjective) is retained, the original spelling is also regularly retained, for example, confidant (n.) confident (adj.).

7. **The** variation between **-sion** and **-tion** is determined by the fourth principal part of the Latin verb from which the word is derived. The last principal part of peto is petitus. Therefore **petition** is spelled **-tion**.

203

B. APPLICATIONS

Explain the spelling of the following words, giving in each instance the rule illustrated:

belligerent
vocative
rebellion
auditory
audible
bellicose
conservative
rebel
occur
laudable
current
annual
biennial
millennium
centennial
carriage

abbreviate
annihilate
illogical
ignorant
important
culpable
curable
portable
separate
temporal
expect
disciple
reign
ascension
autumn
column

acquire
errand
habitable
imperative
notable
tentative
grammar
literal
immortal
inflammable
alleviate
occupant
excitable
constellation
insuperable
expectant

amicable
immure
laboratory
demonstrable
depopulate
benign
ingratiate
affiliate
auxiliary
appellate
effeminate
invalid
resign
preparatory
reparation
separate

TEST SAMPLE: GRAMMATICAL PRINCIPLES IN ENGLISH

Time limit: 35 Minutes.

Name ....

School ....

Teacher ....

Class ....

Period ....

To the teacher: Read the directions aloud with the pupils.

To the pupils: One of the benefits that you should derive from your study of Latin is a clearer knowledge of the grammatical principles underlying English, along with a resulting increase in your ability to speak and write English that is grammatically correct. This is a test of your ability to distinguish between correct and incorrect English in cases where mistakes are frequently made, and of your knowledge of the grammatical principles which apply in such cases. Look at the sample sentence below.

Sample: The general with his staff (was, were) waiting.

Do two things with this sentence. First draw a heavy line around that one of the two words in parentheses which you think is correct. Then from the list of grammatical rules at the end of Part I choose that rule which should lead you to select the correct word. Place the number of this rule in the parentheses after the sentence.

To the teacher: Allow the pupils about a minute for this.

To the pupils: You have drawn a circle around the word *was* and placed the figure 3 in the parentheses after the sentence, since the rule applying is number 3: *A verb agrees with its subject in person and number.* Proceed in the same way with each of the sentences of this test. The test is divided into two parts, each part being followed by its own group of rules. When you have finished with Part I continue with Part II without further directions. Do you all understand exactly what to do? Turn the page and begin.

PART I

1. (Who, whom) do you think is the best player? ( )
2. The other girls and (I, myself) came on the trolley. ( )
3. His knowledge of all kinds of machines, especially of automobile engines, (was, were) the result of long study. ( )
4. Never having seen him before, (he appeared impressive, we were impressed by his appearance). ( )
5. Every way to success is barred against (whoever, whomever) the authorities believe is unworthy. ( )
6. She played (soft, softly) as the curtain rose. ( )
7. (Who, whom) do you believe this man to be? ( )
8. He is one of the fastest runners that (has, have) appeared here in many years. ( )
9. They were curious to know (who, whom) the visitor was. ( )
10. Neither father nor son (act, acts) as if he were guilty. ( )
11. They thought it was (I, me) who had been struck by the car. ( )
12. Let each of us live (our, his, their) own life according to the dictates of conscience. ( )
13. They imagined the fighters to be John and (I, me). ( )
14. Flying in an aeroplane, (the city seemed small, he thought the city seemed small). ( )
15. Can you work as (good, well) as I? ( )
16. Each of you is expected to do (his, your, their) own work. ( )
17. Neither John nor Charles (was, were) there. ( )
18. (Has, have) each of you prepared this lesson? ( )
19. We all arrived home safely, John, Bert, and (I, me). ( )
20. After dinner a friend and (myself, I) set out for the camp. ( )

Grammatical Rules for Part I

1. A pronoun agrees with its antecedent in person, number, and gender.
2. A predicate noun or pronoun agrees in case with the subject.
3. A verb agrees with its subject in person and number.
4. The subject of a finite verb is in the nominative case.
5. A noun or pronoun in apposition agrees in case with the word with which it is in apposition.
6. The subject of an infinitive is in the accusative (objective) case.

7. A participle, being an adjective, must modify a noun or pronoun.
8. Singular subjects connected by *or* and *nor* take singular verbs.
9. The intensive pronoun is always in apposition with a noun or pronoun.
10. A word used to modify a verb, adjective, or adverb is an adverb.

DO NOT STOP. GO RIGHT ON WITH PART II

PART II

1. (That, those) formulae are of the greatest importance.　( )

2. There are many of us (who, whom) he knows to be indispensable for his success.　( )

3. I expected (to have seen, to see) John. *Bryan*　( )

4. (Who, whom) did he give it to?　( )

5. There was no doubt as to (who, whom) the speaker meant. ( )

6. There is the man (who, whom) the Democrats wish to be nominated.　( )

7. He is the best player that (has, have) ever been in school. ( )

8. She liked both of us fellows, but me more than (he, him). ( )

9. We don't like (this, these) kind of clothes.　( )

10. Soon I had finished telling my story to his sister and (he, him).　( )

11. He refused to see John, (who, whom) he believed the other teachers had punished sufficiently.　( )

12. All solid foods are withheld from those (who, whom) such a disease attacks.　( )

13. I should have liked (to go, to have gone).　( )

14. (Who, whom) do historians consider to have discovered America?　( )

15. A person can never feel sure that (his, their) motives are rightly understood.　( )

16. He acted so rashly that he injured himself more than (we, us).　( )

17. I tried to persuade Joan to come with Grace and (I, me). ( )

18. Only a few of the first edition, which has gone out of print, (is, are) left.　( )

19. The main speech was delivered by Mr. Smith, with (who, whom) I know you are acquainted.　( )

20. (This, these) group of players came from abroad.　( )

Grammatical Rules for Part II

1. A pronoun agrees with its antecedent in person, number, and gender.
2. An adjective agrees with the noun it modifies in gender, number, and case.
3. A verb agrees with its subject in person and number.
4. A predicate noun or pronoun agrees in case with the subject.
5. The direct object of a verb is in the accusative (objective) case.
6. The object of a preposition is *not* in the nominative case.
7. The subject of an infinitive is in the accusative (objective) case.
8. A present infinitive expresses the *same* time as that of the main verb; a past infinitive expresses time *before* that of the main verb.
9. The subject of a finite verb is in the nominative case.
10. A noun or pronoun after a comparative agrees in case with the noun with which it is compared.

LATIN-FRENCH WORD STUDY

I. In what form do Latin prefixes In general, in the same form
occur in French?   as in English?

II. Give the Latin prefix contained in each of the following
French words: absorber, admirer, affaire, connaître, défendre,
disparaître, élever, importer, permettre, prévoir, profiter,
revenir, séparer, traverser.

ab, ad, ad, con, dē, dis, ex, in, per, prae, prō, re, sē, trāns

III. Give the Latin prefix contained in each of the following
French words:

1.	déshonneur	dis
2.	entrevoir	inter
3.	parfait	per
4.	poursuivre	prō
5.	souvenir	sub
6.	outremer	ultrā

IV. Give the Latin suffixes contained in the following French
words:

1.	aimé	-ātus
2.	auteur	-tor
3.	oiseux	-ōsus
4.	liberté	-tās

V. From what Latin word does each of the following French
words come, and what vowel changes are illustrated:

1.	père	pater;	a	sometimes becomes	e
2.	mer	mare;	a	" "	e
3.	aimer	amāre;	a	" "	ai
4.	vaut	valet;	al	" "	au
5.	chose	causa;	au	" "	o
6.	six	sex;	e	" "	i
7.	lire	legere;	e	" "	i
8.	plein	plēnus;	e	" "	ei
9.	roi	rēx;	e	" "	oi
10.	bien	bene;	e	" "	ie
11.	ferme	firmus;	i	" "	e

209

12. lettre	lītera;	i sometimes becomes e
13. voie	via;	i " " oi
14. gloire	glōria;	o " " oi
15. seul	sōlus;	o " " eu
16. coeur	cor;	o " " oeu
17. nous	nōs;	o " " ou
18. nombre	numerus;	u " " o
19. rompre	rumpere;	u " " o
20. croix	crux;	u " " oi
21. suis	sum;	u " " ui

VI. From what Latin word does each of the following French words come, and what consonant changes are illustrated?

1. livre	liber	b becomes v
2. avril	aprīlis	p " v
3. chef	caput	p " f
4. neuf	novus	v " f
5. fait	factum	ct " it
6. raison	ratiō	ti " s
7. maître	magister	s is dropped before a consonant and the preceding vowel receives the circumflex accent
8. chose	causa	c becomes ch
9. char	carrus	c " ch
10. espace	spatium	sp " esp
11. étude	studium	st loses s and becomes ét with acute accent

VII. Give the Latin word from which is derived each of the following French words, give the meaning of the Latin word and the meaning of the French word.

French Word	Latin Word	Meaning of Latin Word	Meaning of French Word
1. aimer	amāre	to love	to love
2. ami	amīcus	friend	friend
3. année	annus	year	year
4. arbre	arbor	tree	tree
5. bien	bene	well	well, very
6. bon	bonus	good	good
7. cent	centum	one hundred	one hundred
8. cher	cārus	dear	dear
9. cheval	caballus	horse	horse
10. cinq	quīnque	five	five

French Word	Latin Word	Meaning of Latin Word	Meaning of French Word
11. connaître	cognōscere	to find out	to know
12. croire	crēdere	to believe	to believe
13. croître	crēscere	to grow	to grow
14. dent	dēns	tooth	tooth
15. deux	duo	two	two
16. dieu	deus	god	god
17. dire	dīcere	to say	to say
18. dormir	dormīre	to sleep	to sleep
19. dur	dūrus	hard	hard, dull
20. et	et	and	and
21. facile	facilis	easy	easy
22. fer	ferrum	iron	iron
23. fille	fīlia	daughter	daughter
24. fils	fīlius	son	son
25. fin	fīnis	end	end
26. frère	frāter	brother	brother
27. gens	gēns	tribe	people
28. heure	hōra	hour	hour
29. hier	heri	yesterday	yesterday
30. homme	homō	man	man
31. lait	lāc	milk	milk
32. langue	lingua	language	language
33. lire	legere	to read	to read
34. livre (m.)	liber	book	book
35. lune	lūna	moon	moon
36. maître	magister	master	master
37. mal	male	badly	badly
38. meilleur	melior	better	better
39. mer	mare	sea	sea
40. mère	māter	mother	mother
41. mille	mīlle	one thousand	one thousand
42. mort	mors	death	death
43. mur	mūrus	wall	wall
44. nom	nōmen	name	name
45. notre	noster	ours	our
46. pain	pānis	bread	bread
47. par	per	by, through	by, from
48. patrie	patria	country	fatherland
49. pauvre	pauper	poor	poor
50. père	pater	father	father
51. pont	pōns	bridge	bridge
52. porte	porta	gate, door	door
53. porter	portāre	to carry	to carry
54. premier	prīmus	first	first

French Word	Latin Word	Meaning of Latin Word	Meaning of French Word
55. prix	pretium	price	price, prize
56. reine	rēgīna	queen	queen
57. roi	rēx	king	king
58. sain	sānus	sound, healthy	healthy
59. se	sē	oneself	oneself
60. sel	sāl	salt	salt
61. sept	septem	seven	seven
62. seul	sōlus	alone	alone
63. si	sī	if	if, whether
64. soeur	soror	sister	sister
65. sur	super	above	on
66. tant	tantus	so much	so much
67. tel	tālis	so, such	such
68. temps	tempus	time	time
69. terre	terra	earth	earth
70. tout	tōtus	whole	all, every
71. triste	tristis	sad	sad
72. trois	trēs	three	three
73. un	ūnus	one	one
74. utile	ūtilis	useful	useful
75. valoir	valēre	to be strong	to be worth
76. venir	venīre	to come	to come
77. vérité	vēritās	truth	truth
78. vin	vīnum	wine	wine
79. vingt	vīgintī	twenty	twenty
80. vivre	vīvere	to live	to live
81. voie	via	way	way
82. voir	vidēre	to see	to see
83. voix	vōx	word	voice

VIII. Give the meaning of the following French words and give the Latin word from which each is derived and its meaning:

French Word	Meaning of French Word	Latin Word and Meaning
1. âme	soul	anima, breath, soul
2. appeler	to call, name	appellāre, to call
3. argent	money	argentum, silver
4. autre	other*	alter, the other
5. boeuf	ox	bōs, (bovis), ox
6. boire	to drink	bibere, to drink
7. bras	arm	bracchium, arm
8. celui	this one	ecce, behold + ille, he
9. château	castle	castellum, fortress

French Word	Meaning of French Word	Latin Word and Meaning
10. chercher	to look for	circum, around
11. clair	clear	clārus, clear
12. coeur	heart	cor, heart
13. comprendre	to understand	comprehendere, to grasp
14. conduire	to guide	condūcere, to lead along
15. croix	cross	crux, cross
16. cuisine	kitchen	culīna, kitchen
17. demain	tomorrow	māne, tomorrow
18. devoir	ought, owe	dēbēre, owe, ought
19. école	school	schola, school
20. écrire	to write	scrībere, to write
21. ensemble	together	in + simul, at the same time
22. entre	between	intrā, within
23. être	to be	esse, to be
24. faim	hunger	famēs, hunger
25. faire	to make, do	facere, to make, do
26. femme	woman	fēmina, woman
27. fenêtre	window	fenestra, window
28. fermer	to close	firmāre, to strengthen
29. fleur	flower	flōs, flower
30. genou	knee	genū, knee
31. genre	sort, gender	genus, kind
32. goût	taste	gustus, taste
33. gras	fat	crassus, thick
34. hiver	winter	hībernus, wintry
35. ici	here	ecce, behold + hic, he
36. il	he, it	ille, that, he
37. jeudi	Thursday	Jovis diēs
38. joindre	to join	jungere, to join
39. leçon	lesson	lēctiō, a reading
40. livre (f.)	pound	lībra, balance
41. lundi	Monday	lūnae diēs
42. luire	to shine	lūcere, to shine
43. mardi	Tuesday	Mārtis diēs
44. merci	thanks	mercēs, pay
45. mettre	to put, place	mittere, to send
46. mieux	better (adv.)	melius, better
47. moins	less	minus, less
48. mourir	to die	morīrī, to die
49. mouvoir	to move	movēre, to move
50. naître	to be born	nāscī, to be born
51. neuf	nine	novem, nine
52. nouveau	new	novus, new
53. nuit	night	nox, night

French Word	Meaning of French Word	Latin Word and Meaning
54. on	one (indef. pro.)	homō, man
55. or	gold	aurum, gold
56. ou	or	aut, or
57. oublier	forget	oblīvīscī, forget
58. ours	bear	ursus, bear
59. peindre	to paint	pingere, to paint
60. pas or ne pas	not	passus, step, *i.e. not a step*
61. penser	to think	pēnsāre, to weigh
62. pire	worse	pejor, worse
63. plaire	to please	placēre, to please
64. pomme de terre	potato	pōmum, fruit + terra, earth
65. pour	for	prō, for
66. pourvoir	to provide	prōvidēre, to foresee
67. quand	when	quandō, at what time
68. quatre	four	quattuor, four
69. que	that, than, as	quem, whom, that
70. quel	what, what kind of	quālis, what kind
71. rendre	to give back	reddere, to give back
72. rire	to laugh	rīdēre, to laugh
73. rive	bank, shore	rīpa, bank, shore
74. rompre	to break	rumpere, to break
75. saillir	to gush forth	salīre, to leap
76. s'asseoir	to sit down	adsidēre, to sit down
77. sauver	to save	servāre, to save
78. savoir	to know	sapere, to be wise
79. sentir	to feel	sentīre, to feel
80. servir	to serve	servīre, to serve
81. soir	evening	sērus, late
82. soleil	sun	sōl, sun
83. suffire	to suffice	sufficere, to suffice
84. suivre	to follow	sequī, to follow
85. tenir	to hold	tenēre, to hold
86. vache	cow	vacca, cow
87. vaincre	to conquer	vincere, to conquer
88. vendre	to sell	vēndere, to sell
89. verre	glass	vitrum, glass
90. voisin	neighbor	vīcīnus, neighboring
91. voler	to fly	volāre, to fly
92. vouloir	to wish	velle, to be willing
93. vrai	true	vērus, true

COLLATERAL READING FOR FIRST AND SECOND YEAR LATIN

I. Books containing stories and legends of ancient Rome:

1. HAAREN and POLAND, *Famous Men of Rome*
2. GUERBER, *The Story of the Romans*
3. HARDING, *The City of the Seven Hills*
4. TAPPAN, *The Story of the Roman People*
5. MORRIS, *Historical Tales: Roman*

II. Books telling how the Romans lived:

6. MILLER, *The Story of a Roman Boy*
7. DAVIS, *A Day in Old Rome*
8. SHUMWAY, *A Day in Ancient Rome*
9. HALL, *Buried Cities* (first half: *Pompeii*)
10. CHURCH, *Roman Life in the Days of Cicero*

III. Novels and tales:

11. MACAULAY, *The Lays of Ancient Rome*
12. BULWER-LYTTON, *The Last Days of Pompeii*
13. DAVIS, *A Friend of Cæsar*
14. WELLS, *With Cæsar's Legions*
15. WHITEHEAD, *The Standard Bearer*
16. MITCHISON, *The Conquered*
17. WELLS, *On Land and Sea with Cæsar*
18. WHITE, *Andivius Hedulio*
19. ———, *The Unwilling Vestal*
20. VAN SANTVOORD, *Octavia*

IV. Histories containing brief accounts of Roman history in general:

21. WOLFSON, *Ancient Civilization* (pp. 61-107)
22. HOYLAND, *A Brief History of Civilization* (pp. 117-150)
23. VAN LOON, *Story of Mankind* (pp. 105-130)
24. WEST, *Early Progress* (pp. 237-257)
25. ———, *Modern World* (pp. 9-41)
26. BARNES, *General History* (pp. 203-269)
27. SEIGNOBOS, *History of Ancient Civilization* (pp. 199-288)
28. GREENWOOD, *Our Heritage from the Old World* (pp. 120-176)

29. BOTSFORD, *A Brief History of the World* (pp. 87-153)
30. BREASTED, *Ancient Times* (pp. 484-599)
31. MILLS, *Books of the Ancient Romans*

V. Books on Rome:

32. JOHNSTON, *Private Life of the Romans.*
33. MACGREGOR, *The Story of Rome*
34. PRESTON and DODGE, *Private Life of the Romans*
35. WHITE, WESTON, BRIER, *Plutarch's Lives*

VI. Books on Greek and Roman mythology:

36. BAKER, *Stories of Old Greece and Rome*
37. BALDWIN, *The Story of the Golden Age*
38. BULLFINCH, *Age of Fable*
39. ———, *Mythology*
40. COLUM, *The Golden Fleece*
41. GUERBER, *Myths of Greece and Rome*
42. HAWTHORNE, *Tanglewood Tales*
43. ———, *Wonder Book*
44. SABIN, *Classical Myths That Live Today*

VII. Books pertaining to Greece:

45. DAVIS, *The Victor of Salamis*
46. GAINES, *Gorgo*
47. HALL, *Buried Cities* (second part)
48. HORTON, *In Argolis*
49. SNEDEKER, *The Perilous Seat*
50. ———, *The Spartan*

VIII. Books on Cæsar and his contemporaries:

51. HAAREN and POLAND, *Famous Men of Rome,* "Pompey and Cæsar," pp. 171-202
52. HARDING, *The City of the Seven Hills,* "Julius Cæsar, the Conqueror of Gaul," pp. 184-211
53. CHURCH, *Roman Life in the Days of Cicero,* "Cæsar and Pompey," pp. 151-192
54. HAMILTON, *Ancient Rome: The Lives of Great Men,* "Cæsar," Ch. iii, pp. 141-159, "Pompey," Ch. x, pp. 108-121, "Crassus," Ch. xi, pp. 121-130
55. CLARKE, *The Story of Cæsar*
56. TAPPAN, *Story of the Roman People,* "Rise of Pompey; Cæsar and the Triumvirates," pp. 136-186
57. MOREY, *Outlines of Roman History,* Ch. xxi
58. KIPLING, *Puck of Pook's Hill* (Stories about the Roman occupation of Britain), "The Winged Hat," "Centurion of the Thirtieth," "On the Great Wall"

59. HAMILTON, *Outlines of Roman History,* "Cæsar," Ch. x; "The Triumvirate," Ch. ix
60. GUERBER, *Story of the Romans,* Chs. lviii-lxv, pp. 170-184
61. ABBOTT, *Julius Cæsar*
62. FOWLER, *Julius Cæsar*
63. FROUDE, *Julius Cæsar: A Sketch*
64. OMAN, *Seven Roman Statesmen,* Ch. viii and ix, pp. 234-340
65. WHITE, *Plutarch's Lives,* pp. 326-360

IX. Novels:

66. DAVIS, *A Friend of Cæsar*
67. WELLS, *With Cæsar's Legions*
68. MITCHISON, *The Conquered*
69. WHITEHEAD, *The Standard Bearer*
70. ANDERSON, *With the Eagles*

CLASS RECORD ON COLLATERAL READING

Directions to the Pupil: Place in column 1 the number designating the first book which you read, according to the attached key.[1] Place in column 2 the number designating the second book read, etc. If you discover any other book in the library or elsewhere and read it, add the name to the list and give it a number beyond 69.

Names of pupils	1	2	3	4	5	6	7	8	9	10	11	12	13	14

[1] This refers to the numbered list of books reproduced on preceding pages (215-217).

TEST ON HISTORICAL-CULTURAL BACKGROUND

Time limit: 8 min.

Name ....

Teacher ....

Period ....

Class ....

To the teacher: Read the directions aloud with the pupils.

To the pupils: One of the benefits which you should derive from your study of Latin is an increased understanding of some of the ways in which the Roman civilization has affected that of our own nation. This knowledge you should get both from your classroom and from your reading outside of class. This is a test to determine how much you have acquired in this phase of the study of Latin. Below, you will find a series of statements. After each statement are two words, *True* and *False*. Read each statement through; then decide whether it is a true or a false statement; then underline that one of the two words following it which you think properly describes the statement. For example, read the following sentences:

1. The Roman officials who occupied relatively the same position as our President and Vice-President were called Consuls.   true   false

2. It was the custom of the Roman gentlemen to eat dinner while seated at the table.   true   false

Now decide whether these are true or false statements and underline either *True* or *False* according to your decision.

To the teacher: Allow about thirty seconds for this.

To the pupils: You have underlined the word *True* after Sentence 1, since the statement is a true one, and the word *False* after Sentence 2, since the statement is not true. In the test below some statements are true and some are false. Be sure to underline the correct word to show the truth or falsity of each statement. First go through the test quickly and mark all you know

219

for certain. Then go back and study out the harder ones. Do you all understand exactly what to do?

Number right ......
Number wrong ......
Score ......

Note. To find the score subtract number wrong from number right.

1. Our idea of representative government was taken directly from the Roman system of government.   true   <u>false</u>

2. The alphabet which we use to-day is largely the same as the Roman alphabet.   <u>true</u>   false

3. The union of many states to form one government was a Roman principle adopted by the founders of the United States.   true   <u>false</u>

4. Our modern mode of dress is taken directly from the Romans.   true   <u>false</u>

5. So well did the Romans of ancient times build that some of their edifices still remain in active use to-day.   <u>true</u>   false

6. Women were considered by the ancient Romans as little better than slaves in the household.   <u>true</u>   false

7. The calendar in use to-day is mostly a direct inheritance from Rome.   <u>true</u>   false

8. At night the streets of Rome were extremely dark and treacherous for wayfarers.   <u>true</u>   false

9. A great deal of the mirth and jollity of our Christmas season is due to the spirit which prevailed during the Roman celebration of the Saturnalia.   <u>true</u>   false

10. The books which we use to-day are very similar in form to those used by the Romans.   true   <u>false</u>

11. The Roman day was divided, as is ours, into twenty-four hours of equal length.   <u>true</u>   false

12. When the Roman republic was established, a written constitution was adopted to serve as a basis for all laws which should be made in the future.   true   <u>false</u>

13. The fact that Rome held dominion over so much of the world was a distinct aid in the spread of Christianity.   <u>true</u>   false

14. The two parties prominent in Roman politics were organized upon much the same principles and platforms as the Democratic and Republican parties are to-day.   true   <u>false</u>

15. The Romans did not consider any money-making profession dignified enough for Roman gentlemen.   <u>true</u>   false

16. The Roman religion was, like ours to-day, a monotheism, that is, a worship of one god.   true   <u>false</u>

? 17. The Roman senate was a body of men chosen by the people to make laws.   true   false

? 18. The question of land ownership was a more vital economic problem in the Roman Republic than it is in the United States to-day.   true   false

19. The rulers of the Roman empire were always men of noble Roman birth.   true   <u>false</u>

20. The greatest achievement of the Romans in architecture was the development of the arch and the vault.   <u>true</u>   false

21. The governmental organization of the Catholic church is a direct outgrowth of the Roman imperial system.   <u>true</u>   false

22. Roman law is the basis upon which our modern law system has been built up.   <u>true</u>   false

23. Polygamy was a common practice among the ancient Romans.   true   <u>false</u>

24. The modern wedding procession is a direct inheritance from the Roman custom.   <u>true</u>   false

25. The grammar schools of the Roman Republic were open only to the children of the highest social order.   true   false

26. Concrete for use in building was known to the early Romans.   *true*   *false*

TEST ON LEGENDARY HEROES OF ROME

Time Limit: 5 min.

Name ....

Teacher ....

Period ....

Class ....

To the teacher: Read the instructions aloud with the pupils.

To the pupils: Read the following sample sentence and then look at the five words just beneath it.

"The general who gained over the Romans a victory so costly to himself that it was virtually a defeat was

Hannibal   Pyrrhus   Mithradates   Alaric   Orgetorix."

Now try to decide which of these words or phrases completes the sentence so as to make a true statement. Draw a line under that word.

To the teacher: Allow about half a minute to do this.

To the pupils: In the above sample the line should be drawn under *Pyrrhus* because he was the general who defeated Rome in so costly a victory that it was practically a defeat for him. Below, you will find twelve similar sentences. Underline that word which completes the sentence so as to make a correct statement. Do not ask questions after you have once begun. Do you understand just what to do?

1. The hero who bravely held back the enemy at the bridge was
   Cæsar   Camillus   <u>Horatius</u>   Brutus   Cicero

2. The Trojan who settled in Italy after a long journey was
   <u>Æneas</u>   Ulysses   Priam   Vergil   Ajax

3. Much of the training and inspiration of the Gracchi was received from their mother whose name was
   Lucretia   Julia   Penelope   Publia   <u>Cornelia</u>

4. The Roman hero who left his plow to become dictator of Rome was
   Jason   Cæsar   <u>Cincinnatus</u>   Camillus   Horatius

222

5. The hero who preferred a martyr's death at Carthage to freedom and dishonor at Rome was

Regulus   Scipio   Antony   Horatius   Cæsar

6. The Roman most famous for opposing Greek luxury was

Cæsar   Marius   Seneca   Cato   Atticus

7. A Roman general who ordered his son to be killed for a breach of discipline was

P. Cornelius Scipio   T. Manlius Torquatus   Cæsar
Gaius Laelius   Sulla

8. The Roman hero who proved his fortitude by holding his hand in a burning fire was

Cinna   Tiberius   M. Cassius   Titus Manlius
Mucius Scævola

9. The Roman hero who was recalled from exile to become dictator was

G. Gracchus   Cicero   Cincinnatus   Camillus   Marius

10. The legendary hero of Rome, whose mother and wife persuaded him to give up his advance upon Rome undertaken in a spirit of revenge was

Decius   Coriolanus   Fabricius   Scipio   Marcellus

11. The Sibylline books were purchased and placed in the vault of a temple at Rome by

Æneas   Romulus   Tarquin   Servius   Remus

12. The Roman who feigned idiocy so as to be able later to serve his country was

Junius Brutus   Manius Curius   Gaius Scipio
Servius Tullius   Mucius Scævola.

EXPRESSIONS OF COMMON OCCURRENCE IN ENGLISH, THE MEANINGS OF WHICH ARE DEPENDENT UPON A KNOWLEDGE OF CLASSICAL MYTHOLOGY [1]

1. A fidus Achates — a faithful friend
2. An Achilles heel — a vulnerable spot
3. An Adonis — an exceedingly handsome man
4. Under the ægis of — having the authority of some powerful person or institution back of an action or individual
5. A feast of Alcinöus — a splendid repast
6. An Amazon — a woman of great physical strength
7. Apollo serving Admetus — a highly gifted person forced by necessity to undertake menial work
8. To feed on ambrosia and nectar — to have delicious food and drink
9. An apple of discord — a cause for dispute
10. An Argus-eyed person — one who can see a great deal
11. Argonauts — men who set forth on some adventure involving great risks, usually with the idea of ultimate gain in mind
12. The thread of Ariadne — a clue that unravels a mystery or leads one out of difficulties
13. An Augean task — an enormous and seemingly impossible undertaking
14. An Avernus — hell
15. A bacchanalian revel — a wild orgy
16. A Pyrrhic victory — a victory which is as disastrous as a defeat
17. A Cassandra utterance — words which foretell evil and are not heeded
18. A Cerberus — a forbidding person whom one cannot easily pass
19. A sop to Cerberus — a gift to quiet some one who may be about to cause trouble
20. A Chimerical scheme — a plan that is purely fanciful and outside the range of possibility

[1] Quoted from *Classical Myths That Live Today*, by Frances E. Sabin (Silver, Burdett & Co.).

21. A Circe — a beautiful woman whose charms are difficult to resist

22. Delphic words — words which are mysterious and hard to interpret

23. To cut up didoes — to play tricks

24. Sowing dragon's teeth — proceeding in such a way that troubles are sure to follow from the act

25. Endymion sleep — perpetual sleep in place of actual death

26. An Elysium — heaven

27. A Ganymede — a handsome youth

28. On the knees of the gods — the outcome rests with powers stronger than those possessed by men

29. A case of the Greeks bearing gifts — a fatal gift which is presented under friendly guise

30. When Greek meets Greek — two well-matched contestants

31. Halcyon days — calm and peaceful, untroubled by any care

32. A harpy — an exceedingly greedy person who stops at nothing in order to gain wealth

33. A Hebe — a maiden as beautiful as the cupbearer for the gods

34. To hector — to annoy a public speaker

35. A Helen — a woman of surpassing beauty and charm

36. A Herculean task — one that only Hercules could presumably accomplish

37. Ex pede Herculem — from a detail one can infer the size of the whole

38. One cannot snatch the club from Hercules — it is impossible to steal the power and ability of a great man

39. To drink from the fountain of Hippocrene — to draw inspiration for some literary work (as one might drink from the Muses' fountain on Mt. Helicon)

40. Hydra-headed evils (or difficulties) — evils that continue to grow while one is in the act of repressing them

41. An Icarian adventure — a daring adventure which ends fatally

42. Janus-faced facts — facts which can be interpreted in two ways

43. Winning laurels	acquiring fame through some worthy achievement
44. To look to one's laurels	to take care lest one's position of eminence be lost
45. A Lerna of ills	a great many troubles
46. The waters of Lethe	an experience that brings forgetfulness of care
47. A lotos-eater	one who passes his life in idleness and dreamy ease
48. He is Midas-eared	he is a man without judgment
49. The Midas-touch	the power of making money
50. A Narcissus	one who is fond of admiring himself
51. The shirt of Nessus	a harmful gift
52. An Odyssey	a tale of wild adventure
53. Extending the olive branch	an offer of peace
54. Olympian anger	such wrath as the king of the gods might show
55. To work the oracle	to influence some powerful agency in one's favor
56. A Pactolian flood	a flood of gold
57. A Pæan	a song of thanksgiving for deliverance from danger
58. A Pandora's box	surprises, usually unpleasant, although not always so
59. Mounting Pegasus	attempting to compose poetry or deliver an eloquent oration
60. A Penelope	a wife who remains faithful to her husband in spite of his long absence; also one who displays the traditional virtues of the housewife
61. A Procrustean system	a system which insists that every one shall conform to the same scheme
62. Promethean fire	a gift of value to the world, won through great personal suffering
63. A Protean artist	one who can assume various rôles successfully
64. Between Scylla and Charybdis	a choice between two difficulties
65. A Sinon	a skillful liar
66. A Siren	a beautiful woman who lures one to destruction
67. A task of Sisyphus	one that is never completed

68. The punishment of Tantalus	seeing one's desires near fulfillment and yet never really attaining them
69. A terpsichorean feat	unusual skill in dancing
70. A Titanic effort	an effort recalling the strength of the Titans
71. Wielding the trident	holding the supremacy of the sea
72. A Triton among minnows	one who far outshines his competitors
73. To fight (or work) like a Trojan	to fight with amazing boldness (or work with unusual energy)
74. An Ulysses	one who is clever in devising schemes

TEST ON MYTHOLOGY OF GREECE AND ROME

Time Limit: 5 min.

Name ....

Teacher ....

Period ....

Class ....

To the teacher: Read the directions aloud with the pupils.

To the pupils: Read the sample sentence below.

  The giant who bore the weight of the sky on his shoulders was
    Hesperides   Cyclops   Atlas   Jupiter   Titan

Now decide which of these words completes the sentence so as to make a correct statement. Draw a line under that word or phrase.

To the teacher: Allow the pupils about 30 seconds for this.

To the pupils: In the above example you should have drawn a line under the word *Atlas,* because he was supposed to bear up the sky on his shoulders. In the following test are fifteen sentences similar to the sample above. Choosing from the five words or phrases after each incomplete sentence that one which completes the sentence so as to make a correct statement, draw a line under that word or phrase. Do not ask questions after you have begun. Do you all understand what to do?

1. The man who atoned for his crime by performing twelve super-human tasks was
    Spartacus   Jason   Regulus   Perseus   Hercules

2. The Greek hero who died from a wound in his heel was
    Ajax   Achilles   Hector   Agamemnon   Helios

3. The woman whose curiosity made her open the box containing all human ills was
    Dido   Psyche   Cybele   Pandora   Iris

4. The snaky-locked sisters at the sight of whose faces men were turned to stone were called
    Muses   Harpies   Amazons   Serpentines   Gorgons

228

5. The leader of the expedition after the Golden Fleece was
  Ulysses   Pelias   Jason   Hercules   Æneas

6. The queen of the underworld was
  Minerva   Proserpina   Vesta   Venus   Atlanta

7. The mythical king who was given the Golden touch was
  Jason   Pluto   Crœsus   Midas   Crassus

8. The Roman God of the sea was
  Nereus   Oceanus   Neptune   Triton   Atlantis

9. The monster with a bull's body and a human head was called
  Siren   Cerberus   Satyr   Centaur   Minotaur

10. The sun god of the Greeks and Romans was
  Zeus   Apollo   Phaëthon   Dædalus   Zoroaster

11. The mythical rider of the winged horse was
  Bellerophon   Nereus   Pollux   Perseus   Mercury

12. The priestesses who guarded the sacred fire at Rome were the
  Parcæ   Flamens   Vestals   Sibyls   Omens

For practical purposes the teachers need to be familiar with the correspondences of a group of only nine consonants and four individual consonants.

1. The nine consonants are b, p, f; d, t, th; g, c(k), h(gh). These consist of three groups of three each, a labial group, b, p, and f; a dental group, d, t, and th; and a palatal group, g, c(k), and h. Each of these groups consists of a voiced consonant (sonant), b, d, and g; a voiceless consonant (surd), p, t, and c(k), and an aspirate (spirant), f, th, h(gh). Of these *th* does not occur in Latin (theatrum is borrowed from Greek). The following table summarizes these letters.

	Voiced	Voiceless	Aspirate
Labial	b	p	f (v)
Dental	d	t	(th Eng.)
Palatal	g	c (k)	h (gh, Eng.)

The letter appearing in English cognates of Latin words is regularly the one appearing next after the Latin letter in the horizontal series. Latin voiced consonants appear as voiceless consonants in English, Latin voiceless consonants as aspirates in English, and Latin aspirates as voiced consonants in English. The following illustrations arranged in tables will at once indicate the relative frequency and importance of the correspondences.

Labial Series

1		2		3	
Latin	English	Latin	English	Latin	English
sub	up	pabulum	food	fero	bear
		pater	father	fui	be
		pes	foot	frango	break
		primus	first	frater	brother
		præ	before		
		per	for		
		super	over		
		plenus	full		
		septem	seven		
		pauci	few		
		pro	for		

Dental Series

1		2		3	
Latin	English	Latin	English	Latin	English
duo	two	pater	father		
decem	ten	mater	mother		
tridecem	thirteen	habet	hath		
sedeo	sit	tu	thou		
dens	tooth	tuus	thine		
		tres	three		
		citerior	hither		
		dens			
		(dentis)	tooth		
		octavus	eighth		

Palatal Series

1		2		3	
Latin	English	Latin	English	Latin	English
a*g*er	a*c*re	*c*entum	*h*undred	ve*h*icle	wa*g*on
*g*ens	*k*in	*c*ollis	*h*ill		
fran*g*o	brea*k*	lux			
		(lu*c*is)	li*gh*t		
co*g*nosco	*k*now	nox			
		(no*c*tis)	ni*gh*t		
e*g*o	I (Ger.	*c*ornu	*h*orn		
	Ich)				
		*qu*em	*wh*om		
		o*c*to	ei*gh*t		
		*c*anis	*h*ound		
		*c*ors	*h*eart		
		*c*aput	*h*ead		

2. Important also are the Latin consonants v, qu, and j.

1		2		3	
Latin	English	Latin	English	Latin	English
*v*entus	*w*ind	*qu*artus	*f*our	*j*ugum	*y*oke
*v*olo	*w*ill	*qu*inque	*f*ive		
*v*igilia	*w*ake				
no*v*us	ne*w*				
*v*ehicle	*w*agon				

3. Observe also the loss of *s* in some English cognates:

*s*um	am
*s*ub	up
*s*olvo	loose
*s*uper	over

INDEX